AQUINAS *on the Beginning and End of Human Life*

AQUINAS *on the Beginning and End of Human Life*

Fabrizio Amerini

Translated by Mark Henninger

HARVARD UNIVERSITY PRESS

Cambridge, Massachusetts · London, England

2013

Originally published as *Tommaso d'Aquino: Origine e fine della vita umana,*
copyright © 2009 Edizioni ETS—Pisa www.edizioniets.com

Library of Congress Cataloging-in-Publication Data

Amerini, Fabrizio.
[Tommaso d'Aquino. English]
Aquinas on the beginning and end of human life / Fabrizio Amerini ; translated by
Mark Henninger.
p. cm.
Includes bibliographical references and index.
ISBN 978-0-674-07247-3
1. Thomas, Aquinas, Saint, 1225?–1274. 2. Human embryo—Moral and
ethical aspects. 3. Soul—History of doctrines—Middle Ages, 600–1500. I. Title.
B765.T54A215513 2013
179.7092—dc23   2012041663

To Luisa, my wife

Contents

Abbreviations

CT	Compendium theologiae
DEE	De ente et essentia
De virt.	Quaestiones disputatae de virtutibus
DPN	De principiis naturae
DUI	De unitate intellectus
Exp. Gen.	In Aristotelis libros De generatione et corruptione Expositio
Exp. Met.	In duodecim libros Metaphysicorum Aristotelis Expositio
Exp. Meteor.	In Aristotelis libros Meteorologicorum Expositio
Exp. Phys.	In octo libros Physicorum Aristotelis Expositio
In Jer.	In Jeremiam Prophetam Expositio
QDA	Quaestiones disputatae de anima
QDM	Quaestiones disputatae de malo
QDP	Quaestiones disputatae de potentia
QDSC	Quaestio disputata de spiritualibus creaturis
QDV	Quaestiones disputatae de veritate
Quodl.	Quaestiones de quolibet
SCG	Summa contra Gentiles
Sent.	Scriptum super Sententiis magistri Petri Lombardi
Sent. De an.	Sentencia libri De anima
Sent. De sensu	Sentencia libri De sensu et sensato
Sent. Ethic.	Sententia libri Ethicorum
ST	Summa theologiae
Sup. Cor.	Super primam Epistolam ad Corinthios Lectura
Sup. De causis	Super librum De causis Expositio
Sup. De Trin.	Super Boethium De Trinitate

Sup. Eph.	*Super Epistolam ad Ephesios Lectura*
Sup. Gal.	*Super Epistolam ad Galatas Lectura*
Sup. Ioan.	*Super Evangelium S. Ioannis Lectura*
Sup. Iob	*Expositio super Iob ad litteram*
Sup. Isaiam	*Expositio super Isaiam ad litteram*
Sup. Tim.	*Super primam Epistolam ad Timotheum Lectura*

Preface

THE PURPOSE OF this work is to offer a philosophical reconstruction of Thomas Aquinas's teaching on embryology and an assessment of its possible bioethical implications.[1] As is well known, the term "bioethics" was introduced for the first time in the 1970s to signify the reflection of the medical profession on its limits and on the ethical implications of medical practice and scientific research.[2] Later on, the term acquired different connotations, coming to designate an area of applied ethics that deals specifically with moral problems concerning life and living organisms in general. Strictly speaking, there were certainly no discussions in the Middle Ages of bioethics in this technical, contemporary sense. Nevertheless, the nonappearance of the term "bioethics" and of bioethical discussions and theories similar to those of today does not mean that there was no attention in the Middle

---

1. In this study, the texts of Thomas Aquinas are cited according to the abbreviations given in the list of abbreviations; for the editions of the particular works, see the bibliography. Note that all Latin quotations are taken from the editions indicated in the bibliography, except for those from the Commentary on the *Sentences,* which have been downloaded from the website www.corpusthomisticum .org (accessed May 1, 2012), and whose orthography and punctuation I have freely modified. Keep in mind that all texts of Thomas can be consulted easily at this website. For the dates of Aquinas's writings and a general introduction to his life and works, see Jean-Pierre Torrell, *Initiation à Saint Thomas d'Aquin: Sa personne et son oeuvre* (Fribourg: Éditions Universitaires-Les Éditions du Cerf, 1993). Finally, note that where it is not otherwise indicated, all the translations of Latin texts are mine.

2. The term was introduced for the first time by the oncologist Van Rensselaer Potter in *Bioethics: Bridge to the Future* (Englewood Cliffs, NJ: Prentice-Hall, 1971). For an introduction to contemporary bioethical debates, see Peter Singer, *Practical Ethics* (Cambridge: Cambridge University Press,

Ages to actions and behaviors that directly concerned life, whether human or, more generally, that of animals and plants. From this point of view, it is chiefly within medieval debates about embryology and animal generation that a historian of philosophy can find interesting parallels to contemporary bioethical discussions. In particular, the connection between medieval embryology and contemporary bioethics can be seen in at least two ways. The first is to put certain salient medieval embryological explanations in dialogue with contemporary bioethical debates, asking, for example, to what extent medieval explanations of animal generation can be used today to address questions of contemporary bioethics. The second is more straightforward: to investigate whether the medieval authors had raised and discussed questions that we today consider pertinent and relevant to bioethics.

In this study, the reconstruction of Thomas's embryological teaching is approached from both perspectives. On the one hand, we will see how the explanation of embryogenesis proposed by Thomas Aquinas is no longer tenable today in the terms worked out by the Dominican master. But we will also see how Thomas based his explanation of that process on certain philosophical intuitions and uses certain arguments that could be accepted today. On the other hand, we will show how Thomas strove to work out an explanation of animal generation that was philosophically consistent and rigorous, and how this afforded him the opportunity to treat some of the problems discussed by contemporary bioethicists.

In the Middle Ages, just as both philosophy and law devoted a certain amount of attention to actions and behaviors that impacted human life, so also there was a certain sensitivity to ethical questions connected

---

1979); H. Tristram Engelhardt, *Foundations of Bioethics* (New York: Oxford University Press, 1996); Helga Kuhse and Peter Singer, eds., *A Companion to Bioethics* (Oxford: Blackwell, 1998); John Harris, *Bioethics* (Oxford: Oxford University Press, 2001); Robert Veatch, *The Basics of Bioethics* (Upper Saddle River, NJ: Prentice-Hall, 2003); Helga Kuhse and Peter Singer, eds., *Bioethics: An Anthology* (Oxford: Blackwell, 2006). For an introduction to the specific problem of abortion, on which I shall especially focus in this book, see Leonard W. Sumner, *Abortion and Moral Theory* (Princeton, NJ: Princeton University Press, 1981); Joel Feinberg, ed., *The Problem of Abortion* (Belmont, CA: Wadsworth, 1984); David Boonin, *A Defense of Abortion* (Cambridge: Cambridge University Press, 2003); Michael Tooley, Celia Wolf-Devine, Philip E. Devine, and Alison M. Jaggar, *Abortion: Three Perspectives* (New York: Oxford University Press, 2009).

with medical practice. By checking medieval medical sources, for example, a historian of philosophy can find notable similarities to contemporary bioethical debates, such as important considerations on the status and ethical implications of medical science. Although worthy of further inquiry, our study does not follow this line of investigation. Rather, I consider medieval medical writings only in a limited way, i.e., insofar as they help us understand the embryological teaching of Thomas Aquinas; our viewpoint is philosophical, not medical. One of the aims of this study is to explore how and to what extent certain bioethical questions that interest us today can be approached from an Aristotelian philosophical perspective. In particular, I will investigate how they can be treated if we accept the process of animal generation proposed by Thomas Aquinas, one of the most important theologians and philosophers of the Middle Ages.

As mentioned earlier, bioethical questions are concerned principally with problems that involve the broad notion of life. Although in the Middle Ages there were discussions of moral problems concerning animal and plant life, and the relations of humans with animal and plant life-forms or with nature in general, in this work I am concentrating above all on a particular form of life, that of humans. Among the different life-forms, human life could be considered the most sophisticated, even taken to be, at least in the Middle Ages, the paradigmatic expression of life. It is well known that within the hierarchy of the physical cosmos that the medieval philosophers and theologians inherited from classic Greek philosophy humans occupy the highest level among creatures of the so-called sublunary world, the world of material reality. To be precise, then, this study will analyze the position of Thomas Aquinas concerning the nature of human life, specifically the problem of its beginning and its end.

We are in a very good position today to investigate these questions. Historians of medieval thought have explored extensively Thomas Aquinas's philosophy of human nature, producing excellent studies, from the pioneering work of Bruno Nardi and Sofia Vanni Rovighi to the more recent work of Jan A. Aertsen and Robert Pasnau, to cite only a few. Also the embryology of Thomas has drawn attention in the past few years. More specifically, the relation between Thomas's biological teachings and their possible bioethical implications is beginning to be studied closely. But to my knowledge, a comprehensive and textually founded study dedicated to this aspect of Thomas's philosophy is still lacking. The present work seeks, at least in part, to fill this gap.

In his extensive philosophical and theological writings extending over twenty years (1252–1274), Thomas Aquinas discusses at length the problem of the beginning of human life, while he devotes little attention to the problems of the so-called end of life. Still, as will become clear in this study, Thomas adopts a strict criterion for the definition of human life, such that the conditions required for stating when life begins and ends seem, at first glance, to be the same. In fact, as we shall discuss at the end of this study, when one examines his writings more closely it turns out that there are at least two ways of understanding the symmetry that Thomas seems to establish between the gradual human ensoulment of the human embryo and the gradual loss of human ensoulment of a human being, and these ways are not completely compatible. As a result, while the position of Thomas concerning when human life begins is, when all is said and done, definitive, his position on when human life ends turns out to be elusive and unclear.

Although there have been careful reconstructions of Thomas's theory of human nature, scholars have not agreed on how to interpret certain aspects of this teaching. In particular, there is fundamental disagreement on two points: first, how to interpret the Aristotelian characterization of the soul as act or form of an organic, physical body that has life potentially—a characterization that plays a key role in Thomas's embryological account; second, how to explain the gradual character of the ensoulment of the embryo. Because Thomas's teaching on human nature has received contrasting readings, it is difficult to evaluate philosophically and objectively his own interpretation of Aristotelian embryology. This difficulty is further exacerbated by the strong ideological pressures that mark the contemporary bioethical debate (above all regarding abortion and artificial insemination) and also, for thinkers within the Roman Catholic tradition, because of the figure of Thomas Aquinas himself, whose teaching has so greatly influenced the doctrine of that church today. In an attempt to lessen the ideological pressures that have always played on Thomas Aquinas, some move the debate concerning the beginning and end of human life to that of ascertaining the correct understanding of Thomas's thought and of his interpretation of Aristotelian embryology. But at times they use a tone that arouses opposing reactions and positions. The recent insightful work of Robert Pasnau on Thomas's theory of human nature provides an excellent example of this and has, among other things, provoked the lively reaction of two authoritative exponents of so-called "analytic Thomism," John Haldane and Patrick Lee.[3] Pasnau writes:

> There is an unfortunate tendency to conflate interest in medieval philosophy, especially the work of Thomas Aquinas, with sympathy for the Roman Catholic Church. Inasmuch as the Church's intellectual foundations lie in medieval philosophy, above all in Aquinas, sympathy for his work naturally should translate into sympathy for Catholicism. But the conflation is still unfortunate, because in recent years the Church has identified itself with a noxious social agenda—especially on homosexuality, contraception, and abortion—that has sadly come to seem part of the defining character of Catholicism. So it would be gratifying, for students of medieval philosophy, to see how in at least one of these cases Aquinas provides the resources to show something of what is wrong with the Church's position.[4]

As much as is possible, in this study I have tried to evaluate Thomas's embryological account prescinding from nonphilosophical considerations.

---

3. See John Haldane and Patrick Lee, "Aquinas on Human Ensoulment, Abortion and the Value of Life," *Philosophy* 78 (2003): 255–278, and "Rational Souls and the Beginning of Life: A Reply to Robert Pasnau," *Philosophy* 78 (2003): 532–540. In turn, Robert Pasnau replied to the first article quoted above in "Souls and the Beginning of Life: A Reply to Haldane and Lee," *Philosophy* 78 (2003): 521–531. On this debate see also Denis J. M. Bradley, " 'To Be or Not To Be?' Pasnau on Aquinas's Immortal Human Soul," *Thomist* 68 (2004): 1–39. The debate between Pasnau and Haldane–Lee will be reconsidered in Chapter 8.

4. See Robert Pasnau, *Thomas Aquinas on Human Nature: A Philosophical Study of* Summa Theologiae, *Ia 75–89* (Cambridge: Cambridge University Press, 2002), 100–130, especially 105 (see

In particular, it is not a principal objective of this study to determine whether or not Thomas's teaching is or is not in conflict with the present teaching of the Catholic Church. Nor will I discuss whether the position of the Church regarding the beginning and end of human life is correct or mistaken—as Pasnau, on the other hand, seems to assume; from the point of view I take in this study, this is simply not able to be determined. It should be said, in addition, that the Catholic Church itself seems fully aware that the teaching of Thomas, as that of many Fathers and Doctors of late antiquity and the Middle Ages, does not coincide completely with the final teaching that it has worked out. For example, regarding the question of the beginning of human life, in the Middle Ages it was a rather common and widely shared teaching that the embryo receives a human soul and so becomes a human being only after a certain period of organic development during about the first six weeks. Today such views are referred to as "delayed hominization" of the embryo.

The purpose of this study, therefore, is different and consists, very simply, in offering a reconstruction of Thomas's embryological account. This will show that certain recent attempts to bring Thomas into agreement with the contemporary position of the Catholic Church, especially regarding abortion, are inaccurate from a textual point of view and are not completely convincing theoretically. What is more, they are totally unnecessary for excluding abortion from the acts that are ethically permitted. What is of most interest is the exploration of the philosophical reasons that impelled Thomas to adopt one rather than another embryological explanation (or one rather than another interpretation of Aristotelian embryology). It is certainly legitimate and could be very fruitful to use Thomas's embryological account, or a bioethical theory

---

also what Pasnau says at p. 125). We shall see how a limitation of the interpretation of Pasnau—who considers Thomas's embryology as a theory that allows us to attack the position of contemporary antiabortionists "at its weakest point: at its claim that an unformed mass of cells can genuinely count as a human being" (108)—is that of assuming Thomas's *arguments* are compelling for us as well (106). As we shall see, Thomas's embryology is a proposal that seeks to rationally organize some givens of common sense. None of Aquinas's arguments appears particularly compelling. On the other hand, Pasnau correctly maintains that the *conception* of human life flowing from Thomas's doctrine could be championed also today.

based more or less on Thomas's teaching, in the contemporary debate, but this is beyond the principal scope of this study. Contemporary bioethical or embryological discussions will be kept in the background and referred to only occasionally.

The problem of the status and identity of the embryo is the chief concern of this study, and as Thomas formulates it, this is primarily a problem of *definition.* Answering this question amounts to providing a procedure for identifying the properties necessary and sufficient for a correct definition of human being or human life. Such a procedure should give us a linguistic formula that allows us to distinguish the status of *being a human* from others, both more generic, as *being alive* or *being ensouled,* and more specific and dense in meaning, as *being a person.* It is not, then, a question of "deciding" what is the real or actual status of an embryo, but of arguing for what are the most relevant and appropriate properties for a correct and complete definition of human life. When Thomas discusses the human embryo and human life, he adopts the metaphysical viewpoint rather than the biological. We shall see how for Thomas a metaphysical, and so philosophical, explanation of generation is not eliminable by a purely biological or scientific/medical explanation. Thomas appears to be barely interested in medical questions or in an explanation of the biological details involved in the generation of animals. And this is probably the reason why one finds in his writings discrepancies, second thoughts, and a lack of precision in his explanation and a lack of clarification of some specific, especially scientific, aspects of the process of generation.

In the classification of the sciences, Thomas locates medicine among the so-called practical sciences.[5] So if medicine studies the embryogenetic process, it does it for diagnostic and therapeutic purposes. Medical

---

5. See, for example, what Aquinas says in the Commentary on Boethius's *De Trinitate,* a work dating to the first Parisian teaching of Aquinas (1256–1259). See *Sup. De Trin.,* q. 5, a. 1, ad 4, 140, 277–283: "Cum autem medicina diuiditur in theoricam et practicam, non attenditur diuisio secundum finem,—sic enim tota medicina sub practica continetur, utpote ad operationem ordinata—, set attenditur predicta diuisio secundum quod ea que in medicina tractantur sunt propinqua uel remota ab operatione." This classification has a long tradition. For instance, it was already adopted by Hugh of St. Victor in his *Didascalion,* II, ch. XVI, a work that dates to the first half of the twelfth century.

science, however, does not offer an overall philosophical explanation of this process; it does not attempt to determine the most appropriate conceptual framework for an explanation that describes facets of the process beyond the medical. From Thomas's point of view, only a philosophical explanation in Aristotelian terms can rightly frame the embryogenetic process within a more expansive and theologically grounded notion of humanity. At the same time, Thomas also seems to be aware that a purely philosophical explanation of the process of animal generation cannot determine by itself, in one sense or in another, (bio)ethical and legal questions concerning the beginning and end of human life. For example, an explanation of when an embryo becomes a human being or whether a certain embryo and the human that develops from it are one and the same entity is not strictly tied to any position for or against abortion. Such a connection is made only on the assumption that a human being, or more generally what is termed "human," is sacred and inviolable. All that a philosophical explanation can do is to show that certain natural properties can be considered more fundamental than others insofar as they have more explanatory power than others. Alternatively, a philosophical explanation can state precisely the logical relations that hold among the notions used by a given theory in order to prevent incorrect descriptions and assessments of the facts that the theory seeks to explain. We will see that for Thomas a sound and consistent philosophical account of the embryogenetic process, although it cannot prescind completely from some medical and biological data, nevertheless does not depend on them. This is true to such an extent that advances in science would not be a reason to change the theoretic structure of such an account.

What has been said in the previous paragraphs is important for correctly assessing the scope of this study. In order to avoid any confusion, recall that in this study the theme of the beginning and end of human life is not approached from an ethical perspective but only from a metaphysical perspective. Again, the present study is about Thomas's interpretation of the Aristotelian metaphysics that undergirds his theory of human embryogenesis. The main goals reached by this study—both metaphysical and bioethical—should be assessed from this perspective. Certainly, the metaphysical question of when a human being first comes into existence and later dies informs responses to further ethical questioning on many bioethical issues—such as the moral permissibility of abortion, cloning, embryonic stem cell research, prenatal genetic diagnosis and genetic enhancement, certain assisted reproductive technologies, and decisions concerning irreversibly comatose patients, organ donation, and the like. But although an Aristotelian-inspired metaphysical investigation can generally inform our treatment of such themes, our final response to such bioethically sensitive questions is to a certain degree independent of the metaphysics that has been embraced. This is precisely one of the points for which this study argues. It is no doubt true that in correctly establishing Thomas's position on the value of human life it is crucial to take into account Thomas's ethics. And as for bioethics, a full-fledged moral analysis can help the interpreter of Thomas defend a given bioethical claim, for example, by situating it within a more general theory of a natural law ethic. In this study, however, no discussion of Thomas's ethics will be proposed. The use of Thomas's natural law ethic to derive specific bioethical positions informed by Thomas's metaphysical conclusions goes beyond the scope of the present book. Once again, the purpose of this study is preliminary and limited, namely, the reconstruction of Thomas's metaphysical framework of embryogenesis, the framework into which a properly bioethical analysis could then be inserted. Of course, the metaphysics endorsed by Thomas fixes some boundaries and puts some constraints on possible bioethical choices, even permitting one to draw broad conclusions about the moral permissibility or nonpermissibility of some (bio)ethically significant actions. But only a detailed analysis of Thomas's ethics could provide definitive arguments and justifications for our decisions in bioethical matters according to the spirit of Thomas's teaching. This is, however, the subject of a different study.[6]

This study has eight chapters. Chapter 1, "General Principles of the Embryology of Thomas Aquinas," provides the conceptual tools for a

---

6. For more on Thomas Aquinas's natural law ethic and its connection to bioethics, see John Finnis, *Natural Law and Natural Rights* (Oxford: Oxford University Press, 1980); Anthony J. Lisska, *Aquinas's Theory of Natural Law: An Analytic Reconstruction* (Oxford: Clarendon Press, 1996); Scott MacDonald and Eleonore Stump, eds., *Aquinas's Moral Theory. Essays in Honor of Norman Kretzmann*

correct understanding of the embryology of Thomas. In particular, it explains those aspects of Thomas's teaching on generation and substantial form that are indispensable for understanding his answer to various questions about the status and identity of the embryo. Chapter 2, "The Nature of the Human Soul," develops this theme by discussing some problems connected to Thomas's interpretation of the Aristotelian characterization of the soul as the substantial form or act of an organic, physical body that has life potentially. In Chapter 3, "The Status of the Embryo," I reconstruct Thomas's position regarding the nature of the embryo and the arguments he adopts to reject the thesis that the embryo becomes human from the moment of conception. Chapter 4, "Some Problems," discusses some complications involved in Thomas's explanation of the process of embryogenesis. In Chapter 5, "The Identity of the Embryo," I discuss the position of Thomas concerning the most philosophically significant problem, that of the identity of the embryo during the process of generation. The chapter shows the difficulties that Thomas has defending the unity and numerical identity of the embryo and the continuity between the embryo and the human being. Chapter 6, "Bioethical Implications," discusses possible bioethical implications, especially concerning abortion: those that Thomas himself draws and those that could be drawn from his explanation of the embryogenetic process. Chapter 7, "The Beginning and End of Human Life," examines the position of Thomas regarding the problem of the end of human life and the role played by the definition of a human being as a rational animal in determining when a human life ends. In particular, I ask whether or not Thomas saw a symmetry between the process of human ensoulment of the human embryo and the process of the loss of human ensoulment of a human being. Finally, Chapter 8, "The Contemporary Debate over the Hominization of the Embryo," critically examines some recent attempts to convert Thomas, a proponent of delayed hominization of the embryo, into a supporter of the position of

(Ithaca, NY: Cornell University Press, 1999); Mark C. Murphy, *Natural Law and Practical Rationality* (Cambridge: Cambridge University Press, 2001); Alfonso Gomez-Lobo, *Morality and the Human Goods: An Introduction to Natural Law Ethics* (Washington, DC: Georgetown University Press, 2002); Jean Porter, *Nature as Reason: A Thomistic Theory of the Natural Law* (Grand Rapids, MI: Eerdmans, 2005); and Jason T. Eberl, *Thomistic Principles and Bioethics* (London: Routledge, 2006).

the Catholic Church which holds, as is well known, that the hominization of the embryo takes place at the moment of conception.

A few final clarifications. Although this study is concerned with themes of medieval philosophy, it is not intended exclusively for readers familiar with medieval philosophy. I introduce technical concepts and terms, both philosophical and medical, in a gradual way, explaining them as much as possible in everyday language. It should be expected, however, that alongside general philosophical considerations of Thomas's embryology and theory of human nature, readers will encounter more fine-grained discussions of the writings of Thomas Aquinas. I hope readers will understand that this is indispensable if one wishes to come to a correct philosophical assessment of the position of the Dominican master.

On the other hand, this study is not a strictly historical and contextual reconstruction of the embryological teaching of Thomas Aquinas. Although I do pay close attention to the internal development of the thought of Thomas as well as to the sources of his thinking, one should keep in mind that this work is systematic rather than historical. The teachings of Thomas have been reconstructed by focusing on and discussing his arguments that either clearly or even possibly have bioethical consequences. A further caveat, however, is called for. Despite the intended systematic purpose of the book, the reader will soon come to realize that the style adopted in this book is "aporematic" rather than apodictic or assertive. What motivates this choice is simply respect for Thomas's texts. As the historian of medieval philosophy well knows, the embryological teaching of Thomas is difficult. It may often appear unclear, scientifically inconclusive, or unexplanatory, and in most cases it escapes the interpreter's attempt to project onto it contemporary accounts of human embryogenesis. For these and similar reasons, in this book I have chosen to reconstruct Thomas's reasoning, so to speak, "from the inside," bringing Thomas's conception of human embryogenesis and its difficulties gradually to light, instead of forcing simplifying solutions onto interpretative problems involved in his writings. In particular, in this book I have endeavored to show that Thomas leaves unexplored certain important aspects—both biological and metaphysical—of the human embryogenetic process, and he hesitates or evolves on certain crucial points. Thus, in order to bring out the complexity of Thomas's thought, I have chosen to discuss it in a dialectical way, highlighting one aspect of his complex teaching before highlighting another that may or may not cohere with the former. I hope readers will not be perplexed by this stylistic feature but will be able to follow patiently the thread through the "argumentative labyrinth" I have constructed.

This book is the English translation of *Tommaso d'Aquino: Origine e fine della vita umana* (Pisa: ETS, 2009). Although the present translation faithfully follows the original Italian, it should be noted that the text has been improved and supplemented through exchanges between the author and the translator and by comments of the anonymous reviewers. In particular, the final bibliography and the footnotes have been enhanced and updated.

In conclusion, some acknowledgments. I take this opportunity to sincerely thank Luciano Cova for his valuable suggestions and detailed and constructive comments. My thanks also to Chiara Crisciani, Luca Fonnesu, Paola Bernardini, Gabriele Galluzzo, Sergio Filippo Magni, and the anonymous referees for having contributed in various ways to the discussion and the improvement of issues found in this study. A priceless thanks to Mark Henninger not only for translating this book into English but also for contributing to perfect it with his insightful questions and observations.

A dear and special mention goes to Romana Martorelli Vico, recently and prematurely deceased. I shared with her many important exchanges about the contents of this book, and her works on medieval embryology were an irreplaceable guide for me. I wish to remember here her extraordinary humanity and generosity, as well as her great passion for medieval philosophy. Finally, a warm thanks to all the students that enlivened the course and seminars of mine at Parma, Italy, during which was born the idea to write this book. Of course, the responsibility for the content and any possible errors is entirely mine.

AQUINAS *on the Beginning and End of Human Life*

Introduction

As mentioned in the preface, the term "bioethics" refers to normative and applied ethical theories about actions concerning life, whether human or, more generally, that of animals and plants. A typical way of formulating a bioethical question is the following: Is the act of abortion morally licit? In general, bioethical questions involve decisions about the *boundaries* of human life, its beginning and end, or have to do with questions about the *conditions* for identifying it. Philosophically, these are questions about definition, since defining a thing amounts to providing the necessary and sufficient conditions for identifying a thing, distinguishing it from other things different or similar to it in kind. For example, in the seventeenth chapter of the fifth book of the *Metaphysics*, Aristotle brings together the notions of definition and of limit.[1] The definition of the essence of a thing provides the limits of the knowledge of that thing. Aristotle adds that the limits of knowledge are also the limits of the thing, in that one can be in contact with

---

1. See Aristotle, *Metaphysics*, V, 17, 1022a8–10.

a thing only by knowing it, and when one knows it, one knows what that thing is. To define a thing, therefore, is to delimit it, and this is to list all and only those properties that allow us to determine the contours of that thing.

There is a certain complexity hidden within the question, Is the act of abortion morally licit? One must first clarify what is meant by "licit," and especially "morally licit," and also have at least some intuitive clarity on what is meant by an act, and in particular, what is an act of abortion. This last, obviously, depends on defining what abortion is. It is commonly held that abortion involves the suppression of a human life. Once the principle that what shows signs of human life should be protected is accepted, one's stance for or against abortion depends on the answer to the question of when does human life begin. If the question of abortion were only about establishing when human life begins, one could hold that such a question is simply unanswerable since there seems to be nothing in how things are that forces us to take one property or one biological condition as marking out human life more than another. On the other hand, if one does not make abortion only a question of establishing when human life begins, things become more complicated. For then, a stance for or against abortion begins to include other factors: the moral autonomy of the mother, the degree of intentionality or awareness of the act of conception, whether there was violence involved, the quality and dignity of life, demographic or health considerations about overpopulation of the planet, and so forth. On all these issues it is even more difficult to find a common ground. Furthermore, provisions aimed at regulating abortion could also prescind completely from biological considerations or from answering when human life begins.[2] In fact, one should not assume that abortion involves *only* the question of the beginning of human life, nor that one's stance toward it depends *strictly* on the response one gives to that question.

---

2. A paradigmatic example is given by John Rawls's "political and juridical approach." See his *Theory of Justice* (Oxford: Oxford University Press, 1981). A theoretical account of bioethical questions regarding abortion could be done exclusively in juridical or political terms, i.e., by giving the formal criteria for ordering and assessing behavioral and decisional acts with no commitment to metaphysical or biological disputes about the *real* beginning of human life.

One can be against abortion without recognizing the embryo as any form of human life, as also one can be favorable, in certain cases, toward the interruption of pregnancy while granting that human life begins at conception.

It makes little sense to ask in general whether performing an abortion is licit without first specifying the set of norms to be used in determining whether an act is morally licit, illicit, or indifferent. For example, if one does not accept the possibility of specifying an absolutely fixed or universal system of norms, one could reformulate the above-mentioned question as follows: Is an act of abortion morally *acceptable?* The condition of being acceptable could be distinguished from that of being licit not only in that the former can be interpreted as implying a more subjective stance but also because it could imply a set of norms that is only relatively fixed, i.e., relative to a historical or social context. Not only that, but one could also discuss the acceptability of an act of abortion on the basis of a conception of norms that is conventional.

Two things, then, seem to be required as the basis for a bioethical theory. First, there is needed a set of norms for making moral assessments of certain types of acts. Second, there is needed, at least in a preliminary way, some definition of the basic terms used. Returning to the above-mentioned example, the question of whether an act of abortion is licit or acceptable makes sense only if a given theory or a given community recognizes such an act as the suppression of the *life* of a determinate subject, assuming that such an act of suppression is held to be a threshold not to be crossed or is simply illicit or unacceptable by the same theory or community. But exactly what type of life does an act of abortion suppress? How are we to describe the entity, i.e., the embryo, to which our act is directed? The definitions for being alive and for being human, or even for being a person, are not conceptually interchangeable, and different ways of treating the question of abortion arise from whether one attributes to an embryo only the property of being alive or also that of being human. On the one hand, the inquiry about whether an act of abortion is licit or acceptable reveals that what is at issue is the choice of a criterion for working out a bioethical theory that has normative force concerning abortion. But on the other hand, more fundamentally, the problem of the definitions of "being alive" and "being human" presupposes that a given community be disposed to accept that determinate biological characteristics can be associated with such properties. But what biological characteristics should we use to answer the question, When does human life begin?

Certainly biology makes an important contribution to individuating the natural characteristics to be associated with the general properties of being alive or being human. For example, as the medieval philosophical tradition commonly assumed, being capable of taking nourishment and of growth could be good defining conditions for the property of being alive, just as being capable of movement and of sensation could be good defining conditions for the property of being an animal. And to be capable of rational acts could be an excellent defining condition for the property of being human. These various characteristics, in turn, could be refined in various ways given the biochemical and neurological science we have today. But it is quite clear that the association of select and specific natural characteristics with the general properties expressed by the terms "being alive" and "being human" is an act of choice, and as such the act of choosing one set of natural characteristics rather than another is an act of judgment. It depends on the significance that one assigns to one rather than another class of properties, and that significance has to be justified by rational argument, i.e., proposed and defended philosophically. In the end, the final decision about which biological functions to select and how to associate them with the general properties of being human or being alive turns out to be the result of stipulation, albeit rationally justified. What cannot be conceded, in any case, is that advances in science concerning these biological functions might bring about an abandonment of the imperative to "save the appearances" on which is founded, ultimately, a philosophical explanation.

To make these abstract considerations more concrete consider more closely the case of abortion. In the present-day debate over abortion, legal questions (Is the act of abortion an act of homicide, and so liable to legal prosecution?) are not always clearly distinguished from moral questions (Is the act of abortion morally licit or illicit?). Apart from their specifics, these questions have a feature in common: they both call for a preliminary definition of what is meant by human life. As mentioned earlier, biology can come to our help. For example, it can help us determine *when* the first neural development and nerve connections occur, and it can propose the appearance of such connections as a criterion for distinguishing what is human from what is not (or not yet) human. A move of this sort tends to distinguish the property of being alive from that of being human; before the appearance of such connections, something could be said to be alive, but not (or not yet) human. It is clear, however, that biology cannot defend this criterion as the criterion to be followed in defining human life. For why should the presence of primordial nerve connections, even if they can be likely associated with the presence of pleasure and pain in the embryo, be considered the fundamental condition for defining human life? Someone could require a weaker condition, for example, the presence of basic vital organs which are normally developed later on. Alternatively, one could insist on a more radical condition, such as the act of conception itself or the mixing (or the copresence) of the parents' genetic code, and in this way tend to put on the same plane being alive and being human.

Formulating the debate in this way shows that when we begin to define human life, we usually are working with two factors: (1) the *selection* of certain natural characteristics, i.e., those able to be associated with the presence of nerve connections, to conception in the ovum, to the formation of basic vital organs, and so forth, and (2) the *choice* of such characteristics as the properties relevant for defining human life. Framing the problem in this way, it is evident that emphasis is being placed above all on the *temporality* of the process of generation. A presupposition of the debate is that there is or can be found a discriminating condition—based on verifiable scientific data—with respect to which what undergoes the abortive act is seen as *already* a human being, or as something that *already* has the fundamental characteristics of human life, either completely or only in a partial or imperfect way.

But why must the debate over abortion and the beginning of human life be framed in these terms? Someone could be dissatisfied with this way of posing the problem and suggest another way. One could reject from the start the suppression of an embryo not because what is suppressed is at a certain moment *already* a human being, but because an embryo is potentially exactly that *same* thing that would actually become a human being if it were not suppressed. Reframing the problem in this way places the emphasis above all on the *identity* of the subject or the *identity* of the process involving a determinate subject. In this case, the criterion of the definition of human life is more extrinsic: something has human life not when it has all or some of the natural characteristics that we might associate with being a human, but if it has the potentiality to become a human; that is, if it is the subject of a process that will end (assuming no interruptions or breaks of any sort) in what is a human being. The difficulty then would be not so much the selection of natural characteristics, but rather establishing the continuity or identity of the process or of the subject of the process. This way of framing the problem, obviously, is not completely disconnected from the preceding one, for to establish the identity of the subject requires in any case a selection of characteristics. But in this second way of framing the debate, the characteristics involved are more general. Also in this case, biology can help by providing us with data for determining whether the supposed identity of the subject continues from conception. But again, biology is not able to settle the question of the beginning of human life.

Choosing as the defining condition for being human either (1) the individuation of determinate biological characteristics or (2) the identity or continuity of the subject (or process) is the result of a philosophical decision. Here philosophy can carve out a space, making itself independent of biology, and this in various ways. For example, it can justify the relevance of certain natural characteristics as the basis for working out a normative bioethical theory. It can also make a case for the choice between (1) and (2). In the first way, someone could allow for abortion by distinguishing between before and after in the process of human generation, while in the second way, one could accept abortion only by distinguishing between what is actually a human being and what is only potentially a human being. In any case, such a choice has to be argued for and justified rationally, and neither of the two alternatives can be discounted out of hand.

In Thomas Aquinas's way of approaching this whole question, he shows himself fully aware of the qualifications that we have attempted to introduce in these pages. On the one hand, we shall see how in Thomas's writings both (1) the explanation that insists on the individuation of a set of natural properties and (2) the other that insists on the identity or continuity of the subject (or of the process) are both present and, in the end, are not completely in accord. Although for Thomas the subject of the process of generation remains the same during the whole process since the whole process remains the same, nevertheless such a subject does not retain anything, either formal or material, of the various species to which it gives rise in the process. On the other hand, we will see how in his treatment of abortion Thomas keeps well in mind the difference between the data that medical science is able to furnish us and the philosophical treatment of this data. Scientific, and more precisely, biological considerations can be enormously helpful in coming to a finely considered, judicious assessment of the factors involved in the debate concerning the beginning and end of human life, but such considerations are totally nonessential for determining the criteria for what is meant by "human life." As we will seek to show, Thomas had *philosophical,* i.e., Aristotelian, arguments rather than biological to reject the thesis that human life begins with the insemination of the female matter by the male semen. These arguments hold regardless of the level and type of scientific knowledge that one may have concerning what happens at the moment of conception.

This does not mean, however, that Thomas is neutral, or worse, favorable to abortion. Thomas believes that taken within the natural and ordinary process of conception (the case of a conception induced by violence or brought about by deception could be treated differently) the act of suppression of the embryo is a highly unnatural act, since it stops a process that, without a break in continuity, would lead to the formation of a human being. In his first theological work, his Commentary on the *Sentences* of Peter Lombard, Thomas remarks that even "animals look forward to their own offspring," and so there is no reason why humans should not do the same. Moreover, procreation is the final end of the human species; that is, it is essential for the conservation of the species. The act of abortion, therefore, is morally unjustifiable and, in the end, unacceptable. However, it is not an act that is juridically illicit or criminally punishable, at least not until around the first month and a half of gestation, since, as we shall see, until then the embryo cannot yet be said to be a human being.

One should not be greatly surprised that this teaching conflicts so openly with the present-day doctrine of the Catholic Church. In the first place, it is not an innovation of Thomas Aquinas, but is a position held also by Augustine and was generally shared by most theologians of Aquinas's day. In the second place, this position is nothing but a reformulation of the biological teaching of Aristotle which comes from accepting certain constraints on animal generation and on the soul understood as the substantial form of the body, as we shall show. In this light, Thomas's philosophical account of embryogenesis aims to place two givens within one system. The first given is that the embryo can in no way be considered a human being until the basic vital organs are completely formed, which takes place, on the average, about six weeks into gestation; such a formation is necessary to guarantee the possibility of a correct and complete exercise of those vital functions that can be associated with the human soul, above all the intellectual functions. The second given is that the embryo ought not to be considered as something different, as a subject, from the human being to which it will give rise, for the embryo acquires its own metaphysical identity from the moment of conception. Thomas's philosophical proposal precisely seeks to hold together these two givens: (1) the process of generation taking place in stages, entailing discontinuity of substance, and (2) the identity and continuity of the subject of this process. In the final analysis, the philosophical value of this proposal depends on the success of the attempt to balance the weight of the criterion that is based on natural properties with the weight of the criterion that is based on the identity or continuity of the subject when setting out the definition of what it is to be a human being.

CHAPTER ONE

General Principles of the Embryology of Thomas Aquinas

THOMAS AQUINAS tackles the question of the nature of the embryo at different times in his career and in various contexts. He does not always treat questions of bioethical interest when treating the embryogenetic process. At times one finds bioethical considerations in other contexts, especially theological, as, for example, where Thomas discusses whether certain acts, especially sacramental, that concern the mother affect the embryo, and also where he treats the sacrament of matrimony. Nevertheless, his treatment of embryogenesis and more generally of animal generation constitutes the metaphysical basis for the answers Thomas offers to questions that more directly concern the ethical and theological value of the embryo. Within his treatment of the process of generation, there are two questions in particular that help clarify the status of the embryo. The first is the question of the unicity or plurality of souls and of substantial forms, namely, whether in a human there is only one soul and one substantial form or many. The second concerns the propagation and multiplication of souls, that is, whether the human soul is transmitted from father to child through the semen or is infused by God extrinsically by an act of creation. Obviously, allusions to the nature of the process of generation are found in many works, but below are found the principal passages where Thomas specifically treats embryology.

1. *Scriptum super Sententiis* (Paris, 1252–1256)

I, d. 18, q. 2, a. 1: Whether the human soul is transmitted by the parents *(Utrum anima humana traducatur a parentibus);*

I, d. 18, q. 2, a. 3: Whether the sensible soul exists through transmission *(Utrum anima sensibilis sit ex traduce);*

II, d. 30, q. 2, a. 1: Whether food is truly changed into human nature *(Utrum alimentum transeat in veritatem humanae naturae);*

II, d. 30, q. 2, a. 2: Whether semen is separated because it is generated from food *(Utrum semen decidatur ex eo quod generatur ex alimento).*

2. *Quodlibet* IX (Paris, 1256–1259)

q. 5, a. 1: Whether the vegetable and sensible souls exist through creation *(Utrum vegetabilis et sensibilis anima sint a creatione).*

3. *Summa contra Gentiles* (Naples[?]-Orvieto, 1259–1265)

II, ch. 83: The human soul begins with the body *(Quod anima humana incipiat cum corpore);*

II, ch. 84: Response to the preceding arguments *(Solutio rationum praemissarum);*

II, ch. 85: The soul is not part of the substance of God *(Quod anima non sit de substantia Dei);*

II, ch. 86: The human soul is not transmitted by semen *(Quod anima humana non traducatur ex semine);*

II, ch. 87: The human soul is produced into being by God by an act of creation *(Quod anima humana producatur in esse a Deo per creationem);*

II, ch. 88: Arguments proving that the human soul is caused from semen *(Rationes ad probandum quod anima humana causetur ex semine);*

II, ch. 89: Response to the preceding arguments *(Solutio rationum praemissarum).*

4. *Quaestiones disputatae de potentia* (Rome, 1265–1266)

q. 3, a. 9: Whether the rational soul is brought into being by an act of creation or by the transmission of semen *(Utrum anima rationalis educatur in esse per creationem vel per seminis traductionem);*

q. 3, a. 10: Whether the rational soul is created in the body or outside the body *(Utrum anima rationalis sit creata in corpore vel extra corpus);*

q. 3, a. 11: Whether the sensible and vegetable souls exist through an act of creation or are transmitted by semen *(Utrum anima sensibilis et vegetabilis sint per creationem vel traducantur ex semine);*

q. 3, a. 12: Whether the sensible or vegetable souls are in semen from the moment that the semen is separated *(Utrum anima sensibilis vel vegetabilis sint in semine a principio quando decidatur).*

5. *Quaestiones disputatae de anima* (Rome, 1265–1266)

q. 11: Whether in a human, the rational, sensible and vegetable souls are one substance *(Utrum in homine anima rationalis, sensibilis et vegetabilis sit una substantia).*

6. *Summa theologiae* (1265–1268)

I, q. 90, a. 1: Whether the human soul is something made or is a part of the substance of God himself *(Utrum anima humana sit aliquid factum, vel sit de substantia ipsius Dei);*

I, q. 90, a. 2: Given that the human soul is produced, whether it is created *(Supposito quod sit facta, utrum sit creata);*

I, q. 90, a. 4: Whether the human soul is created before the body *(Utrum sit facta ante corpus);*

I, q. 118, a. 1: Whether the sensitive soul is transmitted with semen *(Utrum anima sensitiva traducatur cum semine);*

I, q. 118, a. 2: Whether the intellective soul is caused from semen *(Utrum anima intellectiva causetur ex semine);*

I, q. 118, a. 3: Whether human souls were created at the same time as the beginning of the world *(Utrum animae humanae fuerint creatae simul a principio mundi);*

I, q. 119, a. 1: Whether some part of food is truly changed into human nature *(Utrum aliquid de alimento convertatur in veritatem humanae naturae);*

I, q. 119, a. 2: Whether semen is from the residue of food *(Utrum semen sit de superfluo alimenti).*

7. Quaestio disputata de spiritualibus creaturis (Rome, 1267–1268) a. 3: Whether the spiritual substance, which is the human soul, is united to the body by some intermediary *(Utrum substantia spiritualis, quae est anima humana, uniatur corpori per medium).*

In addition to these passages, important observations on the nature of the soul and of generation are found in the late commentaries on *De anima* (Rome, 1267–1268) and on *De generatione* (Naples, 1272–1273). The embryological teaching of Thomas is, prima facie, rather simple.[1] In general, Thomas closely follows Aristotle's ideas found in the biological

---

1. A clear and short presentation of Thomas's embryology can be found in Luciano Cova, "Prius animal quam homo. Aspetti dell'embriologia tommasiana," in Chiara Crisciani, Roberto Lambertini, and Romana Martorelli Vico, eds., *Parva Naturalia. Saperi medievali, natura e vita* (Pisa: Istituti Editoriali e Poligrafici Internazionali, 2004), 357–378. See also Gordon A. Wilson, "Thomas Aquinas and Henry of Ghent on the Succession of Substantial Forms and the Origin of Human Life," in Lawrence P. Schrenk, ed., *The Ethics of Having Children* (Washington, D.C.: American Catholic Philosophical Association, 1990), 117–131. Slightly different reconstructions from mine can be found in Stephen J. Heaney, "Aquinas and the Presence of the Human Rational Soul in the Early Embryo," *The Thomist* 56 (1992): 19–48, reprinted in Stephen J. Heaney, ed., *Abortion: A New Generation of Catholic Responses* (Braintree, MA: Pope John Center, 1992), 277–296; Michel Bastit, "L'embryologie de Saint Thomas," *Ethique* 3 (1992): 48–59; William A. Wallace, "Aquinas's Legacy on Individuation, Cogitation and Hominisation," in David M. Gallagher, ed., *Thomas Aquinas and His Legacy* (Washington, D.C.: The Catholic University of America Press, 1994), 173–193, and "St. Thomas on the Beginning and Ending of Human Life," in Abelardo Lobato and Daniel Ols, eds., *Sanctus Thomas de Aquino doctor hodiernae humanitatis* (Vatican City: Editrice Vaticana, 1995), 394–407; Peter Volek, "Thomas Aquinas's Views on the Origins of Humans and Contemporary Embryology," *Filozofia* 62/3 (2007): 203–222. For an introduction to medieval embryology and to that of Thomas in particular, see Jacques Maritain, "Verso un'idea tomista dell'evoluzione," in Jacques Maritain, *Approches sans entraves. Scritti di filosofia cristiana* (Rome: Città Nuova, 1977), vol. 1, 87–153; Michael A. Taylor, *Human Generation in the Thought of Thomas Aquinas. A Case Study on the Role of Biological Fact in Theological Science* (S.T.D. diss., The Catholic University of America, 1982); Jean de Siebenthal, "L'animation selon Thomas d'Aquin: Peut-on affirmer que l'embryon est d'abord autre chose qu'un homme en s'appuyant sur Thomas d'Aquin?," in Société Suisse de bioéthique, ed., *L'Embryon: Un homme* (Lausanne: Société Suisse de bioéthique, 1986), 91–98; Romana Martorelli Vico, *Medicina e filosofia. Per una storia dell'embriologia medievale del XIII e XIV secolo* (Naples: Guerini e Associati, 2002), and "Anima e corpo nell'embriologia medievale," in Carla Casagrande and Silvana Vecchio, eds., *Anima e corpo nella cultura medievale* (Florence: Sismel-Edizioni del Galluzzo, 1999), 95–106; Pamela M. Huby, "Soul, Life, Sense, Intellect: Some Thirteenth-Century Problems," in Gordon R. Dunstan, ed., *The Human Embryo: Aristotle and the Arabic and European Traditions* (Exeter, Devon: University of Exeter Press, 1990), 113–122; and Luc Brisson, Marie-Hélène Congourdeau, and Jean-Luc Solère, eds., *L'embryon. Formation et animation. Antiquité grecque et latine, tradition hébraïque, chrétienne et islamique* (Paris: Vrin, 2008). More generally, for a history of embryology one can consult the classic Joseph Needham, *A History of Embriology* (Cambridge: Cambridge

works, with the aid of Avicenna's interpretation of some parts of these works.[2] Thomas does not in general see human generation as substantially different from animal generation, and so for the sake of brevity, I shall limit myself in what follows to how Thomas treats human generation. The formation of the embryo or fetus—Thomas uses the two terms interchangeably—is the result of the action of the male (the father) on the female (the mother) by means of his semen. In terms of the four Aristotelian causes, the male is the efficient cause of the process, while the mother, through the menstrual blood, is the material cause.[3] Except in cases where Thomas is not concerned to express

University Press, 1959). For emphasis on the importance of Aristotle's biology for Thomas's embryological discussion, see Eric M. Johnston, *The Role of Aristotelian Biology in Thomas Aquinas's Theology of Marriage* (Ph.D. diss., The Catholic University of America, 2008); see there for other bibliographical references.

2. Thomas rarely cites medical and biological sources external to the Aristotelian tradition. He certainly was acquainted with the Latin version of Avicenna's *Canon,* translated from the Arabic by Gerard of Cremona (see, e.g., *Sup. De Trin.,* q. 5, a. 1, ad 4, 140, 251–252), and his so-called *De animalibus,* translated into Latin from the Arabic by Michael Scot around 1230. On the other hand, Thomas did not know Averroes's *Colliget,* which was translated into Latin from the Arabic only in 1285 and used for the first time, to my knowledge, by the Augustinian theologian Giles of Rome. For details on the transmission of the Arab biological and medical works, see Martorelli-Vico, *Medicina e filosofia,* and Cristina d'Ancona, "La trasmissione della filosofia araba dalla Spagna musulmana alle università del XIII secolo," in Cristina d'Ancona, ed., *Storia della filosofia nell'Islam medievale,* 2 vols. (Turin: Einaudi, 2005), vol. 2, 783–843.

3. See *Sent.,* III, d. 3, q. 5, a. 1; *Exp. Met.,* V, lec. 21. Thomas attributes to the female no active role in the process of generation. In particular, Thomas excludes both that the female can actively cooperate in the process and that the female material potentially contains the form of the generated thing. The reasons for excluding both cases are given in *Sent.,* II, d. 20, q. 1, a. 2, and more explicitly repeated in *Sent.,* III, d. 3, q. 2, a. 1: "Cum igitur impossibile sit illud quod est determinatum ut patiens habere virtutem activam respectu eiusdem, oportet quod femina non sit agens in conceptione sed tantum patiens. [. . .] Impossibile est idem esse alterans et alteratum; unde non potest esse quod forma quae est in aliqua materia agat in ipsam, sive sit perfecta sive imperfecta." On the difference between menstrual blood and male semen, and on Thomas's refusal to grant a seed to the female (against the position put forward by some medical doctors), see *Sent.,* III, d. 3, q. 5, a. 1. Nonetheless, again in the Commentary on the *Sentences,* while clarifying in passing the role of the female, Thomas distinguished three actions in the ordinary process of human generation—the preparation of the female matter, the formation and organization of the embryonic body, and some accessory dispositions—, attributing to the female an active, though imperfect, role only in what concerns the initial preparation of the matter, before the arrival of the male semen (*Sent.,* III, d. 3, q. 2, a. 1). Thomas thinks that to exclude the female from having any active role in the process of generation serves to preserve and to give consistency, theologically speaking, to the role of the Virgin Mary as mother, since she does not play any active role at all in the conception and generation of Christ.

himself precisely,[4] he never considers the male semen as a material cause of the generative process.[5] He also clearly excludes this when accounting for the miraculous case of Christ's conception in which there is no male semen and the formative action is taken over by the Holy Spirit.[6] The semen, on the other hand, is the formal cause, and it is in the semen that there exists a vital "spirit" *(spiritus)*, in which is found what the tradition calls a "formative power" *(virtus formativa)*.[7] The final cause, of course, is the generated human.[8]

Given these components then, i.e., a generating agent (the male), a matter that will undergo the process of generation (first the female matter, then the embryonic matter), and what is the result of generation (the human being), the process of human generation takes place in the following way. The male semen is what remains from the final stages of the food's digestion by the father, and as such is not absorbed by the father. According to Aristotelian embryology, this means that the semen does not have of itself a complete species, nor does it constitute a specialized part of the human organism. Since it has not been

---

4. As the following, for example: "Respondeo dicendum quod, sicut supra dictum est, uniuscuiusque speciei generatio naturalis est ex determinata materia. Materia autem ex qua naturaliter generatur homo, est *semen humanum viri vel feminae.* Unde ex alia quacumque materia individuum humanae speciei generari non potest naturaliter" (ST, I, q. 92, a. 4, italics mine). But for a clear distinction, see ST, III, q. 28, arg. 5 and ad 5.

5. See e.g. *Sent.,* III, d. 3, q. 5, a. 1: "Respondeo dicendum quod circa materiam de qua corpus hominis formatum est variae sunt opiniones. Quidam enim dicunt quod corpus humanum formatur ex commixtione seminum, scilicet matris et patris simul, cum sanguine menstruo, ita quod totum hoc sit materia corporis. Hoc autem Philosophus, in XV *De animalibus,* multipliciter destruit, ostendens quod id quod ex viro descendit non est materia humani corporis, sed solum principium activum, et per rationem et experimenta sensibilia, quae magis in rebus naturalibus faciunt fidem: et hoc patet inspicienti verba eius. Similiter etiam ostendit quod semen mulieris nihil facit ad generationem; unde etiam et quaedam mulieres concipiunt sine hoc quod seminent. Sed sanguis qui menstruum dicitur est in mulieribus loco seminis in viris."

6. See e.g. ST, III, q. 31, a. 5; q. 33, a. 4.

7. See e.g. *Quodl.* XII, q. 7, a. 2; SCG, II, ch. 86 and ch. 89; ST, I, q. 118, a. 1. Thomas does not dwell at length on the nature of the "spirit" *(spiritus)* which contains the formative power. Only in one text (QDP, q. 3, a. 9, ad 9) Thomas calls it "corporeal," while in most cases it is simply called "vital" (e.g. *Sent.,* II, d. 18, q. 2, a. 3). In the *Summa theologiae* (ST, I, q. 27, a. 4), Thomas describes a "spirit" as a movement and vital impulse *(vitalis motio et impulsio)*, while in the Commentary on the *First Letter to the Corinthians* of St. Paul (*Sup. Cor,* II, lec. 2) it is described as a vital force *(vis vitalis)*.

8. See e.g. *Exp. Met.,* VIII, lec. 4, n. 1737.

transformed into an organic component by digestion, the semen is undifferentiated with respect to the different types of matter that it could have brought about if it had been absorbed. Today we would say that the semen is totipotent with respect to every possible organic differentiation. Not having by itself a complete species nor being part of the father, it is inanimate and so without any soul. Once detached from the father, the semen begins its formative action on the matter supplied by the mother. The contact between the male semen and the menstrual blood of the female brings about conception and the very first formation of the embryo. More precisely, the semen does not act as such on the menstrual blood but by means of a spirit in which exists, as noted, the formative power that the semen possesses.

Since the semen is inanimate, the formative power of the semen cannot be a kind of soul. Hence, it seems to be a kind of corporeal and material power passed on to the semen by the father's soul at the moment of the semen's detachment from the father at ejaculation. The purpose of the formative power is to modify the menstrual blood of the female in the appropriate ways in order to form the body of the embryo. Such a formation is a process of organization that formally ends with the coming of the human soul. We shall see later how Thomas is careful to distinguish this formative power from the souls of the father and mother, as well as from that of the embryo. For now, we only give two reasons why the formative power of the semen can be neither the father's soul nor part of it. First, the semen is separated physically from the father while the soul is not divisible. Second, the semen does not belong to the ensouled body of the father, and since the human soul is found completely in every part of the body that it vivifies, it follows that the semen is not animated by the soul of the father. From this, Thomas seems to draw the conclusion that the formative power of the semen plays only an instrumental role. As such, it only has a transitory existence for a certain amount of time.[9]

Depending causally on the father's soul, the formative power is a kind of force that brings about movement and transformation, and it is

---

9. See ST, III, q. 62, a. 4.

left by the father in the semen at the moment it is detached. As mentioned, the task of the formative power is to organize the woman's menstrual blood, preparing it for the coming of the soul. Once the soul enters the embryo, the process is then carried out directly by the soul. As a first approximation, the arrival of the soul could be placed at the very moment of conception, since conception indicates nothing else but the very first actualization of the potentiality of female matter to be ensouled, and since the first state of actuality of the matter comes from vegetative ensoulment, the act of conception and the act of vegetative ensouling of female matter coincide. In what follows, we shall make clearer this identification, but it is already apparent from these first indications that the male semen and the inseminated female matter (which constitutes the first embryonic matter) reveal different degrees of potentiality regarding being human. The male semen of itself is not living, since it lacks any soul, and so it is in remote potency to human life; the embryonic matter, on the other hand, right from conception possesses a type of ensoulment, and so immediately is in near potency to human life. Once the embryo has acquired the vegetative soul, it begins to feed and to grow on its own power.[10]

At this point, one might think that the formative power of the male semen disappears since the semen's role of "activation" is entirely finished. But things are more complicated, for Thomas seems to be of the opinion that the formative power has not yet finished its task. The formative power of the semen continues to act on the embryonic matter, endowed now with a vegetative soul, and contributes to its complexification. The simple activities of feeding and growing in size cannot explain the material modification of the embryo and its gradual acquiring of an organic and corporeal physiognomy; hence there is a need to posit the existence of a so-called "program" for material development, that is, to posit a power expressly tasked to structure the matter of a given body. Such a program can only come from the formative power, from something that is directed to produce such a material

---

10. Nutrition and growth require a distinct subject, with a minimal quantity of matter. They are not performed by prime matter. On this, see e.g. *Exp. Gen.*, I, lec. 13.

modification in view of the coming of the human soul. Under the stimulus of the formative power, which still remains in the male semen, the degree of formation and organization of the embryonic matter becomes gradually more complex allowing the embryo to pass from one state of vegetative ensoulment to another state of ensoulment that is both vegetative and sensitive.[11] The remaining action of the formative power, at last, advances the process further until the formation of the principal organs takes place, allowing the embryo to pass from a state of vegetative and sensitive ensoulment to a state of ensoulment that is at once vegetative, sensitive, and intellective or rational. The vegetative and sensitive souls are drawn from the potentiality of the female matter, in the sense that each reveals a state of actuality or a way of ensoulment that the female matter comes to acquire from the moment it is transformed into embryonic matter. On the other hand, the intellective soul is introduced from outside by a direct act of creation. The intellective soul, therefore, is incorporeal and does not act by means of corporeal organs, even if it presupposes a certain organization of the body.

This, in brief, is an introductory overview.

1. Some Constraints on Substantial Generation

The embryological doctrine of Thomas, for which we have just given a first and provisionary reconstruction, is substantially that of Aristotle, modified to take account of the infusion of the human soul by God. As we shall see, this account of the mechanisms of human generation is based on principles that today seem rather difficult to accept, and this

---

11. In Thomas's embryology, the soul is portrayed as the first principle of the kind of being that a given body exhibits. The soul must be distinguished from its capacities or "potencies" *(potentiae)*, which are the faculties through which the soul can exercise its vital functions. As we shall see in chapter two, the soul's potencies are quasi-accidental properties of the soul, although they are entirely determined by the soul itself. There are five potencies of the soul: nutritive, sensitive, intellective, appetitive, and motive. However, such potencies can exercise only three kinds or degrees of vital functions: vegetative (nutrition and growth), sensitive (movement and sensation) and intellective (will and knowledge). In the following, for the sake of brevity, I shall not strictly follow this five-fold division of potencies, but rather speak of three potencies of the soul corresponding to the three kinds of vital acts it exercises. On this division of the potencies and of vital acts, see QDA, q. 13; *Sent. De an.*, II, ch. 5.

to such an extent that not a few interpreters and followers of Thomas have felt the need to reject or at least correct significant aspects of his account. We shall examine this later in detail, along with attendant difficulties. Nevertheless, we can already note that Thomas's account depends on two notions that call for clarification: that of *generation* and that of the soul understood as the *substantial form* of the body. In many ways, Thomas's account is nothing but the logically rigorous application of a few theses concerning these two notions. To have a real understanding of his embryological teaching, then, we must begin with a brief examination of these two notions.

There are essentially four theses that govern Thomas's account of human generation:

(G1) Natural generation, as opposed to the change of qualities or of quantity (alteration) and that of place (locomotion), is a discontinuous process.

(G2) Natural generation is a process and as such takes place over time and is brought to perfection only at the end of the process; hence, what is generated only exists at the end of the process of generation.

(G3) Natural generation is a process and as such requires an external principle of activation and an internal principle of development.

(G4) Every process of generation involves a process of corruption and vice versa.

In the metaphysics of Thomas, natural generation is a phenomenon different from that of creation and alteration. In a process of creation, a substance is posited in being from nothing, while in alteration a substance remains in its proper being, changing only in certain accidental ways or aspects of its being. The genesis of the world is a typical case of the process of creation, while painting a white wall black or moving an object from one place to another are typical cases of alteration. Processes of alteration properly concern the quality and quantity of a substance or its change of place (which is, in fact, for Thomas the only true continuous process).[12] Generation, on the other hand, strictly speaking concerns only the category of substance. Unlike creation, the process of generation requires that there be a pre-existing matter-substrate that remains, but unlike alteration, such matter must be modified in such a way as to posit in being a new substance. The modification of the matter implies that it exchanges the form that it already possesses and acquires a new form. In this way the matter passes from a state that can be described as one of potentiality and privation with respect to the new form to a state that reveals the actual possession of the new form. When a statue is produced from a lump of bronze, for example, the bronze is partially in a state of being and partially in a state of non-being: the lump of bronze possesses being in that it has of itself a certain form (as a lump or block of bronze), but with respect to the form of the statue that it will subsequently acquire, it is in a state of privation or non-being. In this sense, becoming a statue for a lump of bronze can be described as a passage from a privative form to a positive form, from non-being to being, from the absence of the statue-form to the presence of the statue-form. When a lump of bronze becomes a statue, the preceding form and the privation of the final form are both lost. Hence, every process of generation involves a process of corruption and vice versa (G4). We shall see how, taking into consideration suitable differences, the example of the lump of bronze helps us to explain what takes place to the embryonic matter within the process of generation that guides the matter to become a human being.

In general, a process of generation involves three elements: (i) a matter or a material substrate that in some way remains throughout the change of form that it undergoes, becoming part of the new substance that arises from it; (ii) an initial form that is lost; (iii) and a final form that is acquired. Such an account of the process of generation is based, obviously, on a clear distinction between *matter* and *form,* two notions that to a certain degree seek to bring to light two distinct elements of a

---

12. For an explanation of the difference between substantial generation and accidental alteration, see *Exp. Gen.*, I, lec. 10. Doubts about the continuous nature of the movement of alteration can be found in SCG, II, ch. 89: compare n. 1744 b) with n. 1740 d).

generated substance. On the one hand, the fact that the process of generation is described as a change of form implies the postulation of a substrate of the forms, which substrate remains throughout the whole process of change. On the other hand, however, to distinguish the process of generation from that of alteration, it is necessary that every time there is a change of form there is a radical re-identification of the substrate in virtue of which the substrate remains but never exactly identical with itself.

The distinction between matter and form is one of the central themes of the metaphysics of Thomas, and it is a theme that he assumes as fundamental: by definition matter cannot be form and form cannot be matter. It is however difficult to determine the nature of matter for Aquinas. Intuitively, it does not seem too difficult to determine what is the form of an object. But is it possible to say whether there is and, most of all, *what* is the matter of an object beyond this or that form the object assumes? Is it possible to attribute to matter certain properties of its own? Thomas's teaching on the nature of matter is particularly complex, but in essence he seems, finally, to have two convictions. First, the notion of matter refers to a metaphysical component of the object definitely distinct from the form. Second, that component, nevertheless, cannot be determined in itself, that is, its existence and its being known can be drawn only from considerations concerning movement and change, or by analogy with what takes place in the process of constructing an artifact.

According to Thomas, this was also the position of Aristotle who, he believed, had clearly established this point in his *Physics* and in his *Metaphysics,* book seven, where he introduced the principle that matter of itself (καθ'αὐτό) is not some determinate thing, not being of itself classifiable in any of the ten categories, which concern every kind of existing thing. In addition, at the beginning of book eight of the *Metaphysics,* Aristotle clarified this basic intuition by explaining the relationships of the composite, of form and of matter to the two characteristics that define a substance in the proper and primary sense, namely, being some determinate thing (τόδε τι) and being separable (χωριστόν). According to Thomas, Aristotle maintained that the composite is something separable in an absolute sense (ἁπλῶς), and therefore, Thomas glosses, one can affirm with probability that the composite is also some determinate thing in an absolute sense. On the other hand, Aristotle presents the form as that which, being something determinate, is separable by definition (λόγῳ), and so the form is able to be "separated" only by an act by which we conceive of it in separation from matter. Aristotle does not say anything about the type of determination of the form, but the logical connection that he establishes between the two characteristics (already asserted in book five, chapter eight) leads Thomas to say that the form is something determinable only conceptually. Finally, matter is some determinate thing only potentially (δυνάμει), and so one can affirm with probability that it is also separable only potentially.[13] Being of itself lacking in form insofar as it is matter, matter is also lacking in actuality, since it is form that makes a certain thing actually exist as a thing of a certain kind.[14]

As a consequence, Thomas holds that Aristotle understood matter as what is, of itself, purely potential, and this in two senses. First, matter, insofar as it is matter, does not of itself exist as something over and above the forms, as if it were endowed with its own specific characteristics or endowed with a kind of form that is categorically different from the categorical forms that it will subsequently acquire. Second, matter is of itself something that, lacking its own proper form, has the capacity to acquire any form whatsoever. Thomas, following what in his opinion was the interpretation that Averroes had given to this Aristotelian teaching, repeats many times in his writings that the essence of matter lies in its potentiality. Hence, the conclusion of Thomas is that matter of itself is not in act, and so of itself does not exist; from this it follows finally that of itself matter cannot be known.[15]

---

13. Among the numerous places where Aristotle states this, see *Met.*, VII, 3, 1029a20 ff. and VIII, 1, 1042a26 ff. See the corresponding places of Aquinas's Commentary: *Exp. Met.*, VII, lec. 2, nn. 1285–1290; VIII, lec. 1, n. 1687. Thomas extensively illustrates this point when he comments on the first book of the *Physics*, ch. 7.

14. On the nature of matter, see what Aquinas says in the *De principiis naturae* or in his Commentary on I book of the *Physics,* works dating to the beginning and end of Aquinas's career. Not every philosopher relates form and actuality so closely together. Some philosophers, especially belonging to the Franciscan Order, try to prove that matter is endowed with a certain kind of actuality, although it is absolutely deprived of any form.

15. See, for example, the following texts: DEE, ch. 2; *Sup. De Trin.,* q. 4, a. 2; ST, I, q. 86, a. 2, ad 1; and *Exp. Met.,* VII, lec. 10, n. 1496: "Ratio autem huius est, quia materia, quae principium est

To those not familiar with the philosophy of Thomas, this conception of matter may appear obscure and counterintuitive. To avoid confusion, it is necessary to keep in mind that when one speaks of matter in this context, one is referring to the metaphysical component of a substance that is correlative to form. Ordinary matter, which we instinctively think of when we speak of matter, as the bronze of a statue, is not the matter that Thomas is referring to when he speaks of it as pure potentiality. The matter understood as pure potentiality is what Thomas and other medieval philosophers refer to as "prime matter." With this term, borrowed from Aristotle, Thomas intends to refer to that generic and primordial metaphysical substrate, of itself completely lacking in real properties, that is able to assume any form, including that of bronze, precisely because it is lacking in whatever form. Considered in itself, the bronze of a statue is not that primitive matter, but rather a material substance that is the matter for a more complex material substance, namely, the statue, and as such it is a given kind of matter, that is, matter already formed. Bronze's being bronze depends on its never being, of itself, without a certain form, and such a form accounts for a piece of bronze having certain material properties, as malleability, a certain color, etc. In reality, pure bronze does not exist, but is always this or that piece of bronze, some bronze object, the bronze of a statue or of globe. Bronze, understood as a kind of matter, is already the result of the action of a form on prime matter. Considered in relation to a statue, therefore, bronze is matter only insofar as it is a *material* constituent of that statue: insofar as it is a material constituent of the statue, bronze also possesses all those additional qualities that come from the statue-form. In the secondary literature, ordinary matter in the case of living beings often is referred to as "proximate matter" or "functional or organic matter," while prime matter is spoken of as "remote matter" or "non-functional or inorganic matter." Applying these distinctions to the case of a human being, there are three elements that must be considered: prime matter which is absolutely indeterminate;

---

individuationis, est secundum se ignota, et non cognoscitur nisi per formam, a qua sumitur ratio universalis." The idea that matter's essence consists in its potentiality is commonly traced back to Averroes's *De substantia orbis*.

a substantial form (the soul), that acts upon prime matter; and a succession of organic matters that gradually become functionally more complex (as the bones and flesh, organs such as the heart and brain, and organic parts such as the hand).

If every natural matter already possesses a form, it follows that the term "prime matter" designates a metaphysical entity that is completely unverifiable since it is lacking whatever form, but whose hypothetical existence is nevertheless required and necessary to account for the material homogeneity of the world and of the continuity of objects that undergo processes of change. If the objects of our common experience and their changes are described in this way, the form that determines matter must carry out its metaphysical action directly on prime matter. This is precisely what distinguishes the process of generation from that of alteration: while in alteration, the substrate of the forms already has its *identity* in act, in the process of generation the material substrate is lacking in whatever identity. As we shall see better later on, the substrate of the process of alteration is already a substance, while in the process of generation the substrate is only prime matter that gradually acquires different substantial identities. If prime matter cannot exist of itself without a form, it follows that the process of substitution of forms, once set in motion, must be conceived of as uninterrupted.

Now, if matter is absolutely lacking in actuality, an important consequence is that matter does not have, of itself, the capacity to actualize its own potentiality; indeed, if it had such a capacity, that capacity would have to be in act, and so matter would not be absolute potentiality. Therefore, if the process of generation is the passage from prime matter to a substance, such a process needs an agent that enables matter to be transformed into a substance, an agent, that is, that brings to act the potency of matter (G3). Such an agent is initially external.

The notion of prime or primordial matter as pure potentiality leads Thomas to deny that matter virtually includes the forms that in turn actualize it. Matter is not in potency to forms in the sense that it virtually pre-contains those forms that afterwards will specify it. If it were, the form would reveal a state of actuality only of the matter and not of the composite substance, such that matter would be the real subject of the form. But this does not match our experience. When one looks at a bronze statue, for example, one is not inclined to describe it as bronze that has the form of a statue, but as a bronze statue. The reason for this is that the preexistent matter does not persist just as it is in the composite substance, but undergoes a modification by means of the form that radically reconfigures the very identity of the preexistent matter. The form not only specifies a certain matter which is, of itself, already existing, but it also transforms that matter into a determinate substance. In other words, it is not the bronze, already with its identity, that acquires the form of a statue, but it is the form of the statue that gives identity to the bronze, determining it as the material constituent of the statue. The form, then, is the form of a substance (i.e., the statue), not of matter (i.e., bronze).[16]

If this is the profound metaphysical reason for talking of a bronze statue rather than of "statuated bronze," it follows that when it is said that matter is in potency to forms, this should not be understood in the sense that matter has inscribed in its nature the active capacity to acquire a material form. Rather it means that there is nothing in matter's own nature that impedes the acquisition of one or another substantial form. More particularly, this interpretation of the Aristotelian doctrine of generation leads Thomas to reject two theories current at that time. Thomas calls the first the "theory of hidden forms" *(latitatio formarum)*, according to which the forms already actually exist in matter, waiting to be revealed through the process of generation. He calls the second the "theory of inchoate forms" *(inchoatio formarum)*, according to which the forms exist in matter only potentially.[17] He

---

16. On this aspect, see Thomas Aquinas, *Exp. Met.*, VII, lec. 6, nn. 1414–1416. For a detailed reconstruction of Aristotle's account of substantial generation, see Sarah Waterlow, *Nature, Change, and Agency in Aristotle's Physics* (Oxford: Oxford University Press, 1982), and Mary L. Gill, *Aristotle on Substance. The Paradox of Unity* (Princeton, N.J.: Princeton University Press, 1991).

17. For Aquinas's interpretation of these theories, see *Sent.*, II, d. 18, q. 1, a. 2; *Exp. Met.*, VII, lec. 7, n. 1430: "E contrario autem quidam posuerunt propter hanc difficultatem, formas preexistere in materia actu, quod est ponere latitationem formarum"; lec. 8, n. 1442: "sciendum est autem, quod occasione horum verborum, quae hic dicuntur, quidam ponunt, quod in omni generatione naturali est aliquod principium activum in materia, quod quidem est forma in potentia praeexistens in materia, quae est quaedam inchoatio formae" and n. 1442d: "Haec autem opinio videtur propinqua ponentibus latitationem formarum. Cum enim nihil agat nisi secundum quod est in actu: si partes

rejects both of them. For him, the acquisition of a form by matter or the bringing forth *(educere)* of a form from matter is nothing but the bringing of the potentiality of matter into act.[18] In other words, Thomas embraces an "externalist" conception of form, according to which forms come to matter externally and are not included virtually in matter, whether that inclusion is described as a state of latent actuality or as a state of potential germination. Being a statue, then, is not a state that the bronze virtually pre-contained, but rather is a state that the bronze was able to realize. In the case of a human, such an analysis reveals that certain forms that matter will acquire, as vegetative and sensitive ensoulment, are nothing but two states of actualization of the potentiality of matter. Human matter did not pre-contain these states, but was simply made in such a way that it could receive or acquire them. In addition, these two forms of ensoulment are arranged according to an order of growing functional complexity and according to a recip-rocal ordering that is fixed and not reversible. Indeed, once actualized by a form, the potentiality of matter undergoes a double, symmetrical constraint: matter is no longer able to receive any possible form, and the acquired form orients matter toward the acquisition of a further form toward which the already acquired form itself was oriented.

It should be said that it is not in fact easy to distinguish the Domin-ican master's theory from how he understands the "theory of inchoate forms" *(inchoatio formarum)*, and his arguments against these two medieval theories are not entirely convincing, as we shall see below.

---

vel inchoationes formarum quae sunt in materia, habent aliquam virtutem activam, sequitur quod sint aliquo modo actu, quod est ponere latitationem formarum"; *De virt.*, q. 1, a. 11; ST, I, q. 45, a. 8; I–II, q. 63, a. 1. At times Thomas equates the theory of inchoate forms with Augustine's doctrine of "seminal reasons" *(rationes seminales)*. He rejects both of them for the same reasons. See e.g. *Sent.*, II, d. 18, q. 1, a. 2, ad 2; also *De virt.*, q. 5, a. 9, ad 8. For a discussion of the different interpretations of the doctrine of seminal reasons, see *Sent.*, II, d. 18, q. 1, a. 2.

18. See SCG, II, ch. 86, n. 1709: "Omnis forma quae educitur in esse per materiae trasmuta-tionem, est forma educta de potentia materiae: hoc enim est materiam transmutari, de potentia in actum reduci." Usually, Thomas calls the potentiality of matter "passive potency" *(potentia passiva)*, in opposition to the "active potency" *(potentia activa)* of the agent (see e.g. *Sent.*, I, d. 3, q. 4, a. 2, ad 4; d. 42, q. 1, a. 1 and ad 1; II, d. 18, q. 1, a. 2; III, d. 3, q. 2, a. 1, ad 2; SCG, II, ch. 45; QDP, q. 1, a. 1; *Exp. Met.*, V, lec. 14; IX, lec. 1).

Still, it is clear that Thomas is preoccupied with defending a description of generation as the real acquisition of a form rather than the unveiling of a form that the material subject in some way already possessed. According to Thomas, if things were otherwise, there would not be true generation.

It should also be noted that in the metaphysics of Thomas, not every form reveals a state of actuality of matter. In the case of human beings, only bodily and material forms, as the vegetative and sensitive souls, reveal such states.[19] On the other hand, it is well known that throughout his career Thomas firmly maintained the thesis of the immateriality and incorporeality of the rational or intellective soul, insofar as it is a subsistent substantial form, a form, that is, capable of exercising operations that transcend the body. Thomas seeks to prove the immaterial and incorporeal character of the rational soul in various ways, but the main argument that Thomas turns to in defending the rational soul's separateness from the body is the following. Since each thing operates in the way that it exists, if it can be shown that the rational soul carries out an operation that does not occur by means of bodily organs, and if it cannot be demonstrated that such a soul is corporeal, one can conclude that the rational soul has a type of being that does not depend on the body. But since it can be proven that the rational soul is not corporeal nor acts by means of bodily organs—given that the rational soul is in potency to knowing the forms of all things, and hence it itself cannot have the form of any particular thing, for such a form would impede or obstruct it knowing the other forms—it follows that the rational soul has a type of being separate from the body.[20] This conviction of Thomas is also defended by his appealing to the principle that no bodily agent can extend its action beyond the limits of its own nature, and so (independently of the way in which the material formation of humans is

---

19. See e.g. QDP, q. 3, a. 11, ad 11.

20. Thomas formulates the argument in various places. See, for instance, QDA, a. 1; QDP, q. 3, a. 10; ST, I, q. 75, a. 2 ff. This is the first argument that Thomas proposes against the thesis that the rational soul is transmitted through the male semen in QDP, q. 3, a. 9, 22b. The argument presents many problems on which I cannot dwell here. For a discussion, see Robert Pasnau, *Theories of Cognition in the Later Middle Ages* (Cambridge: Cambridge University Press, 1997).

explained) any strictly materialist theory cannot account for the rational activity of the soul, which requires therefore, the positing of a cause belonging to a different metaphysical order.[21]

To summarize, we have seen that an external agent is necessary in order to bring matter from potency to act, and that the form is, usually, a state of actuality of matter. But once any process of generation begins to be actualized, it proceeds on its own, fed by an internal principle of development. In fact, what distinguishes a living organism from an inanimate entity is its possessing an internal principle of movement.[22] On the basis of this principle, Thomas quarrels often in his writings with the Platonic account of generation. More specifically, he maintains that to invoke separated Ideas as principles for the generation of a sensible substance is completely futile. Since what is generated is some determinate thing *(hoc aliquid)* and what is generated must be similar in form to what generates it, what generates must also be some determinate thing. But if separated Ideas were some determinate thing, being separated from sensible substances, they would need another Idea to explain their very existence, and this would generate an infinite regress. Hence, the Ideas are not a determinate thing, but rather refer to *how* things are *(quale quid),* that is, they do not designate a subject, but rather express a property or substantial quality of a subject. As a consequence, Aristotle had rightly pointed out, according to Thomas, how the Ideas are useless in accounting for generation.[23]

In conclusion, a last point to note is that for Thomas form is the final cause of generation, being that towards which generation tends, but it is not, in the proper sense, what is generated. Every process of generation

---

21. See ST, I, q. 118, a. 2; QDP, q. 3, a. 9, 22b: "secunda ratio est, quia impossibile est actionem corporeae virtutis ad hoc elevari quod virtutem penitus spiritualem et incorpoream causare possit; nihil enim agit ultra speciem suam."

22. Thomas extensively deals with this topic in his Commentary on the second book of *Physics*. For a more concise treatment, see *Exp. Met.,* VII, lec. 6, n. 1381 ff.

23. See *Exp. Met.,* VII, lec. 7, nn. 1427–1431. Following Averroes, Thomas assumes that this is the first of three critiques that Aristotle addresses to Plato in book seven of the *Metaphysics*. The other two critiques concern the thesis that the Ideas are separate from sensible substances while expressing at the same time their essence (VII, ch. 6) and the thesis that universal Ideas are substances (VII, ch. 13).

produces composites of matter and form, but strictly speaking, neither matter nor form are generated.[24] Thomas argues that if matter were also generated, either there would be an infinite regress in a series of material substrates, since every process of generation implies a form acting and modifying a given matter, or generation would be indistinguishable from creation. The form, for its part, is by definition that by which something has being. Hence, if it were also generated, there would have to be a second form by which the first form has being, and so on indefinitely. To generate a composite, then, is not so much to produce a new matter and form, but rather to organize a pre-existing matter in such a way that it can receive a form, and this is nothing else, in the majority of the cases, than to actualize the very potentiality of matter. For this reason, a composite does not receive a substantial form because it is in some relation to a separated Idea, but simply because the substantial form actualizes matter, coming to coincide with the realization of this actualization. In the example of the bronze statue, the statue-form is both the formal principle that guides the act of modeling bronze into a statue, and also the expression of the achieved completion of the actualization of the potentiality of bronze-matter to be a statue. In relation to the generated composite, the substantial form, therefore, indicates a certain state of actuality (which in the case of generated living things can be described in terms of biological function); in relation to matter, the form indicates instead the formal principle of actualization of its potentiality. The artist that models the bronze is instead the efficient cause.

2. Some Constraints on Substantial Form

In order to understand the embryological teaching of Thomas, it is necessary to keep in mind these theses on generation. But as was mentioned earlier, his embryological account is also firm on another point: it characterizes the human soul as the substantial form of the body. The notion of substantial form plays a key role in the description of the

---

24. See DPN, § 2; *Exp. Met.*, VII, lec. 6, nn. 1386–1393, and VIII, lec. 3, n. 1716.

process of generation both because it emerges as the principle responsible for the actualization of matter and because it constitutes the final end of generation. For this reason, in addition to the theses concerning generation, the embryological theory of Thomas maintains certain theses concerning the status and function of substantial form. Three are particularly significant for our purposes:

(F1) Substantial form informs prime matter instantly and
     immediately.
(F2) Substantial form is one and indivisible.
(F3) Substantial form does not admit of degrees.

The philosophical formulation of these theses results from the identification of the rational soul with the substantial form of humans, as also from the literal interpretation of the Aristotelian "definition" of the soul as the form or act of an organic, physical body that has life potentially.[25] The reasoning that leads Thomas to develop these theses is rigorous, and we can reconstruct it as follows. As was said, Thomas is of the opinion that the ten Aristotelian categories exhaustively classify all possible and actual existing things; every thing falls under one and only one category. Given this, Thomas assumes that the most general notion of being is subdivided *directly and immediately* into the ten categories of Aristotle and not by means of additional formal differences.[26] The ten categories present all the ways that a thing is or can be. This means that when one describes the kind of being that a thing has, one cannot describe that being in terms of a formal delimitation of the general concept of being. To be clear, one cannot say that a thing somehow just exists, i.e., generally, and then it exists in a given, specific

---

25. Aristotle formulates such a characterization of the soul in the *De anima*, II, 1, 412a19–22, 27–28, and 412b5–6. Aristotelian interpreters have greatly debated this characterization, especially its value as a definition. For the state of the question, see Christopher J. Shields, "Aristotle's Psychology," in Edward N. Zalta, ed., *The Stanford Encyclopedia of Philosophy (Winter 2005 Edition)*, www.plato.stanford.edu (accessed May 1, 2012). For an introduction to the medieval discussions on the nature of the soul and the intellect, see Richard C. Dales, *The Problem of the Rational Soul in the Thirteenth Century* (Leiden: Brill, 1995).

26. See e.g. *Exp. Met.*, V, lec. 9, nn. 889–890.

way. For example, being human cannot be explicated as the formal delimitation of the general notion of being by humanity, nor being white as the delimitation of the general notion of being by whiteness. If being gave rise to the ten categories by additional formal differences (for example, if from "being" came "being human" by virtue of the difference "human"), and if one held that such differences imply modes of being that are different from that mode implied by being considered absolutely, in terms of logic being would be a genus. But if so, the formal differences, which bring about different kinds of being, would have to be external to the concept of being (for a genus, of itself, is none of the opposed differences that divide it), and therefore they would be conceptually a non-being, which cannot be. According to Thomas, one of the greatest virtues of the Aristotelian critique of Plato in the *Metaphysics* was to show that being cannot be a genus. Certainly, Thomas believed that one can isolate *a posteriori* an absolute concept of being that is different from each of the concepts corresponding to the individual kinds of categorial being, but it does not follow that being has its own concept that is different *a priori* from all the concepts corresponding to these kinds of categorial being. In other words, although one can use a notion of generic or undifferentiated being, this does not imply that such a notion refers to a kind of absolute and generic being that things possess before being specified in one way or another.

If being is not a genus, therefore, Thomas argues that the term "being" cannot have a fixed and constant meaning however generic, and so it follows that the concept of being is not univocal for Thomas. But neither is it an equivocal concept, for when we ask about the being of a substance and the being of a quality, in both cases we are looking to individuate the existence conditions of a substance and of a quality. In a certain way, the investigation is the same, and this is possible only if "being" is used in the same sense in the case of a substance and of a quality. If the concept of being is neither univocal nor equivocal, it follows that being is subdivided directly and immediately into the ten kinds of categorial being, and so taken in itself the concept of being can only be analogous, a concept, that is, predicable of the categories according to a certain order of priority and of reference.

A number of points are contained in what we have just said. First, a thing cannot exist without also being either a substance or a quality or an item of one of the other categorial kinds. Second, being (for) a substance is different from being (for) a quality, but being a substance, for a substance, expresses exactly the same thing as is being a quality, for a quality. Third, being a quality, for a quality, requires the being of a substance, for a quality exists to the degree that there is a substance and it is predicated of that substance. Substantial being and accidental being (the latter being taken from the nine non-substantial categories) are the only two possible ways of being, and hence everything that exists can be called either a substance or an accident. More particularly, Thomas believes that a substantial form (as the form of humanity) is what gives absolute being *(esse simpliciter)* to a thing, while an accidental form (as the form of whiteness) is what gives qualified being (*esse tale* or *secundum quid*) to a thing. A substantial form, of necessity, precedes an accidental form.[27]

In the light of this general conception of being, which we have here only summarized, we can easily derive the theses mentioned earlier.[28] Take (F1): Substantial form informs prime matter instantly and immediately. If the substantial form did not directly inform prime matter, there would have to be intermediaries, and these would be either substances or accidents. If they were accidents, then an accidental form would precede a substantial form, and it would be in fact the real

---

27. The distinction between substantial form and accidental form recurs in many places. For a clear formulation, see *Sent. De an.*, II, ch. 1, 71,242–257; ST, I, q. 76, a. 4, and QDA, q. 9, 79–80,139–157: "Dicendum quod inter omnia, esse est illud quod immediatius et intimius conuenit rebus, ut dicitur in libro De causis. Vnde oportet quod, cum materia habeat esse actu per formam, quod forma dans esse materie ante omnia intelligatur aduenire materie, et immediatius ceteris sibi inesse. Est autem hoc proprium forme substantialis quod det materie esse simpliciter—ipsa enim est per quam res est hoc ipsum quod est—. Non autem per formas accidentales habet esse simpliciter, set esse secundum quid, puta esse magnum uel coloratum uel aliquid tale. Si qua igitur forma est que non det materie esse simpliciter, set adueniat materie iam existenti in actu per aliam formam, non erit forma substantialis. Ex quo patet quod inter formam substantialem et materiam non potest cadere aliqua forma substantialis media." See also SCG, II, ch. 68.

28. Aquinas's conception of being is one of the most controversial points of his thought. The question is particularly complex and this is not the place to examine it. For a good discussion, see Rudi A. Te Velde, *Participation and Substantiality in Thomas Aquinas* (Leiden: Brill, 1995), and especially John F. Wippel, *The Metaphysical Thought of Thomas Aquinas. From Finite Being to Uncreated Being* (Washington, D.C.: The Catholic University of America Press, 2000).

substantial form of the prime matter. If they were substances, the substantial form would be reduced to an accidental form, since it would come after those substances, and so it would only give a thing qualified being. From the first thesis springs the second (F2): Substantial form is one and indivisible. If the substantial form immediately informs prime matter, it follows that there cannot be a plurality of substantial forms.[29] If there were more than one substantial form, every form coming after the first would turn out to be accidental, since it would be added to a substance, which is already in being. Such an argument also responds to the suggestion that the substantial form is divided into parts or is found in different subjects. And from this, one obtains the third thesis (F3): Substantial form does not admit of degrees. Because of the immediacy of this union of form and matter, the substantial form cannot undergo a process leading to greater perfection nor undergo any step by step development. Any possible perfecting has to do with the functioning of matter already informed, but not with the fact that it is informed. A modification of matter with respect to form implies the entering of a new substantial form. Following an Aristotelian axiom quite often cited at that time, Thomas compares the species of things to numbers *(species sunt sicut numeri)*: as the addition or subtraction of a unit changes a number, so the addition or subtraction of a perfection changes the form and so the species of a thing.[30] What is more, since a

---

29. The doctrine of the plurality of substantial forms, normally traced back to the *Fons vitae* of Ibn Gebirol (Avicebron), was rather widespread in Aquinas's day. Thomas rejects it on several occasions (see most notably ST, I, q. 76, a. 3), although at the very beginning of his career he himself was in doubt as to whether or not to admit the existence of a "form of corporeity" *(forma corporeitatis)* taken as distinct from and preceding the substantial form of man. On this, see Marie-Dominique Roland-Gosselin, *Le "De ente et essentia" de s. Thomas d'Aquin: texte etabli d'apres les manuscrits parisiens. Introduction, notes et études historiques* (Paris: Vrin, 1948). On medieval theories of the plurality of forms, one finds still useful the work of Roberto Zavalloni, *Richard de Mediavilla et la controverse sur la pluralité des formes* (Leuven: Editions de l'Institut Supérieur de Philosophie, 1951).

30. See, for example, SCG, II, ch. 44; IV, ch. 41, n. 3789 a); ST, I, q. 47, a. 2; III, q. 52, a. 1: "Ut igitur huius rei veritas manifestetur, considerandum est quod illud secundum quod sortitur aliquid speciem, oportet esse fixum et stans, et quasi indivisibile, quaecumque enim ad illud attingunt, sub specie continentur; quaecumque autem recedunt ab illo, vel in plus vel in minus, pertinent ad aliam speciem, vel perfectiorem vel imperfectiorem. Unde Philosophus dicit, in VIII *Metaphys.*, quod species rerum sunt sicut numeri, in quibus additio vel diminutio variat speciem. Si igitur aliqua forma, vel quaecumque res, secundum seipsam vel secundum aliquid sui, sortiatur rationem

substantial form transforms the entire matter in a substance, Thomas argues that the substantial form has to be the proper form of the whole body and each of its parts.[31] Hence, the substantial form cannot be divided if the body is divided. Every separation of a part from the whole implies that that part ceases to be formed and, if the form is a soul, ceases to be animate.

The combination of these theses helps us to understand why Thomas denied that the substantial form is already present in the male semen, and also why he held that it is not transmitted or even infused into the embryo at the moment of conception.[32] It is not necessary, for the moment, to explore further these theses; for our purposes, it is sufficient that they have been introduced. We shall return to them in the following chapters, showing their role in the explanation Thomas gives of the embryogenetic process.

---

speciei; necesse est quod, secundum se considerata, habeat determinatam rationem, quae neque in plus excedere, neque in minus deficere possit"; *De virt.*, q. 5, a. 3; *Exp. Gen.*, I, lec. 8.

31. See, for instance, ST, I, q. 76, a. 8.

32. The two cases, however, do not overlap. Even granting that the human soul is not transmitted to the embryo by the male semen, this does not exclude that it can be infused by God at the moment of conception. We shall see in the following what reasons Thomas has for also excluding this second case.

CHAPTER TWO

The Nature of the Human Soul

IN CHAPTER I, we discussed certain theses concerning generation and substantial form that are particularly helpful for understanding the way in which Thomas develops Aristotelian embryology. Before passing on to a more detailed examination of his position concerning the status of the embryo, we must first clarify the nature of the human soul, especially the way in which Thomas interprets Aristotle's general characterization of the soul in the second book of his *De anima*, namely, as "the form or act of an organic, physical body that has life potentially." In this chapter, I will not offer a comprehensive reconstruction of all the aspects and problems connected with this theme; that would require a separate work given the complexity of the question and its importance, both philosophical and theological.[1] I intend, instead, to

---

1. For an introduction to Aquinas's philosophical anthropology, see Sofia Vanni Rovighi, *L'antropologia filosofica di san Tommaso d'Aquino* (Milano: Vita e Pensiero, 1972); Robert Pasnau, *Thomas Aquinas on Human Nature: A Philosophical Study of Summa Theologiae, 1a 75–89* (Cambridge: Cambridge University Press, 2002); Jan A. Aertsen, *Nature and Creature: Thomas Aquinas's Way of Thought* (Leiden: E. J. Brill, 1988); and John F. Wippel, *The Metaphysical Thought of Thomas Aquinas:*

bring to light only certain consequences and difficulties of the Thomistic conception of the human soul, points that will take on their full significance when we evaluate Thomas's position regarding a number of significant bioethical questions.

1. The Unity of the Human Being and the Soul as the Substantial Form of the Body

Often in theology, even in medieval times, a human being is described as a union or composition of soul and body.[2] The idea of the union of soul and body can lead to thinking of the soul and the body as entities independent from one another, each with its proper being and identity, the union of which needs explanation in some way. Thomas is well aware of this dualistic vision of a human being, rather widespread among the theologians of his time, and he repeatedly rejects it in his works with various arguments. Why is such a dualistic description unable to capture the deepest essence of our human nature?

Without entering into the details of the various arguments of Thomas, some of which, however, will be examined later, his central point is that such an explanation cannot give an adequate account of the intrinsic and essential *unity* of a human being. Already Aristotle, at the end of the eighth book of his *Metaphysics,* had noted that every description aimed at presenting the soul as something independent of the body gives rise to the problem of explaining what it is that keeps them together.[3] Take the

---

From Finite Being to Uncreated Being (Washington, DC: Catholic University of America Press, 2000). More recently, see Massimiliano Lenzi, "Alberto e Tommaso sulla natura dell'anima umana," *Archives d'histoire doctrinale et littéraire du Moyen Âge* 74 (2007): 27–58, and *Anima, forma e sostanza: Filosofia e teologia nel dibattito antropologico del XIII secolo* (Spoleto, Italy: CISAM, 2011).

2. On this view, see the following contributions by Eleonore Stump: "Non-Cartesian Substance Dualism and Materialism without Reductionism," *Faith and Philosophy* 12 (1995): 505–531, esp. 512 ff.; *Aquinas* (London: Routledge, 2003), ch. 6; and "Forms and Bodies: The Soul," in Maria C. Pacheco and José Meirinhos, eds., *Intellect and Imagination in Medieval Philosophy,* 4 vols. (Turnhout, Belgium: Brepols, 2006), vol. 3, 1379–1387. For different proposed interpretations, compare Pasnau, *Thomas Aquinas on Human Nature,* 408, and Fernand van Steenberghen, *Thomas Aquinas and Radical Aristotelianism* (Washington, DC: Catholic University of America Press, 1980), 73–74.

3. See Aristotle, *Metaphysics,* VIII, 6, 1045b7 ff.; see Aquinas's Commentary in *Exp. Met.,* VIII, lec. 5, n. 1767.

example, discussed by Aristotle, of letters and a syllable. What distinguishes a syllable from a vowel and a consonant—as "ba"—is the arrangement of those letters; that is, the fact that such letters, i.e., "b" and "a," are neither written nor pronounced separately. If one were to describe that arrangement of letters as an element of the same kind as the vowel and the consonant, one would have to introduce a new element to account for the union of that arrangement with the letters, and this way of reasoning would be repeated indefinitely. The upshot is that the arrangement of the letters is not, for Aristotle, something different from the letters that are arranged in a given way; nonetheless it is what distinguishes a syllable from a sum of two letters.

With necessary provisos, this argument can be adapted to the case of the relation between soul and body. On the one hand, if the (human) soul were taken as an entity separate from the body and of the same metaphysical type as the body, one would have to introduce a third element of connection, and in this way one would risk an infinite regress. But on the other hand, if such a third element of connection were not introduced, it would remain inexplicable how such heterogeneous entities as the soul and body could be united together and how one could save the intrinsic unity of a human being. For Thomas, the greatest drawback to thinking of the soul as somehow extrinsically related to the body, as for example, what moves is related to what is moved, is that there is no way to avoid considering a human as an entirely accidental unity. At first look, this result does not seem to be particularly problematic, but conceding that the soul and body form an accidental unity can have unexpected consequences. In the first place, the body would already possess a form that identifies it as a human body before and independently of the action that the soul exercises upon it. In the second place, if the union of the soul with the body were not essential, then in principle nothing would stop the body from receiving over time different souls, or being ensouled with a number of souls, or even that the same soul could ensoul, simultaneously or successively, different bodies. Obviously, one could accept these consequences, but it is clear that doing so would involve various complications, both philosophically and theologically. For example, one would have serious problems in explaining the transtemporal identity of a human being and in safe-guarding individual moral responsibility.

Theologically, the idea that the soul is a substance independent of the body—such that ensouling a body would be more of a function (*officium*) of the soul than of its essence—raises the problem of accounting for why the soul at a certain moment is united to the body. In his writings, Thomas considers various accounts, but maintains that every attempt to understand the soul as a spiritual substance existing of itself is doomed. In the tradition, the way most often followed is to hold that souls were created before the bodies and that only subsequently were united to bodies, a position, derived distantly from Origen, condemned by the Catholic Church. Setting aside its heterodox character, Thomas holds that this position encounters difficulties in explaining the numerical differentiation of souls, since it is matter that brings about the numerical multiplication and differentiation of forms.

But the greatest theological problem Aquinas seems to see is that this position is entirely unsuccessful in explaining the reason why souls are united to bodies. On the one hand, one cannot say that to be united or able to be united with the body is part of the nature of the soul, for then, unless there is some hindrance, every soul would be naturally united to a body from the beginning of its existence. Besides, what is part of the nature of a thing is a perfection of that thing. But if the soul were already perfect without being united to a body, such a union would be a perfection only for the body, but not for the soul. But if the union were a perfection also for the soul, one would have to admit that God had made things in an initial state of imperfection. On the other hand, if being united or able to be united with a body were not part of the nature of the soul, any union with the body would have to be the result of an act of will. But this cannot be, since to desire and choose a body is not in the power of the soul, as neither is it in its power to leave a body (setting aside that such a desire would be irrational, since souls would desire something for which they had no need);[4] nor would souls

---

4. See ST, I, q. 118, a. 3.

have been able to have this power or desire if they had been created before any body. Souls could not be united with bodies even by the will of God, for then, either souls would be taken from a state of perfection to a state of imperfection, or on the other hand, once again, if to be united to a body were for them a perfection or were natural, there is no reason why (again, unless there be some hindrance contrary to nature) souls are not united immediately to a body. Nor, finally, can one say that souls are united to bodies because of humans' sin, for then the union of the soul with the body would not be provided for immediately by God but would depend on an accidental and subsequent cause.[5]

Besides attacking it from a theological perspective, Thomas also rejects the conception of the soul as a spiritual subsistent substance with philosophical arguments. As was said, if the soul were a substance separated from the body, we would be unable to account for the metaphysical essential unity of soul and body. A second argument given by Thomas is that we would also be unable to account for the psychological connection between the intellective function of the soul and its sensitive function. The soul's sensitive function requires bodily organs since it deals with the external sensorial world, so it requires the soul be united to the body. On the other hand, the intellective function, even presupposing the sensitive function, performs acts that do not need specific bodily organs. If the soul in its entirety were a substance separated from the body, either we would have to allow, in opposition to common experience, that the soul is able to receive sensations separately from bodily organs (granted that it is one and the same soul that exercises sensitive and intellective acts), or we would have to allow that the intellective function is completely disconnected from the sensitive function. For these and similar reasons, Thomas thinks that describing the soul as a complete substance, which can be classified *per se* under a species, is untenable. If the soul cannot be taken as a separate spiritual substance, it follows that it must be taken as a *form*. Specifically, Thomas argues that the soul must be seen as the *substantial form* of the body.

Many studies have shown that Thomas had developed his teaching

---

5. These arguments recur in various places. For a clear formulation, see QDP, q. 3, a. 10, 70–71.

of the soul as the substantial form of the body in opposition to the then current theological doctrines dominant at the University of Paris, which doctrines were Platonic and Augustinian in character in that they held that the soul is a subsistent spiritual substance.[6] But as one can easily imagine, to deny that the soul is a separate substance and instead emphasize its character as a form can have the drawback of making the soul equivalent to other forms that are material and bodily, and theologically this could lead to a type of materialism regarding the soul and imply its mortality and corruptibility. Thomas was fully aware of these possible consequences. But in the face of this, he does not return to a description of the soul as a separate spiritual substance. Instead, his move is to establish an intermediate status for the soul between being a separate spiritual substance and being a material form. To do this, Thomas weakens the notion of subsistence or separate existence, distinguishing between what subsists in the full sense, and so is classifiable under a species for it is a complete substance, and that which subsists in a lesser sense, since it carries out operations that do not depend on another nor can be attributed to another, and so is not classifiable under a species except by reduction for it is not a complete substance.[7]

---

6. See especially the studies by Bernardo-Carlos Bazán, "Pluralisme de formes ou dualisme de substances?" *Revue philosophique de Louvain* 67 (1969): 30–73; *Préface,* in Sancti Thomae de Aquino *Quaestiones disputatae de anima, Opera Omnia,* t. 24, 1 (Rome: Commissio Leonina-Les Éditions du Cerf, 1996), 1*–102*; and "The Human Soul: Form and Substance? Thomas Aquinas's Critique of Eclectic Aristotelianism," *Archives d'histoire doctrinale et littéraire du Moyen Âge* 64 (1997): 95–126.

7. Technically, Thomas introduces this specification by discussing the idea that the soul is "some determinate thing" *(hoc aliquid)*. To defend his point, Thomas distinguishes two senses of the expression "some determinate thing" and states that only the first is true of the soul: "Ad primum ergo dicendum quod hoc aliquid potest accipi dupliciter, uno modo, pro quocumque subsistente, alio modo, pro subsistente completo in natura alicuius speciei. Primo modo, excludit inhaerentiam accidentis et formae materialis, secundo modo, excludit etiam imperfectionem partis. Unde manus posset dici hoc aliquid primo modo, sed non secundo modo. Sic igitur, cum anima humana sit pars speciei humanae, potest dici hoc aliquid primo modo, quasi subsistens, sed non secundo modo, sic enim compositum ex anima et corpore dicitur hoc aliquid" (ST, I, q. 75, a. 2, ad 1). See also QDA, q. 1, 7, 191–192 and 197–199. In general, "to subsist" *(subsistere),* for Thomas, is said of a determinate being (see *Sent.,* I, d. 23, q. 1, a. 1). On this, see also *Sent.,* I, d. 17, q. 1, a. 2, ad 1; *Sent. De an.,* II, ch. 1; ST, I, q. 75, a. 2, ad 1. Worries about the characterization of the soul as "some determinate thing" were raised by Albert the Great. See *Commentarius in quattuor libros Sententiarum,* II, d. 17 C, a. 2, ad 2; *Summa de Creaturis,* p. 1, tr. 1, q. 2, a. 2, ad diff. 3, ad 1. But see also Thomas Aquinas, *Sent.,* II, d. 17, q. 1, a. 1, ad 1; Bonaventure, *Commentaria in quattuor libros Sententiarum,* II, d. 17,

Armed with this distinction, Thomas argues that that which completely subsists and is able to be classified under a species is neither the soul nor the body (namely the form and matter, which only come under the category of substance "reductively," that is, as principles or essential parts of a substantial composite), but the human understood as composed of both. With respect to the "strong" sense of subsisting, the soul is only a part of what subsists, and as a part the soul does not exist in act in the whole that subsists and in which it exists, nor is the soul separable from the whole. Nevertheless, the soul has some claim to being subsistent because, as was discussed in the first chapter, the soul is able to engage in an operation in separation from bodily organs and it cannot be demonstrated that the soul is corporeal.[8] As a consequence, the final position of Thomas is nuanced and qualified, consisting in two claims: (1) the soul is not completely subsistent and classifiable under a species; nonetheless (2) the soul is something that is subsistent and somehow classifiable under a species. What is the importance of this distinction for a theory of human nature that describes the soul as the substantial form of the body?

Up until now, we have seen the arguments that Thomas uses to reject the idea that the soul is a (separate spiritual) substance and that he concludes that the soul is a form. In a successive step, we have seen that Thomas defends the thesis that the soul nevertheless has a kind of substantiality by distinguishing two senses of subsistence. At this point, Thomas endeavors to show that describing the soul as the substantial form of the body is philosophically consistent, and this is the most problematic and controversial point in his strategy. Thomas's greatest difficulty is in reconciling two theses that seem irreconcilable: on the one hand, the thesis that the soul is the form of the body, and on the other hand, the thesis that the soul's intellectual operation takes place in separation from the body. Throughout his career, Thomas undertook at length to demonstrate that these two ideas are consistent.[9] This is not

---

a. 1, q. 2, arg. 6. For further discussions of this question, see the following works of Aquinas: *Sent.*, II, d. 1, q. 2, a. 4, d. 17, q. 2, a. 1; SCG, II, chs. 56–59; ST, I, q. 75, a. 2 and q. 76, a. 1; QDP, q. 3, aa. 9 and 11; QDSC, a. 2; DUI, ch. 3; CT, I, chs. 80 and 87.

8. On the incorporeality of the soul, see ST, I, q. 75, a. 1.

9. Extensive treatments can be found in ST, I, q. 76, a. 1, and in DUI.

the place to dwell on the details of this aspect of Thomas's philosophy of human nature and the arguments he brings forward in support of it. For our purposes, we can confine ourselves to noting that his attempted resolution of the problem takes place in two stages. First, Thomas demonstrates that it can be proven that the soul is the substantial form of the body. Second, he reconciles the two theses by confining the character of the soul as separate to its ability to exercise acts, such as intellectual acts, that take place in separation from the body.

Regarding the first point, Thomas elaborates the following argument: that by virtue of which something primarily operates is the form of that to which that operation can be attributed. But something operates insofar as it is in act, and so that by virtue of which something is in act is that by virtue of which it operates. In the case of living beings, the soul is that by virtue of which something primarily lives, and to live is the act of a living body; therefore, the soul is that by virtue of which something primarily performs vital operations. But because that by virtue of which something primarily operates is its form, it follows that the soul is the form of the body to which are attributed the vital operations.[10] As to the second point, Thomas rejects the "Averroistic" conclusion that if something is separated from the body as to its operating *(in operari)*, it is also separated from the body as to its being *(in esse)*. Rather, he understands the separate character of the soul in a weaker way. For Thomas, the separate character of the soul means two things: first, that what can be counted as the form of the body has *a power* that transcends the body, that is, a power that is not performed by any bodily organs; second, that the soul has a noncorporeal nature.

Earlier we said that Thomas's principal argument is that if the soul is the form of a given body and it is in some way subsistent, then the soul is a *subsistent substantial form* of a given body. This argument has certain consequences, two of which should be highlighted. (1) Insofar as it is the *substantial form* of a body, for a soul to be just is to animate a body. In this sense, Thomas closely follows Aristotle in holding that a soul and to be (for) a soul are not different, since to be (for) a soul is

---

10. The argument is briefly but clearly presented in ST, I, q. 76, a. 1 and extensively examined in *Sent. De an.,* II, chs. 1–3.

precisely to be the form of a body: a soul, that is, just *is* a given body's being animated.[11] If this is the essence of the soul, the soul cannot lose its inclination to animate a body even if it becomes separated from the body, and this gives an acceptable philosophical sense to the resurrection of bodies at the end of time, when souls and bodies will once again be perfectly united.[12]

(2) Insofar as the soul is a *subsistent* substantial form, it has a kind of being that neither depends upon nor is caused by the body. This does not mean, however, that the soul is entirely identical with its being, that is, that it is none other than its being. The soul cannot undergo a process of corruption; nonetheless being can be removed from the soul. One of the pillars of Thomas's philosophy of human nature is that the soul, conceived as a form, is not composed in its turn by matter and form; hence, it cannot naturally lose its being, since as form it is act and as act, of itself it possesses being. To be corrupted, it would have to lose its form, but since it does not possess any form other than itself, the soul cannot be corrupted. Only material beings can be corrupted properly speaking because once form is taken away what remains is matter, which, insofar as it is pure potentiality, cannot be in act.[13] For Thomas, corruptibility is found only within the process of generation of material beings. The soul, as immaterial, is incorruptible since it is purely actual.

---

11. In some places Thomas notes that the property of being able to be united to a body is part of the soul's essence (see, e.g., QDA, q. 3, ad 15 and ad 19; q. 7; ST, I, q. 75, a. 7, ad 3). Note, however, that such a statement does not mean that the body itself is part of the soul's essence, nor does it mean that the soul's essence precisely consists in its being united to a body (QDP, q. 3, a. 11). The inclusion in the soul's essence of the possibility or capacity to be united to a body allows Thomas to reject the following argument: if the soul is "some determinate thing," it is necessary that it be individual; hence, it is individual either in virtue of something else (*ex alio*) or in virtue of itself (*ex se*). In the first case, since the soul is the form of the body, the soul would be individual in virtue of the body, so that once the body is corrupted, the soul no longer would be individual. In the second case, either the soul is a simple item, and so the soul would be formally and therefore specifically different from another, or it is a complex item, and so the soul could not be the form of the body. Hence, Thomas concludes, it is impossible for the soul to be simultaneously the form of the body and "some determinate thing." Thomas's qualification seeks to reconcile these two features. Philosophically, it is a development of what Avicenna stated in *Liber de anima*, tr. 5, ch. 3.

12. On the imperfect state of the separate soul, see *Sent.*, IV, d. 49, q. 1, a. 4, q.la 1. Thomas deepens this theme in the *Quaestio disputata de spiritualibus creaturis*, which dates to 1267–1268.

13. See ST, I, q. 50, a. 5; QDA, q. 6.

The idea that being belongs to the soul of itself and therefore is somehow inseparable from it seems to make the soul very similar to God. But the two cases, quite distinct for Thomas, should not be confused. The fact that the soul of itself *has* being does not mean that the soul of itself *is* being or that it is entirely its being. As any created substance, the soul has a certain composition that distinguishes it from God. In particular, the soul, *qua* spiritual entity, is composed of being and essence.[14] In its case, the essence is completely exhausted by its being a form and an act, while its absolute being is logically complementary to its essence. Since being is to a certain extent determined, as was said, by the very principles of the essence, and since the soul, essentially, is nothing other than a form, absolute being necessarily accompanies the soul's essence. In other words, once created, the soul receives a being that it cannot lose, but nevertheless the soul is not this being. What does it mean, then, to say that being belongs to the soul of itself *(per se)*?

The distinction between God and the soul, between what is of itself being and what has of itself being, seems to imply that being is not said of the soul of itself in the first of the two ways of *per se* predication that Thomas takes from Aristotle, that is, essential predication, and this for two reasons.[15] First, as was said earlier, being is not a genus and so being cannot be part of the essence of anything, and second, if being were part of the essence of the soul, the soul would exist necessarily and independently from the moment in which it is created. In Thomas's world, however, only God is being essentially and is his very essence. It follows that Thomas probably believes that being belongs to the soul of itself in the second way of *per se* predication, that is, as something that is necessarily (with respect to the actual world in which the soul exists) inseparable from the soul even if it is not part of the soul's essence. This is because the soul, in the end, with respect to the only truly existing

---

14. Thomas illustrates in great detail this composition in DEE, ch. 4, and in the *De substantiis separatis*. On this, see Gabriele Galluzzo, "Aquinas on the Genus and Differentia of Separate Substances," *Documenti e studi sulla tradizione filosofica medievale* 18 (2007): 343–361.

15. According to the medieval authors' understanding of Aristotle's doctrine of *Posterior Analytics*, I, 4 and *Metaphysics*, V, 18, B is predicated *per se* of A either (1) if B is part of the essence of A, or (2) if B is necessarily entailed by A. For example, "animal" is predicated *per se* of "man" in the first sense, while "being capable of laughing" is predicated *per se* of "man" in the second sense.

realities which are composites, is nothing other than a form of substantial being and the fundamental part or principle of the composite.

Distinguishing between "what has of itself being" and "what is of itself being" helps Thomas also to differentiate between the incorruptibility and the perpetuity of the soul. The fact that the soul has no potentiality for nonbeing does not mean that the soul is not able to cease to be. The act of annihilating a soul, as also the act of granting it existence separated from the body (which, although it is impossible according to the natural order of things, is not logically contradictory), is the prerogative of God alone, and in no case can such an act deprive the soul of the being that belongs to it of itself. Clearly, to speak of two senses of *per se* predication of being presupposes that in the case of the soul two different kinds of being are ultimately involved. On the one hand, there is the being of the soul that is nothing else than its essential being, and such a being expresses the soul's being as a certain type of being of the body. On the other hand, there is being understood as actual or existential being which God can confer on and remove from the soul. A certain type of created being, therefore, is part of the essence of the soul, since the essence of the soul expresses a certain type of created being (i.e., the body's being animated), and this explains why for Thomas, following Aristotle, a soul and to be (for) a soul are exactly the same thing.[16] But on the other hand, souls receive an additional being from God on whom depends, among other things, their individuation and numerical multiplication as on an efficient cause.[17]

---

16. See, e.g., *Exp. Met.*, VIII, lec. 3, n. 1709.

17. See *Sent.*, II, d. 19, a. 1; SCG, II, chs. 79–81; QDA, q. 14; ST, I, q. 75, a. 6; CT, I, ch. 84; *Exp. Met.*, VIII, lec. 3, n. 1709. For God's role in the numerical individuation and multiplication of souls, see DEE, ch. 4, 377–378, lin. 178–201; QDP, q. 3, a. 10, *secunda ratio*, 71a. As is well known, with respect to the material cause, souls are distinguished according to the different bodies they bring into existence and ensoul, although the "formal" cause of their numerical individuation and multiplication, occasioned by their union with a given body, consists in what Aquinas calls an unrepeatable relationship or proportion *(commensuratio, proportio, habitudo)* each soul bears to its body (see especially QDA, q. 1, ad 5; q. 3; q. 6, ad 4 and ad 13). The souls' relationship with the bodies, which formally individuates souls without distinguishing them specifically, is part of the souls' essence (see QDA, q. 3, ad 20); this explains why Thomas thinks that the soul united to the body is more perfect than the separated soul (see QDA, q. 17, ad 1 and q. 1, ad 10; ST, I, q. 51, a. 1 and q. 89, a. 1). Thus, for Thomas, the numerical individuation and multiplication of souls is not caused by bodies, although it is occasioned by them, so that it can be deduced from them. Borrowing from Avicenna

To summarize, souls are incorporeal and incorruptible, and so once created do not lose their being and so are immortal. Nevertheless, they cannot be considered as eternal on account of their composition of being and essence.

2. The Identity of the Being of the Soul and the Being of the Body: Some Problems

The fact that the soul is described as a subsistent substantial form has another consequence. As we said in the first chapter, matter insofar as it is matter is something that is purely in potency. In the case of humans, the body is the material aspect, and so if the body, as matter, is that which is purely in potency to the soul, then the soul is that by way of which a given matter can come to be in act and become a body of a given (i.e., human) type. Now many times Thomas rejects the idea that the soul and body each have a distinct being and identity because of the difficulties (noted earlier) concerning the unity of a human being. As something in potency, the human body does not have its own being before the coming of the rational soul, nor can it continue to have its being after the rational soul leaves the body. A body is a human body as long as it is animated: just as there is neither a human nor a human body, except in potency, before the coming of the rational soul, similarly a dead body is no longer a human nor a human body except

---

(*Liber de anima*, tr. 5, ch. 3), Thomas introduces this piece of doctrine by claiming that the souls' individuation depends on the bodies as to its beginning but not as to its end. See, for instance, the following texts: *Sent.*, I, d. 8, q. 5, a. 2, ad 6; *Sent.*, II, d. 17, q. 2, a. 1; DEE, ch. 5; SCG, II, chs. 73–75, ch. 81, nn. 1620–1621, chs. 82 and 87; QDSC, a. 9; QDP, q. 3, a. 10, ad 16; CT, I, ch. 85; and especially ST, I, q. 76, a. 2. The idea that souls are numerically distinguished by virtue of bodies and that they maintain this individuation even after they are separated from bodies seems to conflict with Thomas's principle that in each thing there is a correspondence between being and being one (see QDA, q. 1, ad 2, 10,350–359). In addition, this idea implies that the body exerts some influence on the soul. This problematic consequence is highlighted by Siger of Brabant, among others. From a different point of view, it seems to me that there is no strong opposition between what Aquinas says in his early writings and what he says in his late works. For an opposed reading, see Bernardo-Carlos Bazán, app. font. ad lin. 354–359, in QDA, q. 1, 10. Note, however, that Thomas's reason for denying that the matter is the direct cause of the numerical individuation and multiplication of the soul, as stated in the late QDA, q. 1, ad 1, 10, lin. 342–346, was already affirmed by Thomas in DEE, ch. 5, 378, lin. 59 ff.

equivocally.[18] From this point of view, if a body as matter cannot have its own being, it must be that the being of the body (and so of a human understood as a composite of soul and body) is in every way the same as the being of the soul: the being that the human body has and the being that the soul has are exactly one and the same being.[19] The identity of being of soul and body, a consequence of the fact that the soul is that which brings it about that a certain matter can become a certain type of body, is however only partial. The being of the soul continues to transcend the body, since the soul is endowed with a capacity, i.e., the intellectual capacity, that transcends the body, as was said.

The teaching of Thomas, though philosophically thought-provoking and well-founded as an interpretation of Aristotle, contains many difficulties which go beyond the scope of this study. Here, I mention only three that are especially relevant to bioethical questions connected to determining the human nature of the embryo.

One of the points most criticized by Thomas's opponents at the time, such as Siger of Brabant, concerns the idea that the soul is the form of the body with respect to the soul's being, but it transcends the body in its power and operation. Since Thomas himself considers the soul's powers as quasi-accidental properties of the soul, which although they are not essential, still derive *(fluunt)* from it, it is strange that an accident, or in any case a faculty of the soul, be endowed with a being more noble than that of its subject. According to his adversaries, the way Thomas distinguishes between the essence and powers of the soul can lead to two consequences, both problematic. It could lead to making

---

18. See SCG, II, ch. 89, n. 1752; ST, I, q. 76, a. 8; *Sup. Iob,* ch. 20. The idea that a dead human body is no longer a human body except equivocally stems from Aristotle; see, e.g., Aristotle, *Metaphysics,* VII, 10, 1035b22 ff. As we shall see in what follows, the state of what precedes the substantial form and of what follows it are different, for in the first case we find a thing that is in potency to being human, while in the second case a thing that is deprived of the potentiality for being human. Following Aristotle, Thomas expresses this asymmetry by pointing out that the succession of generation and corruption in a human being happens according to a certain irreversible order of potentialities and actualities. Thus, in order for a cadaver again to have the potentiality for being human it is necessary for it to become again prime matter, from which the process of generation can begin again. See, e.g., SCG, III, ch. 144, and *Exp. Met.,* VIII, lec. 4, nn. 1750–1754 (the source is Aristotle's *Metaphysics* VIII, 5, 1044b29 ff.).

19. See SCG, II, ch. 68, n. 1450; SCG, II, ch. 69, nn. 1461–1462; QDA, q. 2.

the intellective power a separate substance, or, inversely, to reducing the intellective power to an organic power. In fact, precisely in light of the relation, admitted by Thomas, between the way in which a thing operates and the type of being that it has, the restriction of the soul's separate character only to its intellective operation seems illegitimate.

A second point, brought forward and analyzed by his adversaries, concerns instead the sequence of the constitution of a composite. The soul plays a primary role in defining a certain matter as a body of a certain type. From this viewpoint, the body should play no role in the multiplication and numerical differentiation of souls. This is even truer since matter cannot act upon the soul, and so the body can in no way be what directly individuates and numerically distinguishes souls. However, if one does maintain that it is not the body as such that individuates and distinguishes souls, but rather a certain "disposition" toward bodies that souls possess, then (1) either the individuation of souls depends on something accidental, in that such a disposition is thought to be outside the soul's essence, or else one must admit (2) that this disposition toward a body is something essential to the soul. But both alternatives seem to conflict with the teaching of Thomas. In the first case, if the individuation of souls came about through something extrinsic to the essence of the soul, then once the body no longer exists, the disposition of the soul toward *that* body should also cease. In the second case, souls would be able to differentiate themselves before being united to bodies. But if what is essential to a soul is a formal property of the soul, then souls should differentiate themselves formally, and so specifically.[20]

---

20. See QDP, q. 3, a. 10, 71a: "*Secunda ratio est Avicennae.* Cum enim anima non sit composita ex materia et forma [distinguitur enim et a materia et a composito in II *de Anima*], distinctio animarum ab invicem esse non posset nisi secundum formalem differentiam, si solum secundum se ipsas distinguerentur. Formalis autem differentia diversitatem speciei inducit. Diversitas autem secundum numerum in eadem specie ex differentia materiali procedit: quae quidem animae competere non potest secundum naturam ex qua fit, sed secundum materiam in qua fit." For an introduction to the problem of the substantiality of the soul and to the debate between Siger and Thomas, see Bernardo-Carlos Bazán, "The Human Soul: Form and Substance?"; Van Steenberghen, *Thomas Aquinas,* 29–74; and Antonio Petagine, *L'aristotelismo difficile: L'intelletto umano nella prospettiva di Alberto Magno, Tommaso d'Aquino e Sigieri di Brabante* (Milan: Vita e Pensiero, 2004), to which I refer for further bibliographical references.

The greatest problem, however, involves explaining how in actual fact the soul's being is communicated to the body. Thomas thinks that the corporeal organs, insofar as they are animated organs, are the subject of the lower vital operations, that is, the vegetative and sensitive operations. Once these organs are corrupted, these operations do not remain. On this basis, Thomas holds that, unlike the souls of humans, those of animals are not incorruptible, since an animal is animated only by a sensitive soul. The fact that it is not the soul directly, but the corporeal organs by means of the soul that exercise sensitive operations is also the reason why we say that the eye sees on account of the soul, and not that the soul sees. Strictly speaking, Thomas is of the opinion that the soul does not have vegetative or sensitive functions or states; at most, the soul can become aware of some vegetative and sensitive states of the body when they occur. It is not the soul that sees or that feels pain, but the body; in an Augustinian fashion, the soul only becomes aware of these corporeal states.[21]

The fact that the soul does not exercise vegetative and sensitive acts is proof, for Aquinas, that the essence of humans cannot be reduced to the soul. This reduction, which according to Thomas is upheld by the Platonists and certain philosophers who draw from Averroes's teaching, would be valid only if the soul were capable of having sensations without using sense organs. But because this is not the case, since we know from experience that impairment of a corporeal organ ends the capacity of the soul dependent on that organ for having sensations, it follows that it cannot be the soul that is the subject of sensitive acts, but rather the individual corporeal organs animated by the soul.

Now as they are organic parts of an organic whole, that is, as parts

---

21. There is an extensive discussion among the interpreters on whether or not Aquinas granted sensitive operations to the soul. On this, see Peter O. King, "Why Isn't the Mind-Body Problem Mediaeval," in Henrik Lagerlund, ed., *Forming the Mind: Essays on the Internal Senses and the Mind/Body Problem from Avicenna to the Medical Enlightenment* (Berlin: Springer Verlag, 2007), ch. 10; the article can be also consulted online at www.individual.utoronto.ca (accessed May 1, 2012). For more on the body/mind problem in the Middle Ages, see Robert Pasnau, "Mind and Hylomorphism" and Peter O. King, "Body and Soul," in John Marenbon, ed., *The Oxford Handbook of Medieval Philosophy* (Oxford: Oxford University Press, 2012), 486–504 and 505–524, respectively (see there for further bibliographical references).

functionally defined with respect to the whole, what can be said functionally of individual organs and individual sense faculties can also be said of the entire living organism. And so the sense functions of an organ can be attributed by extension to the entire human being. As one can say that it is not the soul that sees, but the eye on account of the soul, so one can say that it is not the eye that sees, but the human being that sees on account of the eye.[22] It is clear, however, that this is true only for the lower vital functions, the vegetative and sensitive functions. While the subject of the vegetative and sensitive acts is a determinate corporeal organ and, by extension, the entire human being, the subject of the higher vital functions, as thinking and willing, is the soul. On the one hand, Thomas is clear in holding that the soul is the *principle* of all the powers and all their vital operations, both those that have their proper subject in a corporeal organ (the vegetative and sensitive operations) and those that have their proper subject directly in the soul (voluntary and intellective operations). On the other hand, Thomas maintains that only the vital operations of a cognitive and volitional type exist in the soul as their proper subject.[23] The reason for this is that there are no corporeal organs specifically tasked with thinking and willing. We have already mentioned some of Thomas's arguments defending this conclusion. Even if these arguments seem inconclusive or unable to prove the separate character of the intellective soul anymore than that of the sensitive soul, nevertheless it is beyond question that, for Thomas, the soul is the subject of the acts of thinking and willing.

At this point, a difficulty could arise for Thomas. If the soul is the subject of the acts of thinking, then it becomes highly problematic whether such acts can be attributed to the whole human being. How an activity proper to the soul, namely, thinking, is communicated to the human being might be explained by the fact that the soul has its own being and it communicates its being to the body to such an extent that the body's being animated, i.e., being alive, is nothing other than the soul's being. When all is said and done, the soul can also be considered

---

22. See ST, I, q. 75, aa. 2–4.
23. See *Sent.*, IV, d. 44, q. 3, a. 3, q.la 1; ST, I, q. 76, a. 8, ad 4, and q. 77, aa. 5–6.

a part of the human being. But there lurks a problem. The soul, indeed, is not a part of the human being in the way that the eye is a part; for while the soul is what allows each part of a human to be functionally defined, it itself is not able to be functionally defined in virtue of something else. Once one accepts that the soul is not a functionally defined part of a human being, as is the eye, one must admit that the relation between some corporeal organ and the intellective soul is identical to that between the entire human being and the intellective soul; for the human being, taken as a whole, can be considered as one corporeal organ or, at any rate, as a collection of corporeal organs. As the intellective soul operates without using a specific organ (even if this does not mean that the intellective soul can completely do without corporeal organs, since the intellective faculty requires a correct and continuous functioning of the imaginative and sensitive faculties, which are corporeal faculties), so the entire human being cannot also be considered an organ for thinking. In fact, it is a human being and each of its parts that is defined with respect to the soul and not vice versa. In light of all this, how can one say that it is the individual human being that is the subject of the acts of thinking?

The question becomes all the more pressing if one recalls that Thomas, against the so-called "Latin Averroists" and their teaching on the unicity and separate character of the human intellect, had focused his entire polemic precisely on a defense of the cognitive experience of the individual human being.[24] It is clear, however, that it is one thing to say that it is the human being that thinks by virtue of the soul, and another to say that it is the soul that thinks or that the human being thinks insofar as it is a soul. The problem is that a human being, understood as a composite, does not have a being that is different from that of the soul. If so, then the soul remains the subject of the acts of thinking, and even if the being of the soul is identical with the being of the human being, it cannot properly be said that it is the human being, understood as a composite, that thinks. The whole human being can be said to think only in an indirect way, insofar as its being is identical

---

24. See, e.g., SCG, II, ch. 73; ST, I, q. 76, a. 1; CT, I, ch. 86; DUI, ch. 3; *Sent. De an.,* III, ch. 7.

with that of the soul, which is the true thinking subject. This is the only possible conclusion if one wants to maintain the continuity of the subject of the acts of thought. In fact, it is the soul that continues after the death of the body and not the human being, and therefore the soul is the subject to which all moral responsibility should be ascribed; hence, it must be the soul that is the real subject of the acts of thinking and willing. Nevertheless, it is well known that Thomas spends a great part of his philosophical project in demonstrating that it is the individual human being that is the subject of the acts of thinking and not the intellective soul, whether it is located within or without the human being.[25]

Beyond the difficulties to which Thomas's philosophy of human nature gives rise, the notion of the soul as the substantial form of an organic, physical body will greatly influence Thomas's account of Aristotelian embryology, as we shall see. In particular, the role played by the soul in the process of the constitution and identification of matter as an organic body will be key for understanding why, from Thomas's point of view, positing human ensoulment of the embryo at the moment of conception is philosophically unfeasible.

---

25. See especially his *De unitate intellectus*. For further complications and discussion about the state of the human soul after death, see Eleonore Stump, "Resurrection, Reassembly, and Reconstitution: Aquinas on the Soul," in Bruno Niederberger and Edmund Runggaldier, eds., *Die menschliche Seele: Brauchen wir den Dualismus?* (Frankfurt: Ontos Verlag, 2006), 153–174, and "Resurrection and the Separated Soul," in Brian Davies and Eleonore Stump, eds., *The Oxford Handbook of Aquinas* (Oxford: Oxford University Press, 2012), 458–466. See also Christina van Dyke, "Human Identity, Immanent Causal Relations, and the Principle of Non-Repeatability: Thomas Aquinas on the Bodily Resurrection," *Religious Studies* 43 (2007): 373–394.

The Status of the Embryo

THE THESES ABOUT generation and substantial form, which we have introduced in the preceding chapters, place a series of constraints on the account of the embryological process. As a consequence, for Thomas a philosophical explanation of this process must take into account certain elements: first, that metaphysically human ensoulment can be portrayed as the substantial form of a physical body endowed with organs; second, that human ensoulment is what allows us to identify an organic body as a human body; third, that generation is attained only at the end of the process of formation of the primary vital organs; and fourth, that the male semen is not ensouled. As we have mentioned, Thomas's account of the embryological process developed primarily through the rejection of two positions concerning the origin of the human soul: the position of Origen that the human soul is created before it is infused into the body, and the traducianist position that the human soul is passed on from father to child. In the last chapter, we saw some of the reasons that led Thomas to reject the thesis of the pre-creation of the human soul. In the first chapter, we saw that he opposed the idea that the semen has some form of ensoulment. One of the arguments for this was that the semen is not an organic part of the human being, and if not a part, then it is lacking any soul. In this, Thomas follows Aristotle very closely, conceiving of semen as what remains from the final stages of the food's digestion, not having given rise to differentiated organic parts.[1] If the semen had been assimilated, it would not have been able to keep its capacity to generate an entire human being, but only the capacity to generate the organic part corresponding to what assimilated it. Because of this, the semen has to be organically undifferentiated, maintaining the potentiality to generate any organic part. In the abstract, we could avoid this conclusion of Thomas by supposing that the semen, even if assimilated, still preserves the capacity to generate all organic parts insofar as it is differentiated, *qua* semen, from all organic parts. For Thomas, however, such a defense would be plausible only if one understands the semen as a kind of "little animal" in act.[2] But such a "preformist" theory is unacceptable for Thomas, since it would reduce generation simply to a process of separation and quantitative growth; on the hypothesis that the semen is a small human being in act, the generation of a human being would, in fact, be only a process of augmentation of its corporeal mass that ends with the attainment of a suitable quantity.

1. The Origin of the Human Soul

Once Thomas excludes both that human souls are created before they are associated with a body and that they are passed on naturally with

---

1. See Aristotle, *De generatione animalium,* I, 18, 726a26–27. On the nature of semen as the "superfluous" *(superfluum)* from the final stages of digestion, see *Sent.,* II, d. 30, q. 2, a. 2; QDP, q. 3, a. 12; ST, I, q. 119, a. 2. Such a description of the semen, however, does not lead Thomas to equate the semen to other organic residue, such as urine or sweat. The reason is that the semen, albeit superfluous from digestion for the individual, is nonetheless nonsuperfluous and essential for the preservation of the human species, whereas urine and sweat are not. On this, see *Sent.,* II, d. 18, q. 1, a. 1, ad 3; SCG, III, ch. 122.

2. See ST, I, q. 119, a. 1: "Non autem est possibile quod accipiatur pro semine id quod iam conversum est in substantiam membrorum, per quandam resolutionem. Quia illud resolutum, si non retineret naturam eius a quo resolvitur, tunc iam esset recedens a natura generantis, quasi in via corruptionis existens; et sic non haberet virtutem convertendi aliud in similem naturam. Si vero retineret naturam eius a quo resolvitur, tunc, cum esset contractum ad determinatam partem, non haberet virtutem movendi ad naturam totius, sed solum ad naturam partis. Nisi forte quis dicat, quod esset resolutum ab omnibus partibus corporis, et quod retineat naturam omnium partium. Et sic semen esset quasi quoddam parvum animal in actu; et generatio animalis ex animali non esset nisi per divisionem."

generation, the only possibility remaining for one who wishes to continue to work with the notion of soul is to hold that human souls are
infused into the body immediately at the moment of their creation. But
when are human souls created? Philosophically, the options reduce only
to the following: God creates human souls as soon as either (1) the body
begins to be formed, or (2) the body has completed its formation (or at
least has completed it as far as its principal parts are concerned). Before
examining these options, Thomas excludes one way of responding that
might seem to reconcile both, namely, the position of those who hold a
plurality of souls. Thomas discusses many times in his career "whether
the vegetative, sensitive and rational souls are substantially one soul" or
"whether in a human being there are other souls, essentially different
from the rational soul." Over and over Thomas uses various arguments
to defend the position that there is only one substantial form and one
soul, but there are three basic ones and they concern (1) identity, (2)
predication, and (3) functional coordination of the different souls. We
will briefly look at each.

Let us start with the supposition that in a human being there are
three really distinct souls, each located in a separate organ and tasked
with a different function. On this supposition, a human being would
be alive through a vegetative soul (located in the liver), and be an animal
through the sensitive soul (located in the heart), and be human through
the rational soul (located in the brain).[3] Thomas contests this supposition. For him, the first disadvantage of this picture is that a human
being would turn out not to be a unity by itself, for what accounts for
the being of a thing is what accounts also for its being one. Nor can
someone avoid this by saying that it is the unity of the body that gives
unity to the three souls, since the unity of the body depends on the
unity of the soul and not vice versa.[4]

The second argument follows from the first. If there were a number
of souls, then it would be impossible to predicate essentially distinct
forms of one and the same subject. For example, suppose again that

---

3. See SCG, II, ch. 58; *Sent. Ethic.,* I, ch. 19; ST, I, q. 76, a. 3; *Sent. De an.,* III, ch. 1 ff.
4. See QDA, q. 11, 99–100, 218–230; ST, I, q. 76, a. 3, *respondeo,* "primo."

Socrates is a man and an animal through distinct forms; that he is, as said above, a man through the rational soul and an animal through the sensitive soul. But then there is no possibility of giving a stable and homogeneous metaphysical basis for the standard essential predications when one predicates substantial properties of Socrates. The statements "Socrates is a man" and "Socrates is an animal," for example, would continue to be explicated as predications *per se* in the proper sense (since "being a man" and "being an animal" would express parts of the essence of Socrates), but "a man is an animal" could only be explicated as predication *per accidens,* since "being an animal" does not belong to the essence of "being a man." At most, it would be predication *per se* of the second kind, on the condition that one grants that the sensitive soul is ordered to the intellective or rational soul as matter or what is material is ordered to form or to what is formal.[5] But in this last case, one could not avoid making the intellective soul an accidental form. For, as was said above, a substantial form is what transforms matter into a given material substance. If this function were carried out by one of the souls that preceded the rational soul or even by a primal form of corporeity (understood as the form that fixes the identity and extension of a body before it is ensouled), then the intellective soul would confer on the human only accidental being.[6]

The third argument, finally, focuses upon the functional coordination of the distinct souls: to associate distinct activities with distinct souls would have the drawback that intense activity on the part of one soul could impede or damage the activity of another soul that depends upon it.[7]

Not all of these arguments of Thomas seem to be compelling. The second argument, in particular, is decisive only if the objector accepts the classic version of Aristotle's theory of predication, but it is not

---

5. See QDA, q. 11, 99, 194–217; ST, I, q. 76, a. 3, *respondeo,* "secundo." As was already noted in Chapter 2 (note 15), in a *per se* predication of the first kind (e.g., "man is animal") the predicate is part of the essence of the subject, while in a *per se* predication of the second kind (e.g., "man is capable of laughing") it is the subject that is part of the essence of the predicate. In a *per accidens* predication, neither is the subject part of the essence of the predicate nor vice versa.

6. See QDA, q. 11, 100, 231–245; QDP, q. 3, a. 9, 67a–b B); ST, I, q. 118, a. 2, ad 2.

7. See QDA, q. 11, 100–101, 258–260; ST, q. 76, a. 3, *respondeo,* "tertio."

conclusive if the objector develops another theory of predication with different ontological commitments. Also, the third argument, only sketched by Thomas, can easily be evaded by introducing certain constraints on the interdependence among the different souls. In the end, the only argument with some force seems to be the first that focuses upon the intrinsic unity of the human being, as has been seen already a number of times. But also this one works only if the adversary takes as valid Thomas's characterization of substantial form and his identification of the intellective soul with the substantial form of the human being and at the same time intends to present the doctrine of the plurality of forms as a plausible interpretation of Aristotle's philosophy of human nature.

In any case, granted that in humans there cannot be a real layering of souls, the main problem for Thomas is to establish when the coming of the rational soul precisely occurs. Since the possibility of defining a body as human depends on the rational ensoulment of that body, determining when the rational soul arrives is equivalent to determining when human life begins. Thomas seems to think that the problem is inescapable because whether one holds that the rational soul is infused at the moment of conception or is infused afterwards, one must admit and account for the fact that in the embryo, right from the moment of conception, certain "vital operations" *(opera vitae)* can be observed.[8] But if something manifests operations that can be associated with life, it must be ensouled and so have a vital principle that animates it. And so, if one admits that the embryo manifests vital operations, one could conclude that the embryo somehow has a soul right from the moment of conception. The question is then the following: What is the factor responsible for the vital operations that the embryo exhibits right from the moment of conception?

Thomas does not undertake to examine all the ways of explaining this fact in every one of his writings that concern embryology. The most complete treatment is found in *Quaestiones disputatae de potentia,* question 3, article 9, ad 9 (from his Roman stay, 1265–1266), and I will

---

8. See QDA, q. 11, arg. 1, 95, 3–9; QDP, q. 3, a. 9, arg. 9, 64b.

take this as the main text to guide us. Earlier, Thomas had considered parts of the positions mentioned in *Quaestiones de potentia* in his *Summa contra Gentiles,* book II, chapter 89 (dated probably to 1260–1263), and he again considered them later in *Quaestiones disputatae de anima,* question 11, ad 1 (composed between 1265 and 1266) and in the *Summa theologiae,* part I, question 118, article 2, ad 2 (edited almost certainly between 1265 and 1267).

When Thomas worked out his own account of Aristotelian embryology, the possibilities for examining or directly observing what occurs within the mother's womb were obviously rather meager. He himself recognizes these limits when he points out in his Commentary on the *Sentences* (book IV, distinction 1, question 2, article 6, the second minor question, ad 2) that the thesis that the embryo in the mother's womb does not possess a being distinct from the mother can be maintained within the limits of what is possible to human cognition *(quantum pertinet ad humanam cognitionem).* Data drawn from experience (above all spontaneous abortions, as Isidore of Seville had mentioned in his *Etymologies,* direct observations of the effects of pregnancy, and gynecological considerations),[9] together with reports obtained from postmortem examinations that doctors in special circumstances carried out, led easily to the conviction that the embryo in the womb of the mother exercised certain basic vital operations, as movement, growth, and nourishing itself. Putting aside whether and how such a conviction could be verified with scientific tests and empirical observations, what is of interest from the viewpoint of the history of philosophy is that at the time of Thomas this datum was assumed in almost every embryological account, whether or not the account admitted or denied the

---

9. See Isidore of Seville, *Etymologiae,* XI, ch. 1, ed. W. M. Lindsay (Oxford: Clarendon Press, 1911), n. 143: "Primum autem aiunt cor hominis fingi, quod in eo sit et vita omnis et sapientia; deinde quadragesimo die totum opus expleri; quod ex abortionibus, ut ferunt, collecta sunt." I cite the text from the website www2.hs-augsburg.de/~Harsch/Chronologia/Lsposto7/Isidorus/isi_eto0.html (accessed May 1, 2012). See also Thomas Aquinas, *Sent.,* III, d. 3, q. 5, a. 2, ad 3: "Minimum autem quantitatis in uno individuo est in primo instanti suae figurationis et animationis; quae quantitas adeo parva est quod parum excedit quantitatem formicae, ut dicit Philosophus, quod in quadragesima die muliere pariente abortum inventum est corpus prolis omnia membra distincta habere, quamvis in quantitate esset sicut magna formica."

existence of the soul of the embryo. To medieval philosophers, there was no problem admitting that the embryo *manifests* some vital operations; this is the point of departure for their different accounts of the embryological process. Rather the problem, for many medieval thinkers, was the inference from such operations to admitting the existence of a principle of ensoulment. What is in question is the following inference: "if a thing manifests vital operations, then such a thing has a soul."

2. Ensoulment of the Embryo: Opposing Positions

The point of departure for the debate, therefore, comes from the conviction that the embryo manifests certain vital operations, a fact on which there seemed to be substantial agreement. Once this is admitted, two general hypotheses can be advanced to explain this fact:

(A) According to Thomas, one can say that the embryo has no internal principle of ensoulment, and that the vital operations are from an *external* principle. With respect to this, there are two possibilities. Someone could say that the principle of ensoulment is the soul of the father.[10] Alternatively, one could say that it is the soul of the mother.[11] If one accepts this explanation, one must conclude that the ensoulment of the embryo is only apparent because it is directed by another.

(B) Alternatively, someone could hold that the embryo has an *internal* principle of ensoulment.

---

10. This explanation can be traced back at least to Bonaventure. See, e.g., *Commentaria in quattuor libros Sententiarum*, II, d. 31, a. 1, q. 1, in *Sancti Bonaventurae Opera Omnia*, t. 2 (Quaracchi, Florence: ex Typographia Collegii S. Bonaventurae, 1885), 742a. Thomas recalls this argument in QDP, q. 3, a. 9, arg. 5. See also QDA, q. 11, 101, 267–271: "Quidam enim dicunt quod in embrione ante animam rationalem non est anima, set quidam uirtus procedens ab anima parentis, et ab huiusmodi uirtute sunt operationes que in embrione apparent, que dicitur uirtus formatiua."

11. See, e.g., QDP, q. 3, a. 9, ad 9, 67b D): "Alii vero dicunt, quod embrio non habet animam, quousque perficiatur anima rationali: operationes autem vitae quae in eo apparent sunt ex anima matris"; QDA, q. 11, 102, 321–323: "Non enim uirtus actiua que est in semine potest esse a matre, licet hoc quidam dicant"; ST, I, q. 118, a. 2, ad 2: "Aliqui dixerunt quod operationes vitae quae apparent in embryone, non sunt ab anima eius, sed ab anima matris, vel a virtute formativa quae est in semine."

Thomas rejects hypothesis (A). That it is not the soul of the father that makes the embryo ensouled is derived from what was said about the semen not being ensouled. In addition, Aquinas notes that it would be impossible for the soul of the father to act at a distance, given that the semen is detached from him. It seems, however, more difficult to reject this role for the soul of the mother. In order to understand Thomas's position we must keep in mind that for Thomas what distinguishes a living organism from a nonliving organism is the capacity of the living to move itself. This is rather plausible. When someone moves a table, for instance, one cannot attribute the action of moving to the table because the table itself is not performing that action. Similarly, one could not say that the embryo moves or feels, if it is the soul of the mother that makes it move or feel. What is more, properly speaking one could not even say that it is the soul of the mother that makes it move or feel, for in this case, the embryo would not in fact move or feel however much it seemed to move and to receive sensations. If it were the mother's soul that ensouled the embryo, in a trivial way the embryo would be no more than a part of the mother and all the actions that we attribute to the embryo should be more properly attributed to the mother (even when the rational soul is added, since the embryo continues to be materially united to the mother, receiving nourishment from her).[12] In addition—Thomas observes—if the embryo were ensouled by the mother's soul, the embryo could not be called an organism of the animal kind since every animal requires a body and a

---

This variant is usually referred back to the *Summa Halensis,* II-1, inq. 4, tr. 3, q. 1, tit. 2, ch. 6. Among others, it is endorsed by the Dominican Roland of Cremona. On this, see Richard C. Dales, *The Problem of the Rational Soul in the Thirteenth Century* (Leiden: Brill, 1995), 36–37; Odon Lottin, *Psychologie et morale au XIIe et XIIIe siècle,* 2 vols. (Leuven: Abbaye du Mont César, 1949), vol. 1, 465, 19–22; and Bernardo-Carlos Bazán, "La Corporalité selon saint Thomas," *Revue philosophique de Louvain* 81 (1983): 369–409, esp. 391, note 52. Note that Albert the Great in *De animalibus,* XVI, tr. 1, ch. 2, ed. A. Borgnet, in Alberti Magni *Opera Omnia,* t. 12 (Paris: Vivès, 1891), 136, attributes this position, without any further qualification, to "some medical doctors" *(quibusdam medicorum).*

12. See QDP, q. 3, a. 9, ad 9, 67b D): "Sed hoc non potest esse: nam in hoc viventia a non viventibus differunt, quia viventia movent se ipsa secundum operationes vitae, quod de non viventibus dici non potest; unde non potest esse quod nutriri et augeri, quae sunt propriae operationes viventis, sint in embrione a principio extrinseco, scilicet ab anima matris. Et praeterea virtus nutritiva matris assimilaret cibum corpori matris, et non corpori embrionis; cum nutritiva deserviat individuo sicut generativa speciei. Et iterum sentire non posset esse in embrione ex anima matris."

soul.[13] But if the embryo were not an animal, we would not be able to attribute to it vital operations, which, through experience, we also cannot attribute to the mother. Thus, if the embryo is really performing acts of moving and sensing, Aquinas concludes, it must have an intrinsic principle of ensoulment.[14]

Hence, there remains only hypothesis (B). Thomas offers five different ways of understanding this hypothesis:

(B1) Someone could say that the human or rational soul is already entirely present in act in the male semen, and so is in the embryo, in its complete species, and hold, nevertheless, that the soul of the embryo is not able to exercise all its operations right from the start because of the lack of organs *(propter organorum defectum);* gradually, as the organs are formed under the impetus of the formative power, the soul begins to exercise all its functions.[15]

---

13. See SCG, II, ch. 89, n. 1736.

14. See SCG, II, ch. 89, n. 1736; QDP, q. 3, a. 9, ad 9, 67b D); QDA, q. 11, ad 2, 102, 321–325; ST, I, q. 18, a. 2: "Nam *vitae* nomen sumitur ex quodam exterius apparenti circa rem, quod est movere se ipsum" and ad 2, 100a: "Ad secundum dicendum quod opera vitae dicuntur, quorum principia sunt in operantibus, ut seipsos inducant in tales operationes"; QDSC, a. 3, ad 13, 383a: "Ad decimum tertium dicendum quod in embryone apparent quaedam opera vitae, sed quidam dixerunt huiusmodi opera esse ab anima matris. Sed hoc est impossibile, quia de ratione operum vitae est quod sint a principio intrinseco, quod est anima."

15. See SCG, II, ch. 89, n. 1737; QDP, q. 3, a. 9, ad 9, 66b A): "Ad nonum dicendum quod circa embrionis vitam sunt aliqui diversimode opinati. Quidam namque assimilaverunt in generatione humana progressum animae rationalis progressui corporis humani, dicentes quod sicut corpus humanum in semine est virtualiter, non tamen habens actu humani corporis perfectionem, quae in distinctione organorum consistit, sed paulatim per virtutem seminis ad perfectionem huiusmodi pervenitur; ita in principio generationis est ibi anima, virtute quadam habens omnem perfectionem quae postea apparet in homine completo, non tamen eam habens actu, cum non appareant animae actiones, sed processu temporis paulatim eam acquirit; ita quod primo apparent in ea actiones animae vegetabilis, et postmodum animae sensibilis, et tandem animae rationalis. Et hanc opinionem tangit Gregorius Nyssenus in libro quem fecit *de Homine.*" This explanation must be understood in the first way indicated at 67a: "Sed haec opinio non potest stare, quia aut intelligit quod ipsa anima secundum speciem suam existat a principio in semine, nondum habens perfectas operationes propter organorum defectum." See also ST, I, q. 118, a. 2, ad 2: "Et ideo alii dicunt quod illa eadem anima quae primo fuit vegetativa tantum, postmodum, per actionem virtutis quae est in semine, perducitur ad hoc quod fiat etiam sensitiva; et tandem perducitur ad hoc ut ipsa eadem fiat intellectiva, non quidem per virtutem activam seminis, sed per virtutem superioris agentis, scilicet Dei deforis illustrantis. Et propter hoc dicit Philosophus quod intellectus venit ab extrinseco."

(B2) Alternatively, someone could say that the human or rational soul is present in the male semen only virtually or potentially; that is, in the semen there is a power, virtue, or a form that does not yet have the complete species of the soul, but it will become a soul in act as soon as the formative power of the semen disposes the matter, rendering that power or form capable of carrying out also the vegetative, sensitive, and finally rational functions.[16]

(B3) Someone else could say, on the other hand, that the relation between the vegetative soul, which is rooted in the semen, and the sensitive soul, as also the relation between the sensitive and the rational soul, is a relation of potency to act.[17]

(B4) In addition, someone could say that the sensitive soul and the rational soul are added to the vegetative soul, which is present in the semen, in such a way that there are in humans three substantially different souls.[18]

---

16. See SCG, II, ch. 89, n. 1740; QDP, q. 3, a. 9, ad 9, 66b A) (see the previous note). This explanation must be understood in the second way indicated at 67a: "[. . .] aut intelligit quod in semine a principio sit aliqua virtus vel forma, quae nondum habet speciem animae; sicut nec semen habet speciem humani corporis, sed paulatim producitur [*so in the edition, perhaps for* perducitur] per actionem naturae ad hoc quod ipsa eadem sit anima primo quidem vegetabilis, secundo sensibilis et deinde rationalis"; QDA, q. 11, 101–102, 281–292; ST, I, q. 118, a. 2, ad 2. This interpretation is close to the one of Albert the Great. For references, see below, note 31; see also Luke Demaitre and Anthony A. Travil, "Human Embryology and Development in the Works of Albertus Magnus," in James A. Weisheipl, ed., *Albertus Magnus and the Sciences: Commemorative Essays 1980* (Toronto: Pontifical Institute of Mediaeval Studies, 1980), 405–440.

17. See QDP, q. 3, a. 9, ad 9, 67b C): "Unde *alii dicunt,* quod anima vegetabilis est in potentia ad animam sensibilem et sensibilis est actus eius; unde anima vegetabilis quae primo est in semine, per actionem naturae perducitur ad complementum animae sensibilis; et ulterius anima rationalis est actus et complementum animae sensibilis; unde anima sensibilis perducitur ad suum complementum, scilicet ad animam rationalem, non per actionem generantis sed per actum creantis; et sic dicunt quod ipsa rationalis anima in homine partim est ab intrinseco, scilicet quantum ad naturam intellectualem; et partim ab extrinseco, quantum ad naturam vegetabilem et sensibilem."

18. See QDP, q. 3, a. 9, ad 9, 67a–b B): "Alii vero dicunt quod in semine primo est anima vegetabilis, et postmodum ea manente, inducitur anima sensibilis ex virtute generantis, et ultimo inducitur anima rationalis per creationem, ita quod ponunt in homine esse tres animas per essentiam differentes. *Sed contra* hoc est quod dicitur [in libro de Eccles. dogmatibus, cap. *XV*]: *neque duas animas dicimus esse in uno homine sicut et Iacobus et alii Syrorum scribunt, unam animalem qua animatur corpus et immixta sit sanguini, et alteram spiritualem quae rationem ministret.* Et *iterum* impossibile est unius et eiusdem rei esse plures formas substantiales: nam cum forma substantialis faciat esse non solum secundum quid, sed simpliciter, et constituat hoc aliquid in genere substantiae, si

(B5) Someone could say, finally, that in the embryo there is only a material and organic formative power and that there is no soul to be found in the embryo.[19]

In different works, Thomas presents these interpretations in various ways. For example, in the *Summa contra Gentiles,* (B1) and (B2) are clearly distinct, while in the *Quaestiones de potentia* he sets forth as the first position that traditionally taken from *De hominis opificio* of Gregory of Nyssa, and then he interprets it in two ways corresponding to (B1) and (B2). In any case, the philosophical intuition articulated by the different accounts is clear: there is already present in the semen the formal continuant of the generative process, whether it is the vegetative soul itself or the formative power. In (B1), human generation is understood as a process of gradual *realization* of a form that is already completely present in the male semen, while in (B2) it is seen as a gradual *perfecting* of a form that is present in the male semen only virtually or potentially. (B3) is a variant on (B2) that is introduced only in the *Quaestiones de potentia,* and Thomas himself struggles to distinguish it from the preceding cases. The different positions in Thomas's various works do not always overlap, and the situation also becomes more complicated by the fact that at times identical arguments are used to attack apparently different theses.

Putting aside the differences of context and formulation, the idea that Thomas wants to attack is that the human soul is found, in whatever form, already at the start of the process of generation. If it were,

---

prima forma hoc facit, secunda adveniens, inveniens subiectum iam in esse substantiali constitutum, accidentaliter ei adveniet; et sic sequeretur quod anima sensibilis et rationalis in homine corpori accidentaliter uniantur. Nec potest dici quod anima vegetabilis quae in planta est forma substantialis, in homine non sit forma substantialis, sed dispositio ad formam: quia quod est de genere substantiae nullius accidens esse potest, ut dicitur in I *Physic* [COM. 17]"; ST, I, q. 118, a. 2, ad 2: "Dicunt ergo quidam quod supra animam vegetabilem quae primo inerat, supervenit alia anima, quae est sensitiva; et supra illam iterum alia, quae est intellectiva. Et sic sunt in homine tres animae, quarum una est in potentia ad aliam." This is the common position of the supporters of the plurality of forms (for example, Philip the Chancellor in the *Summa de bono*).

19. See QDP, q. 3, a. 9, ad 9, 67b E): "Et ideo *alii dicunt,* quod in embrione non est anima ante infusionem animae rationalis, sed est ibi vis formativa, quae huiusmodi operationes vitae in embrione exercet"; QDA, q. 11, 101, 267–271 (I have cited this text above at note 10).

Thomas thinks we would have difficulties explaining the passage from the sensitive soul to the rational soul. If we did admit that the rational soul was an "evolution" from the sensitive soul (even if by means of an external agent), then either the rational soul would be corporeal and so mortal (since the vegetative soul and the sensitive soul are such), or else vice versa, the vegetative and sensitive souls would be immortal (like the rational soul). If we did admit, on the other hand, that the rational soul was of a different type, then either we would fall into (B4), the position of the plurality of forms, which as mentioned earlier Thomas holds to be unfeasible, or we would have to admit that the rational soul takes the place of the sensitive soul, the position that Thomas will finally adopt.

3. Two Different Intuitions concerning the Ensoulment of the Embryo

The schema that Thomas introduces in his *Quaestiones de potentia* is rather complicated, and to make it clearer, we can present it in the following way. Intuitively, there are two ways of explaining the fact that the embryo manifests vital operations.

1. A first way is simply to deny that the human or rational soul is the principle responsible for the vital operations manifested by the embryo. If someone wanted to hold that the human or rational soul is only added subsequently and at the same time wanted to deny a plurality of souls, he/she would have to argue that there is not any soul before the coming of the rational soul. Technically, this type of move consists in distinguishing the soul from what in the tradition is called the formative power *(virtus formativa)*, and this is position (B5) in the schema outlined above. Thomas does not always treat this as a separate position. In the *Quaestiones de potentia*, for example, he does distinguish (B5) from (A), while in the *Quaestiones de anima* the two positions tend to coalesce. The two positions, however, are not entirely interchangeable. In contrast to position (A), that denies that the embryo is ensouled of itself since it is ensouled by the mother or father, (B5) admits that the evolution of the embryo is guided by an internal principle, but at the same time it maintains that such a principle is not a soul. The formative

power is different from the soul in two respects: first, it is communicated to the embryo by one of the parents and is not introduced from outside; and second, it is, so to speak, a program of development that concerns exclusively the material side of the embryo. In his *Summa contra Gentiles,* Thomas assumes that the formative power plays an important role in animal generation, remaining numerically identical throughout all the phases of the formative process of the embryo.[20] Such a power is directed to the formation or material organization of the body. Ontologically speaking, Thomas denies that the formative power has as its subject the semen, as Bonaventure held.[21] More precisely, Thomas identifies its subject with something fluid present in the male semen *(spiritus, quoddam spumosum).*[22] While recognizing the existence of a formative power of the semen, which he incorporates into his account, Thomas nevertheless denies that such a program of

---

20. See SCG, II, ch. 89, n. 1743: "Haec igitur virtus formativa eadem manet in spiritu praedicto a principio formationis usque in finem." In the *Summa contra Gentiles* the temporal duration of the formative power is not determined: the end of the embryo's formative process could coincide with the coming of the rational soul, or, even if less probable, with the birth of the fetus. In QDP, q. 3, a. 9, ad 16, Thomas adds a clarification, stating that the "spirit" in the male semen remains even after the coming of the rational soul, although the formative power becomes then a "regulative power" *(virtus regitiva):* "Ad decimumsextum dicendum, quod virtus formativa quae in principio est in semine, manet adveniente etiam anima rationali; sicut et spiritus in quos fere tota substantia spermatis convertitur manent. Et illa quae prius fuit formativa corporis fit postmodum corporis regitiva. Sicut etiam calor qui fuit dispositio ad formam ignis manet forma ignis adveniente, ut instrumentum formae in agendo" (68b). On the notion of formative power, for which the Aristotelian source is *De generatione animalium,* 2, 733b31–734a16, 736a32–b27, 740b24–741a2, see the apparatus of sources in QDA, q. 11, ad 1, 101, ad lin. 271. Thomas also relates the notion of formative power to Avicenna (see, for instance, *Sent.,* II, d. 18, q. 2, a. 3; probably, Thomas has in mind Avicenna's *De animalibus,* IX, ch. 3, and XV, ch. 2, rather than his *Canon,* I, fen. I, doctr. 6, ch. 2) and to Averroes's Commentary on the *Metaphysics [In Metaphysicam Commentarium,* VII, t.c. 31 (Venice: apud Junctas, 1572), t. 8, f. 181E–F]. Thomas does not mention, however, Averroes's Commentary on the *De generatione,* II, ch. 3 (Venice: Apud Junctas, 1572), t. 62, f. 75K, where Averroes traced this notion back to Galen.

21. See Bonaventure, *Commentaria in quattuor libros Sententiarum,* II, d. 31, a. 1, q. 1.

22. See SCG, II, ch. 89, n. 1742: "Sed, cum ipsa [*scil.* virtus formativa] fundetur sicut in proprio subiecto in spiritu cuius est semen contentivum, sicut quoddam spumosum, operatur formationem corporis prout agit ex vi animae patris, cui attribuitur generatio sicut principali generanti, non ex vi animae concepti, etiam postquam anima inest; non enim conceptum generat seipsum, sed generatur a patre"; also ST, III, q. 33, a. 1, ad 4. Thomas regards the formation of the body as the principal natural result of the act of conception (see ST, III, q. 33, a. 1). On the notion of *spiritus spumosus,* see Aristotle, *De generatione animalium,* 2, 735b32–34, 736a14. On this, see Thomas Aquinas, *Sent.* II, d. 18, q. 2, a. 3: "Subiectum autem et organum huius virtutis est spiritus vitalis inclusus in semine;

development is the explanatory factor of the vital operations (as movement, sensitive receptivity, and growth) that the embryo exhibits. He
gives two arguments for this denial.

The first is that such a power would not be able to explain an array
of vital operations that differ in species, since such a power is only one
in species. The second and philosophically more persuasive argument is
that such a power is posited to explain the formation of the body, but
to explain how the body *is formed* is not the same as explaining how the
body *functions*. The formative power of the semen, for example, can
modify the matter of the mother so that it forms organs, but such
organs could well remain nonfunctioning, just as similarly not all corporeal organs in any condition whatsoever can support the vital operations to which they are tasked. Organic formation is only a necessary
condition for the biological functioning of the embryo, but formation
and functioning are not the same process. Hence, no formative power
ascribed to the semen is able to account for the functioning of the
formed body.[23] For these reasons, Thomas maintains that the action of
the formative power is limited to modifying the matter. Nevertheless,
by so doing it triggers the actualization of the potency of the matter,
that is, its ensoulment.

---

unde ad continendum huiusmodi spiritum semen est spumosum et haec est causa albedinis eius.
Huic autem spiritui coniungitur virtus formativa, magis per modum motoris quam per modum
formae, etsi forma eius aliquo modo sit"; SCG, IV, ch. 46, n. 3. Thomas dwells on this notion at
more length in the ST, I, q. 118, a. 1, ad 3: "Ad tertium dicendum quod illa vis activa quae est in
semine, ex anima generantis derivata, est quasi quaedam motio ipsius animae generantis, nec est
anima, aut pars animae, nisi in virtute; sicut in serra vel securi non est forma lecti, sed motio
quaedam ad talem formam. Et ideo non oportet quod ista vis activa habeat aliquod organum in
actu; sed fundatur in ipso spiritu incluso in semine, quod est spumosum, ut attestatur eius albedo.
In quo etiam spiritu est quidam calor ex virtute caelestium corporum, quorum etiam virtute agentia
inferiora agunt ad speciem, ut supra dictum est."

23. See QDP, q. 3, a. 9, ad 9, 67b–68a E): "Sed hoc etiam esse non potest: quia cum appareant
esse in embrione ante ultimum complementum, diversae operationes vitae, non possunt esse ab una
virtute: unde oportet quod sit ibi anima habens diversas virtutes"; QDA, q. 11, ad 1, 101, 267–276:
"Quidam enim dicunt quod in embrione ante animam rationalem non est anima, set quedam uirtus
procedens ab anima parentis, et ab huiusmodi uirtute sunt operationes que in embrione apparent,
que dicitur uirtus formatiua. Set hoc non potest esse omnino uerum, quia in embrione non solum
apparet formatio corporis, que posset attribui predicte uirtuti, set etiam alie operationes, que non
possunt attribui nisi anime, ut augeri, sentire, et huiusmodi." Note that in the *Quaestiones de anima*,
Thomas only hypothetically attributes the formative function to such a power (*posset attribui*: lin.

2. At this point, if someone held that Thomas's arguments were convincing, he/she could change position and concede that the human or rational soul is already present in the embryo from the moment of conception. Here an opponent has two possibilities: to claim either (a) that the human soul is present in a complete and perfect way already in the male semen, or (b) that the human soul is present in the male semen actually, but imperfectly, or in an entirely potential way.

Thomas rejects both options. Obviously, from Thomas's point of view, the first is the less sustainable answer. The main reason is that if one takes literally the Aristotelian characterization of the soul as the form of an organic, physical body that has life potentially, one finds oneself having to admit that the primary organs of the body must be already formed before the coming of the soul. Thomas's point is exactly that: a living body becomes human when and only when it has an organic structure that is able to support all the functions of the soul.

Given the way in which Thomas interprets, especially in his Commentary on the second book of *De anima,* the Aristotelian characterization of the soul, in order for there to be a human being, it is not enough to require that the body be in potency to having the capacity to actually exercise the highest vital functions (i.e., the intellectual functions)—a capacity that, at the time that the body is in potency to it, the body still does not have. This condition would be too weak, for the embryo just conceived is certainly in potency to having the capacity to exercise rationality, but it is clear that the embryo, insofar as it is in potency to the possession of a capacity, does not possess rationality in act, and even less the possibility to exercise it. Hence, the embryo is not in condition to actually exercise rationality, nor is it in condition to be able to exercise it.

On the other hand, it seems too much to require that the body be in

---

274). In the *Summa contra Gentiles,* the admission of a formative power as the explanatory factor of the embryo's vital operations is not explicitly considered. There Thomas discusses the role of the soul of the mother as the explanatory factor of the embryo's vital operations. But as was said, in that context Thomas rejects the appeal to the mother's soul by pointing to the fact that in that case the embryo would not be an animal, given that each animal is composed of a body and a soul, rather than to the fact that otherwise the embryo would not be independent of the mother (SCG, II, ch. 89, n. 1736).

condition to actually exercise intellectual, i.e., rational, functions. This, on the other hand, seems too strong a condition, for even after the primary organs are formed, the embryo is certainly not able to actually exercise intellectual functions. What is required seems to be only that the organic body has in act *the capacity to be able to exercise* intellectual functions, even if in fact it does not exercise them nor is able yet to exercise them in a complete and perfect way. As soon as that capacity is acquired, the embryo becomes a human being and immediately nothing stops it from being able to begin to exercise intellectual functions.[24] At the beginning, the exercise of this capacity is obviously imperfect. But that does not mean that the embryo does not possess in act such a capacity. The imperfection concerns the exercise of the capacity, not its possession, and the entire subsequent generative process after the infusion of the rational soul can be described as a process of perfecting the organs regarding the possibility, for such a capacity, to exercise perfectly those intellective acts that by nature it can carry out. In Thomas's way of speaking, it is not required that a human body already possess "second act," i.e., that it actually carry out intellectual acts; it is sufficient that it possess "first act," i.e., that it possess the capacity to carry out such acts. In other words, it is sufficient that it possess the actual capacity to exercise intellectual acts, not the actual exercise of such acts.[25] From this point of view, neither the male semen nor the embryo just conceived can have a rational soul since they do not have a material organization adequate for being able to support possible intellectual acts.

I have just reconstructed the principal argument of Thomas for rejecting the possibility of the embryo's possessing human ensoulment from the moment of conception. As one can see, this argument is

---

24. The exercise of a potency or capacity is, for Thomas, the final goal of certain active potencies or capacities, like the intellective ones (see *Exp. Met.*, IX, lec. 8, n. 1862).

25. See, for example, what Thomas says in his Commentary on *De anima*, I, 412b5–6 (CH. 2). For a different assessment of this threefold condition of potentiality in Aquinas, see Norman M. Ford, *When Did I Begin? Conception of the Human Individual in History, Philosophy and Science* (Cambridge: Cambridge University Press, 1991); Jason T. Eberl, "The Beginning of Personhood: A Thomistic Biological Analysis," *Bioethics* 14.2 (2000): 134–157; and Norman M. Ford, *The Prenatal Person: Ethics from Conception to Birth* (Oxford: Blackwell, 2002). This point is well illustrated in Robert Pasnau, *Thomas Aquinas on Human Nature: A Philosophical Study of* Summa Theologiae, Ia 75–89 (Cambridge: Cambridge University Press, 2002), 114 ff.

nothing other than an application of the thesis (F1) "substantial form informs prime matter instantly and immediately," while taking the soul as the substantial form and the first actuality of a body. The substantial form is introduced into the matter immediately, but only after the matter has reached a level of sufficient organization with respect to the capacity that it must have to be able to support the functions that depend on the form.

The idea that the human soul, i.e., the rational soul, is present in act already in the male semen, in any case, encounters further difficulties. In his writings, Thomas discusses at least four.

The first difficulty is that this idea inverts the logical order that holds between generation and what is generated. If the male semen were already rationally ensouled, it would have the substantial form of a human being. In this case, the transformations described as substantial generation, which follow the semen's being detached from the father and the insemination of the female menstrual blood, would have to be treated as a case of alteration because in these circumstances everything that happens after conception would be nothing else than a process of quantitative growth of the corporeal mass and the qualitative differentiation of the organic parts. If this were the case, everything that follows the formation or the detachment of the semen from the father, or even the conception of the embryo, would be logically nonessential for generation. Even an adversary would admit that generation is not said to be finished when the semen is formed or detached, or the embryo has been conceived. The purpose of nature is not to form semen or to conceive embryos and stop there. It is clear that to generate a thing is to suitably transform matter so that it receives the substantial form of that thing. The introduction of the substantial form, then, must follow and achieve generation, not precede it.

The second difficulty is that if the rational soul were already in act in the male semen, generation would take place simply by the detachment of the semen from the father, as with a segmented worm, where two new individuals are generated when it is divided. The third difficulty is that the rational soul would turn out to be divisible, being divided as the male semen is detached from the father. Finally, the fourth difficulty concerns involuntary ejaculations of semen in which there would be a proliferation of rational souls.

Setting aside the severe conciseness of the last three arguments and their argumentative weakness, these last difficulties have force only if one thinks that the human soul is already present in act in the male semen, right from the moment of its formation. They have no hold, however, for one who thinks that God infuses the rational soul just at the moment of conception. Only the third difficulty could be adapted to this case, as long as it is shown that the cellular division subsequent to conception is equivalent to a real material division. In some circumstances, as in monozygotic twin births, this takes place, and it is not by chance that this case, not imagined by medieval thinkers, is considered in the contemporary debate as one of the principal counterexamples to the thesis of the immediate hominization of the embryo.

Thomas formulates these four difficulties in the *Summa contra Gentiles.*[26] In his *Quaestiones de potentia,* the arguments for rejecting this position are tied above all to the Aristotelian conception of the semen, that is, to the twofold idea that (1) the semen is not assimilated by the father as one of his organic components, and so the semen cannot be ensouled by the father's soul, and that (2) the semen is in remote potency to life, being itself at the same time lacking life.[27] In other places, as the *Summa theologiae,* Thomas deals with the same theme from another point of view, asking if the semen is able to generate a rational soul.[28] In these texts, his arguments come from a simple application of (G1)

---

26. See SCG, II, ch. 89, nn. 1737–1741.

27. See QDP, q. 3, a. 9, ad 9, 67a I: *"Prima autem pars huius divisionis destruitur: primo* quidem per auctoritatem Philosophi. Dicitur enim in II *de Anima* [com. 10], quod potentia vitae quae est in corpore physico organico, cuius actus est anima, non est abiiciens animam, sicut semen et fructus; ex quo datur intelligi quod semen est ita in potentia ad animam quod anima caret. *Secundo,* quia cum semen nondum sit ultima assimilatzione membris assimilatum (sic enim eius resolutio esset corruptio quaedam) sed sit superfluitas ultimae digestionis, ut dicitur in XV *de Animalibus* [lib. I *de Gener. animal.,* cap. XIX], nondum fuit in corpore generantis existens anima perfectum; unde non potest esse quod in principio suae decisionis sit in eo anima. *Tertio,* quia dato quod cum eo decideretur anima, non tamen potest hoc dici de anima rationali, quae cum non sit actus alicuius partis corporis, non potest deciso corpore decidi."*

28. See ST, I, q. 118, a. 2.

"Natural generation, as opposed to the change of qualities (alteration) and that of place (locomotion), is a discontinuous process," and (G2) "Natural generation is a process and as such takes place over time and is brought to perfection only at the end of the process; hence, what is generated only exists at the end of the process of generation," or of (F3) "Substantial form does not admit of degrees." But the principal argument to which he returns is that no corporeal power is able to generate what is not corporeal. We will leave this point for the moment and return to it later.

We now return to the other alternative, that is, to the second possibility mentioned above, (b), that the human or rational soul is present in the semen actually, but imperfectly, or in an entirely potential way. This answer is more difficult to characterize. There are two ways of understanding the virtual presence of the rational soul in the male semen, and this probably explains why in the *Quaestiones de potentia* Thomas distinguishes two positions, (B2) and (B3). In the first case, the virtuality of the soul consists in the fact that in the male semen there is something that takes the place of the soul in the sense that although it itself is not a soul, it is able to carry out certain functions characteristic of the soul, and in the course of the process it will itself become a soul. In the second case, what is in the male semen is only in potency to the soul, and so the human soul expresses a mode of realization or actualization of such a power. If in the first case the emphasis is placed above all on the identity between the power that is in the semen and the soul, the second case highlights that each soul reveals a state that perfects and completes the one preceding. Putting aside such fine distinctions, what causes difficulties for Thomas in this position is the idea that (1) there is a formal continuant in the process of human generation, and (2) that such a continuant remains numerically identical throughout the whole process, even though it can undergo a process of perfectioning or completing.[29]

---

29. See QDP, q. 3, a. 9, ad 9, 67a II and 67b C): "*Secundam etiam partem divisionis praedictae* patet esse falsam. Cum enim forma substantialis non continue vel successive in actum producatur, sed in instanti (alias oporteret esse motum in genere substantiae, sicut est in genere qualitatis) non potest esse quod illa virtus quae est a principio in semine, successive proficiat ad diversos gradus

Given the texts of Thomas, it is not easy to determine what, for the adversaries, this continuant might be. At times in his writings there are variations that suggest different positions are in play. For example, in the *Summa contra Gentiles,* it seems that it is the formative power of the semen that gradually, as the organs are formed, becomes first the vegetative soul, then the sensitive soul, and finally the rational soul.[30] In other works, as the *Quaestiones de anima,* the formative power of the semen seems to play instead only the concomitant role of what allows the human soul, which exists in potency in the semen, to become in act vegetative and then sensitive (while the passage from sensitive to rational soul is always due to an external agent).[31]

However it may be, Thomas is of the opinion that positing a formal continuant gives rise to a range of problems. Most of the problems are connected, once again, with the stipulations Thomas makes upon the nature of a substantial form. If one assumes that the same, numerically identical form becomes in succession the individual souls of a human,

---

animae. Non enim forma ignis in aere hoc modo inducitur ut continuo procedat de imperfecto ad perfectum; cum nulla forma substantialis suscipiat magis et minus; sed solum materia per alterationem praecedentem variatur, ut sit magis et minus disposita ad formam. Forma vero non incipit esse in materia nisi in ultimo instanti alterationis. [. . .] *Sed hoc nullo modo potest stare:* quia vel hoc ita intelligitur quod natura intellectualis sit alia anima a vegetabili et sensibili, et sic redit in idem cum secunda opinione: vel intelligitur ita quod ex istis tribus naturis constituatur substantia animae in qua natura intellectualis erit ut formale, et natura sensibilis et vegetabilis erit ut materiale. Ex quo sequitur quod cum natura sensibilis et vegetabilis sint corruptibiles, utpote de materia eductae, substantia animae humanae non possit esse perpetua. *Sequitur* idem etiam inconveniens quod inductum est contra primam, scilicet quod forma substantialis successive educatur in actum"; ST, I, q. 118, a. 2, ad 2; QDSC, a. 3, ad 13, 383a.

30. See SCG, II, ch. 89, n. 1740: "Neque etiam dici potest, quod quidam dicunt: etsi a principio decisionis in semine non sit anima actu, sed virtute, propter deficientiam organorum, tamen ipsammet virtutem seminis, quod est corpus organizabile, etsi non organizatum, esse proportionaliter semini animam in potentia sed non actu. [. . .] Secundum enim hanc positionem, sequeretur quod aliqua virtus eadem numero nunc esset anima vegetabilis tantum, et postmodum anima sensitiva."

31. See QDP, q. 3, a. 9, ad 9, 66b A) and 67b C); QDA, q. 11, ad 1, 101–102, 281–292: "Dicunt igitur aliqui quod licet in embrione prius sit anima uegetabilis quam sensibilis, et sensibilis quam rationalis, non tamen est alia et alia anima; set primo quidem reducitur semen in actum anime uegetabilis per principium actiuum quod est in semine; que quidem anima in processu temporis magis ad ulteriorem producitur [*so in the edition, perhaps for* perducitur] perfectionem per processum generationis, et ipsamet fit anima sensibilis; que quidem ulterius producitur [*so in the edition, perhaps for* perducitur] in maiorem perfectionem a principio extrinseco, et fit anima rationalis";

such a form must undergo a process of becoming more perfect, which goes against (F3) "Substantial form does not admit of degrees." As has been mentioned many times, every change that perfects a form is a formal change, and every formal change produces a change in species; no form, however, can remain numerically one and the same in different species. In the second place, such a form would have to come into act not immediately, but successively, which goes against (F1) "Substantial form informs prime matter instantly and immediately." For Thomas, every interruption of a process of substantial generation brings it about that every form acquired by the subject after such a break is an accidental form. In the end, the starting hypothesis, i.e., positing a formal continuant, would make of the generative process a continuous process, as alteration, and so it would no longer be an authentic process of generation.[32]

As we have mentioned previously, these arguments are persuasive only if the adversary accepts Thomas's doctrine of substantial form. Beyond pointing out to a hypothetical adversary that what is being proposed is a poor interpretation of Aristotle (which is obviously a different question), someone could find nothing particularly perplexing in the idea that the process of generation is a continuous process like that of alteration, or that a form fully reaches its potential only over time. The desire of Thomas to reject this position is surely linked to scruples about Aristotelian exegesis, but it also arises from a preoccupation to specify exactly the logical relations holding between the notions involved in an account of the embryogenetic process.

A clear example of such a preoccupation is given by another argument which recurs at times in Aquinas's writings. Thomas observes that if it were precisely the virtue of the male semen, i.e., the formative power, to become the vegetative and then the sensitive soul of the

---

ST, I, q. 118, a. 2, ad 2. The position referenced in this citation of Thomas seems to be that of Albert the Great; see *In De animalibus,* XVI, tr. I, ch. 11, 157; *Summa de creaturis,* II, q. 17, a. 3, A. Borgnet, ed., in Alberti Magni, *Opera Omnia* t. 35 (Paris: Vivès, 1896), 155; *De natura et origine animae,* tr. I, ch. 4, A. Borgnet, ed., in Alberti Magni *Opera Omnia,* t. 9 (Paris: Vivès, 1890), 385.

32. These arguments recur in SCG, II, ch. 89, n. 1740; QDP, q. 3, a. 9, ad 9, 67a II; ST, I, q. 118, a. 2, ad 2.

human being, the process of generation would be circular since what generates would also be the generated thing and vice versa, and so the generation would be reduced to a process of nutrition and growth.[33] This argument operates under the stipulation that by "what generates" one means "what acts in the process of generation to generate something," and hence it is something opposed to "the generated thing." Accordingly, what generates, as efficient cause, and the generated thing, as final cause, must be distinct items. Otherwise, if the formative power of the male semen of what generates became the soul of the generated thing, at a given time the soul of the generated thing would be also what generates and, worse, it would generate itself. In this case, the process of generation, activated by the soul of the generated, would not be differentiable from a process of nutrition and growth.

Once again, the last argument does not appear particularly decisive. More persuasive, instead, are Aquinas's considerations regarding the theological consequences of this position. Theologically, the main problem for this position, as was said, is to explain how it is possible to pass from a corruptible soul, like the vegetative and the sensitive soul, to an incorruptible soul, such as the rational soul. Thomas highlights this difficulty with different arguments. In the *Summa contra Gentiles,* for example, Thomas invokes the principle that what is formally corruptible by nature cannot make a thing incorruptible by nature. We have already noted this argument: if the vegetative and sensitive souls become rational, the rational soul becomes corruptible since the vegetative and sensitive souls are corruptible by nature.[34] In the *Quaestiones de potentia* and, with greater precision, in the *Summa theologiae,* Thomas Aquinas resorts to a variant on the above argument: if one holds that the rational soul is really different from the vegetative and sensitive souls (since the former is subsistent, as Thomas explains in the *Summa*), then such a position is not in fact different from the doctrine of the plurality of forms (B4), even though the supporters of such a position

---

33. A version of this argument can be read in ST, I, q. 118, a. 1, ad 4.
34. See SCG, II, ch. 89, n. 1741; also QDA, q. 11, ad 1, 102, 292–299.

would like to distinguish it from the pluralist doctrine. On the other hand, if one argues that it is not really different, then the rational soul turns out to be corruptible, a conclusion that must be avoided.[35] One could attempt to avoid this final consequence by holding that the vegetative and sensitive souls, when they become rational, become incorruptible, but this conclusion too cannot be accepted.[36]

In the light of these critiques, what is the final position of Thomas? The conclusion he reaches in the *Summa contra Gentiles* is that the formative power *is not itself* the soul of the embryo nor does it *become* the soul of the embryo.[37] For Thomas the formative power, passed on by the father's semen, is a corporeal power whose only task is to manage the material formation and organization of the body. It remains throughout the whole process, at least until the coming of the rational soul. But since for Thomas the species of what is formed changes during the process (in fact the embryo performs vital operations—vegetative, sensitive, and intellective functions—that are of different species), it follows that, once it is conceded that one and the same form cannot perdure and be gradually perfected, the only possibility is to assume that in the process of generation there is a succession of species, and this requires an alternation of generation and corruption because (G4) "every process of generation involves a process of corruption, and vice versa." And so, before the coming of the rational soul, embryos are formed to last a short period of time. As soon as they are conceived, embryos possess a vegetative ensoulment. Once they reach a more perfect form of organization, these embryos corrupt and embryos specifically more complex take their place. In this way, embryos in their first phases are entities that are transitory and almost instrumental, produced to give life to more articulated and functionally sophisticated embryonic forms and, finally, to a human being. Early embryos do not possess a fixed species, but are like "entities on the way toward a species" *(entia in via ad speciem):* they express preliminary, provisional

---

35. See QDP, q. 3, a. 9, ad 9, 67b C); ST, I, q. 118, a. 2, ad 2.

36. See CT, I, ch. 91; DUI, ch. 1.

37. See SCG, II, ch. 89, n. 1742: "Non igitur ipsamet virtus quae cum semine deciditur et dicitur *formativa,* est anima, neque in processu generationis fit anima."

forms and preparatory phases of the species toward which they are tending. With respect to the species that the embryo gradually exhibits, the generative process is highly discontinuous. Before becoming or giving way to a human being, Thomas says that the embryo acquires at least four different species: that of the semen, that of the menstrual blood, that of a plant, and that of an animal.[38] This discontinuity distinguishes the generation of living, animate organisms from the generation of the simple elements (as air or water), in which a new form is acquired immediately with the corruption of the preceding form:

> Although the generation of simple bodies does not proceed according to an order, since each of them has a form immediately in prime matter, in the generation of other bodies, on the other hand, there must be an order to the generations on account of the many intermediate forms between the first form of an element and the last form to which the generation is ordered. And so there are many generations and corruptions in succession, one after the other. Nor is it a difficulty that something of what is intermediary be generated and immediately after be interrupted, because these intermediary entities do not have a complete species, but are like entities on the way toward a species *(in via ad speciem)*. Therefore, they are not generated so that they may remain, but rather that through them may come what is generated last. Nor is it surprising that the entire transformative process of generation is not continuous, but there are many intermediate generations. . . . The vegetative soul, therefore, which firstly inheres when the embryo lives the life of a plant, is corrupted, and a more perfect soul succeeds,

---

38. Thomas does not single out these four species in every place where he deals with embryology. Moreover, such a sequence is not always explained by Thomas and in itself, as we shall see, is highly problematic. Indeed, Thomas holds at the same time that the material that gives rise to the embryonic process is the female's matter and that the male's semen cannot be considered as a material part of the embryo. But if the first form of the embryo is that of the semen, this entails either that the material subject undergoing the process of generation is the male's semen and not the female's menstrual blood (this consequence would in a way hold even if one would admit that the male's semen mixes or merges with the female's menstrual blood), or that the semen, once united to the menstrual blood, immediately disappears, but in this case a change of the material subject should be granted. Thomas, however, rejects both conclusions.

which is at the same time both nutritive and sensitive, and then the animal lives the life of animal. But once this is corrupted, the rational soul succeeds it, being introduced from outside, although the preceding souls had come about in virtue of the semen.[39]

This account of the embryological process describes the succession of souls in terms of a *replacement* of substantial forms. On the reading that Thomas gives of the fifth chapter of the *Categories,* one of the properties of a substance is that it does not admit of degrees.[40] Thomas shares this Aristotelian intuition, and as a result he sees substantial forms, as opposed to accidental forms, as being entities having a point-like or number-like character, as also Aristotle himself suggests in the *Metaphysics.*[41] The Aristotelian image of species as numbers leads to the

---

39. See SCG, II, ch. 89, nn. 1743–1745: "Licet enim generatio simplicium corporum non procedat secundum ordinem, eo quod quodlibet eorum habet formam immediatam materiae primae; in generatione tamen corporum aliorum, oportet esse generationum ordinem, propter multas formas intermedias, inter primam formam elementi et ultimam formam ad quam generatio ordinatur. Et ideo sunt multae generationes et corruptiones sese consequentes. Nec est inconveniens si aliquid intermediorum generatur et statim postmodum interrumpitur: quia intermedia non habent speciem completam, sed sunt ut in via ad speciem; et ideo non generantur ut permaneant, sed ut per ea ad ultimum generatum perveniatur. Nec est mirum si tota generationis transmutatio non est continua, sed sunt multae generationes intermediae. [. . .] Anima igitur vegetabilis, quae primo inest, cum embryo vivit vita plantae, corrumpitur, et succedit anima perfectior, quae est nutritiva et sensitiva simul, et tunc embryo vivit vita animalis; hac autem corrupta, succedit anima rationalis ab extrinseco immissa, licet praecedentes fuerint virtute seminis." This way of describing animal generation stays unchanged across Thomas's career. See, e.g., *Sent.,* II, d. 18, q. 2, a. 3; QDA, q. 11, 102, 300–315; and especially QDP, q. 3, a. 9, ad 9, 68a F): "In generatione autem animalis apparent diversae formae substantiales, cum primo appareat sperma, et postea sanguis, et sic deinceps quousque sit forma hominis vel animalis. Et sic oportet quod huiusmodi generatio non sit simplex, sed continens in se plures generationes et corruptiones. Non enim potest esse quod una et eadem forma substantialis gradatim educatur in actum, ut ostensum est. Sic ergo per virtutem formativam, quae a principio est in semine, abiecta forma spermatis, inducitur alia forma; qua abiecta, iterum inducatur alia: et sic primo inducatur anima vegetabilis; deinde ea abiecta, inducatur anima sensibilis et vegetabilis simul; qua abiecta, inducatur non per virtutem praedictam sed a creante, anima quae simul est rationalis sensibilis et vegetabilis. Et sic dicendum est secundum hanc opinionem quod embrio antequam habeat animam rationalem, vivit et habet animam, qua abiecta, inducitur anima rationalis. Et sic non sequitur duas animas esse in eodem corpore, nec animam rationalem traduci cum semine" and ad 10; ST, I, q. 118, a. 2, ad 2; QDSC, a. 3, ad 13.

40. See Aristotle, *Categories,* 5, 3b33 ff. On this property, see Thomas Aquinas, *Sent.,* I, d. 8, q. 3, a. 3; ST, I, q. 93, a. 3, ad 3; *Exp. Phys.,* VII, lec. 8.

41. See Aristotle, *Metaphysics,* VIII, 3, 1043b34–1044a10.

thesis, for Thomas, that the species of substances cannot undergo any process of perfecting, nor undergo an increase or decrease of their substantial form. There is not and there cannot be a human being that is more of a human being than another once the species "human being" is completely realized, even if there can be comparisons among species, since a human is superior to a horse. But once substantial forms exist, they can be eliminated only by substituting other substantial forms for them.

Someone could lessen the impact of this curious teaching of Thomas—that sees the generation of a human as a process that contains within it innumerable subprocesses of generation and corruption, advancing by jumps in species—by proposing that the succession of forms in the embryo is not temporal but only conceptual or logical, that the replacement takes place only by an act of mental abstraction. As a matter of fact, some passages can lead to this interpretation.[42] But it seems to me that the majority of passages support a temporal reading of the succession of forms.[43]

Taking up again a doctrine rather common in his day, and even proposed by Augustine, Thomas determines that in fact the entry of the rational soul takes place at the fortieth or forty-sixth day for males and at the ninetieth day for females, but in any case after the primary vital organs are formed.[44] The replacement, then, has to be understood

---

42. See, e.g., *Sent.,* II, d. 4, q. 1, a. 3, ad 1: "Ad primum ergo dicendum quod secundum Augustinum in illa distinctione operum quae in principio *Genesis* memorantur non designatur successio temporis, sed ordo naturae tantum, secundum quod in via generationis est imperfectum ante perfectum et in eodem potentia ante actum, quamvis actus simpliciter praecedat potentiam."

43. Among other passages, see DPN, § 4, 44, 51–68: "Cum ergo nature operatio procedat ab imperfecto ad perfectum et ab incompleto ad completum, imperfectum est prius perfecto secundum generationem et tempus, sed perfectum est prius in complemento: sicut potest dici quod uir est ante puerum in substantia et complemento, sed puer est ante uirum generatione et tempore. Sed licet in rebus generabilibus imperfectum sit prius perfecto et potentia prior actu, considerando in aliquo eodem quod prius est imperfectum quam perfectum et in potentia quam in actu, simpliciter tamen loquendo oportet actum et perfectum prius esse, quia quod reducit potentiam ad actum actu est, et quod perficit imperfectum perfectum est. Materia quidem est prior forma generatione et tempore, prius enim est cui aduenit quam quod aduenit." For other evidence, see Chapter 8, note 4.

44. In the case of the male, the vacillation depends on whether one strictly follows the Aristotelian doctrine (*Historia animalium,* VII) or one also brings into account certain considerations of Augustine. The temporal difference between males and females instead depends on the different

as temporal and, so understood, offers the basis for a qualified answer to the question of the animation of the embryo: the embryo receives rational, and so human, ensoulment only after the fundamental primary organs (above all, the heart and the brain) are formed. Nevertheless, one can safely say that the embryo just conceived is alive and already has some form of ensoulment, namely, vegetative.[45] The semen, on the other hand, once formed possesses only a virtue of the soul, i.e., the formative power, which continues to act also when the matter of the mother is transformed into a living embryo. The function of the formative power is to contribute to the formation and organization of the embryonic body.

---

factors that can influence the conception, both external to the process (such as climatic and environmental conditions) and internal (such as the force of the male semen, the resistance or coldness of the female matter, and the like), on which see *Sent.,* II, d. 20, q. 2, a. 1, ad 2; *Sent.,* II, d. 30, q. 2, a. 2 and ad 4; *Sent.,* III, d. 11, q. 1, a. 1; QDV, q. 5, a. 9, ad 9; QDA, q. 5; and especially ST, I, q. 92, a. 1, ad 1. A clear and complete temporal quantification of the embryogenetic process can be found in the Commentary on the *Sentences.* See *Sent.,* III, d. 3, q. 1, a. 1, q.la 2, ad 1; q. 5, a. 2: "In aliis [*scil.* a Christo] autem haec successive contingunt, ita quod maris conceptio non perficitur nisi usque ad quadragesimum diem, ut Philosophus in IX *De animalibus* dicit, feminae autem usque ad nonagesimum. Sed in completione corporis masculi videtur Augustinus superaddere sex dies, qui sic distinguuntur secundum eum in *Epistola ad Hieronymum.*" For the forty-sixth day, see Thomas Aquinas's Commentary on *John's Gospel:* "Quamvis autem Iudaei intentionem suam referrent ad templum materiale, tamen, secundum Augustinum, potest referri ad templum corporis Christi: quia, sicut ipse dicit in *Lib. LXXXIII Quaest.,* conceptio et formatio humani corporis perficitur quadraginta quinque diebus hoc modo. Primis enim sex diebus corporis humani conceptio, quasi lactis habet similitudinem; novem vero diebus sequentibus convertitur in sanguinem; duodecim inde diebus solidatur in carnem; sed decem et octo reliquis diebus formatur usque ad perfecta lineamenta omnium membrorum. Isto ergo numero sex, novem, duodecim et octodecim in unum coacto, exurgit numerus quadraginta et quinque, cui addito uno propter sacramentum unitatis, sunt quadraginta sex" (*Sup. Ioan.,* ch. 2, lec. 3, n. 409).

45. See SCG, II, ch. 58, n. 1344: "Sed secundum animam intellectivam dicimur *homines,* secundum sensitivam *animalia,* secundum nutritivam *viventia.*"

CHAPTER FOUR

Some Problems

THE POSITION OF THOMAS, which we have reconstructed in the previous chapters, is characterized by a certain originality. His views are different from those of other theologians of his time in that he holds both that Aristotle and his great Arab interpreters, especially Avicenna, were in favor not only of the delayed ensoulment of the embryo (a position that was, in the end, widely shared) but also of a "discontinuist" conception of human generation.[1] On the one hand, Thomas's teaching appears quite logically rigorous, for he correctly draws all the consequences that follow from his assuming the theses concerning the nature of generation and of substantial form that we have shown earlier. As the Dominican master frames the question, the idea that in generation there is a replacement of forms appears to be the only one possible. On the other hand, despite the apparent simplicity

---

1. See *Sent.,* II, d. 18, q. 2, a. 3, ad 4; *Exp. Gen.,* I, lec. 8 (I quote the text in Chapter 7, note 25). Absolutely speaking, Thomas's position is not new. Already William of Auvergne in his *De anima* explained the succession of souls as a succession in which the subsequent soul replaces the preceding one, reabsorbing its functions. I wish to thank Luciano Cova for pointing out this aspect to me.

both of the formulation of the doctrine and the general theoretical framework within which the doctrine is elaborated, this account of embryogenesis gives rise to difficulties of which Thomas himself seems aware, as is shown by the arguments he brings forward against his position. Among the many difficulties, it is helpful for our purposes to look at three in particular.

1. Discontinuity of Generation and Immediate Ensoulment

A first point concerns the relation between the discontinuity of the process of generation and the immediate human ensoulment of the embryo. Someone could maintain that Thomas's analysis of the mechanisms of human generation of itself does not express a position contrary to the thesis of the immediate hominization of the embryo. On the one hand, it has been noted that the arguments brought forward against the thesis that the rational soul exists in act already in the male semen concern the status of the soul before conception. Thomas never discusses the question of the infusion of the human soul at the moment of conception, but always the presence of the human soul in the semen and its possible transmission from the father to the embryo. Since the mother plays no formal role in the process of human generation, it is plain that, from Thomas's perspective, the start of the process of generation cannot be fixed at the moment of conception but at the moment of the semen's formation and detachment from the father. This being the case, many of the arguments noted earlier appear ineffectual against one who believes that conception is the occasion for which God waits to infuse the rational soul in the embryo. On the other hand, the arguments used to deny that the substantial form is introduced over time and that it undergoes a process of perfecting or completion also do not seem to have force against the thesis of the immediate hominization of the embryo. The only truly decisive argument seems to be that based on the Aristotelian characterization of the soul: if one agrees in describing the soul as "the act or form of an organic, physical body that has life potentially," the lack of formed organs could be a good reason for rejecting the moment of conception as that in which the rational ensoulment of the embryo takes place.[2]

In what follows, we will return again for a closer look at this argument, but we can already anticipate it here, based on what has already been said previously. For Thomas, the clause "that has life potentially," which appears in the Aristotelian characterization of the soul, does not refer to the condition of what is completely deprived of life, as the semen, nor does it refer to the condition of what is already alive though still in potency to all or some superior vital operations. For Thomas, the clause "that has life potentially," rather than indicating the status of being about to become ensouled, in which status an organic body is, indicates that the body, just as it is ensouled in act by the soul, is in potency to exercising the operations connected with such an ensoulment.

Thomas's argument that the human or rational soul cannot be infused at the moment of conception, for then it would undergo a process of perfecting which is contrary to (F3) that the "substantial form does not admit of degrees," has been particularly debated in the literature. Some interpreters of Thomas, for example, the editor of his *Quaestiones de anima,* Bernardo-Carlos Bazán, have criticized Thomas's idea that the rational soul cannot be infused at the moment of conception because of the lack of formed organs. The view that the rational soul is introduced at the moment of conception and does not exercise all its functions for lack of organs does not necessarily imply that the soul undergoes a process of perfecting. What is refined over time is not the nature of the soul, but the completeness of the exercise of its capacities:

> Independently of the incompatibility of this conception (i.e., delayed hominization of the embryo) with contemporary biology and with the doctrine of the Church, one can draw attention to certain philosophical weaknesses in the position of Thomas. . . .

---

2. It is evident that, absolutely speaking, this is a weak argument, for one could easily neutralize it by rejecting the Aristotelian characterization of the soul. Indeed, one could simply characterize the soul as "the act or form of a *potentially* organic, physical body that has life potentially."

Saint Thomas labors under a hypothesis without foundation. He believes that if one affirms the existence of the rational soul from the first instant of the embryonic process, while holding the gradual appearance of operations as the development of the organs allows, one ends up affirming at the same time the theory of the degrees of one and the same form. We do not see this following as a consequence. One can perfectly affirm that the rational soul exists in the embryo and that it does not exercise all its operations for want of the necessary organs, as is the case with the mentally sick.[3]

Taken in the abstract, there is no doubt that the arguments of Thomas can be criticized, and we ourselves have drawn attention a number of times to their lack of both demonstrative and persuasive force. Most of them operate under the stipulations introduced and accepted by Thomas. But it seems that a type of criticism such as that of Bazán, which is probably influenced by certain contemporary concerns to defend the immediate hominization of the embryo, does not capture the heart of Thomas's proposal nor in itself is it a convincing critique, given Thomas's presuppositions.

In the light of the arguments of Thomas, the inconsistency of the thesis of the immediate rational ensoulment of the embryo is unavoidable, and there is no philosophical weakness in drawing this conclusion. We have seen how for Thomas generation is a kind of movement directed to giving matter, which is in a state of privation of form, a specific substantial form. If generation reached its full realization at conception, everything that follows conception would end up being

---

3. See Bernardo-Carlos Bazán, "La Corporalité selon saint Thomas," *Revue philosophique de Louvain* 81 (1983): 391–392, note 54: "Indépendamment de l'incompatibilité de cette conception [that is, the delayed hominization of the embryo] avec la biologie actuelle et avec la doctrine de l'Église, on peut mettre en relief certaines faiblesses philosophiques dans la position de Thomas. . . . saint Thomas travaille sur une hypothèse sans fondement. Il croit que, si l'on affirme l'existence de l'âme rationnelle dès le premier instant du processus embryonnaire, tout en soutenant l'apparition progressive des opérations au fur et à mesure que le développement des organes le permet, on tombe par là même dans l'affirmation de la théorie des degrés d'une même forme. Nous ne voyons pas cette conséquence. On peut parfaitement affirmer que l'âme rationnelle existe dans l'embryon et qu'elle n'exerce pas toutes ses opérations, faute d'organes nécessaires, comme c'est le cas chez le malade mental."

accessory and inessential to the generation.[4] This, however, seems to conflict with our common experience and with the very view of substantial generation as a process that results in a substance. The argument of Thomas, evidently, presupposes a specific view of the nature of substantial form. On the one hand, if the embryo were rationally ensouled right from conception, right from conception the embryo ought to have the capacity to be able to exercise intellectual functions. But if, on the other hand, this is not necessary, since it is evident that without formed primary organs the embryo cannot have the capacity to be able to exercise any intellective function, then either the rational ensoulment of the embryo takes place subsequently or, if the initial ensoulment of the embryo is exactly the same as the final ensoulment, then the same and numerically identical form undergoes perfecting or enrichment of its functions. This conclusion appears unavoidable because, with respect to the corporeal matter, the perfecting of a form is expressed by the type of actuality that the form determines in that matter, an actuality that is expressed in terms of the capacity that the composed material substance possesses to be able to exercise certain vital functions. If this is the case, the substantial form would inevitably undergo a process of perfecting if it were infused into the body right at the initial moment of generation, since the embryo just conceived not only does not actually exercise the capacity to reason but it does not even actually possess such a capacity to be able to exercise reason. For Thomas, the natural potentiality to develop, through its own process of self-development after conception, such a capacity to exercise reason cannot be taken therefore as a sufficient basis to argue that a human embryo is informed by a rational soul from the very beginning of its self-developmental process. For something to be a human being, such a capacity to exercise reason must be possessed in act.

Later we will see other difficulties tied to the thesis of the immediate rational ensoulment of the embryo. For now, we can take it as proven

---

4. See SCG, II, ch. 89, n. 1738: "Omnis autem generatio substantialis praecedit formam substantialem, non eam sequitur: si quae vero transmutationes formam substantialem sequuntur non ordinantur ad esse generati, sed ad bene esse ipsius. Sic igitur generatio animalis completur in ipsa decisione seminis: omnes autem transmutationes sequentes essent ad generationem impertinentes."

that for Thomas rational ensoulment of the embryo requires the presence of sufficiently developed vital organs, and this is the only solution philosophically allowable once one assumes that the trait that is characteristic of the human soul is its being the act or form of an organic, physical body.

2. Formation versus Functioning of the Embryo

It is helpful to dwell upon a second aspect, the relation between the formative power and the soul of the father, on the one hand, and the formative power and the material of the mother, on the other. We have seen how Thomas rejected two extreme positions: the first affirmed that in the male semen the human soul was already present, with the soul having the task of guiding the development of the embryo, while the second denied that in the male semen there is in any way a soul, explaining the embryo's vital operations by appealing to the formative power. In the *Summa contra Gentiles,* where one finds the first extended theoretical systematization of Aristotelian embryology, Thomas says nothing more about this power except, as mentioned earlier, that it has as its subject a certain spirit present in the male semen, and that it brings about the formation of the body by dint of the father's soul.[5] Thomas never clarifies the nature of this spirit, nor does he explicate the relation between the formative power *(virtus formativa)* and the soul of the father, which is the principal agent of generation, confining himself to restating the Aristotelian doctrine of *De generatione animalium.* In the Commentary on the *Sentences,* which precedes by a few years the *Summa contra Gentiles,* Thomas opaquely describes this formative power as "that which is left in the semen by the operation of the father's formal power acting in the semen," which is the cause of the relation of resemblance between the father and the child.[6] But also in this case,

---

5. See SCG, II, ch. 89, n. 1742.

6. See *Sent.,* II, d. 30, q. 2, a. 2: "Similiter etiam virtus activa non est ex parte materiae, sed magis ex parte formalis principii. Unde causa assimilationis filii ad patrem non est convenientia in materia, ut oporteat membrum fieri de materia quae ex membris patris resolvitur, cum etiam sit similitudo filii ad patrem in illis ex quibus nullo modo semen deciditur, sicut in unguibus et capillis; sed causa similitudinis est virtus formativa, quae in semine relinquitur ex operatione virtutis formalis ipsius patris agentis in semen."

the way in which the formal power of the father is transmitted to the semen is left unexplored.

Working with Aristotelian examples, in the *Summa theologiae* Thomas presents the formative power as a *movement* rather than as a *form* of the spirit, as an extension of the father's soul rather than as an exercise of a faculty of the spirit that is contained in the semen; he therefore concludes that there is no organ specifically tasked for it.[7] The soul of the father is the principal agent of human generation. However, since the semen cannot be ensouled and the soul is not divisible, the formative power in the semen that is detached from the father cannot be identified with the soul of the father. Thomas confines himself to describing the formative power as a power of a soul or of the soul *(virtus animae)*.[8] Thomas's idea is that the father, as a noble agent, can act in such a way that his effects extend a great distance and remain over time, still continuing to persist even if the father no longer exists. When the semen is detached from the father, then, the semen becomes endowed with a force that brings about moving and transforming, which force is nothing else but a formal power that the semen, in an entirely unique way, comes to possess. Such a power is able to mimic the functions of the father's soul, formally reproducing it in the embryo.

The opacity of many aspects of this account and the use of generic expressions without precise reference can give the impression that Thomas's explanation is nothing more than *ad hoc* or, worse, an explanation that explains nothing. The varying and imprecise formulations that at times appear in his works are apt to enhance this impression. In the *Quaestiones de anima,* question 11, for example, coming some years after the *Summa contra Gentiles,* Thomas affirms that the formative power is not sufficient to explain the vital operations of the embryo, since the formative power only explains the formation of the embryonic body, not its functioning, and so one must appeal to the soul. But then he notes that it would be problematic if one wished to connect the primordial vital operations to the formative power, identifying at the same time such a power not so much with the soul, since the soul is not yet

---

7. See ST, I, q. 118, a. 1, ad 3. See also *Sent.,* II, d. 18, q. 2, a. 3; QDM, q. 4, a. 3; QDA, a. 11, ad 2.

8. See QDP, q. 3, a. 9, ad 11, 72a; QDA, q. 11, ad 3, 102, 330–332: "Ad tertium dicendum quod illa uirtus habet rationem anime, ut dictum est; et ideo ab ea embrio potest dici animal."

perfected, but with a power of the soul *(virtus animae)*.[9] Now, Thomas here recognizes that the vital operations of the embryo are due to the soul or to a soul.[10] In the *Summa contra Gentiles* and in the *Quaestiones de potentia* question 3, article 9, ad 9, he attributed them instead to a power of the soul. Given these conflicting texts, one can ask whether the power of the soul *(virtus animae)* to which he refers in the *Quaestiones de anima* reveals a rethinking of his earlier position, or rather a criticism against those who identify such a power with a power of the parent's soul. At first look, in the *Quaestiones de anima* Thomas does not seem to change his own position, and if this were so, then in order to make sense of the varying terminology found in these texts, an interpreter could hold that Thomas is really discussing two different cases: whether the semen, just detached from the father, already contains a soul or a power of the soul, and whether such a power remains also in the embryo. Thomas's different responses could be explained in the light of this distinction: the semen from the moment of its being formed and detached from the father contains a power of the soul, but once such a power has allowed the actualization of the vegetative faculty of the matter, the embryo is in every respect ensouled and therefore able to live.[11]

But on closer look, things are not so simple: the formative power remains a rather mysterious entity. The expression "power of the soul" *(virtus animae)* could refer to three things: (1) a virtuality of the parent's soul that remains in the semen; (2) a corporeal and material power that mimics the functions of a soul; (3) a virtuality of the rational soul that the embryo will acquire only over time. Each of these alternatives involves problems. On both (2) and (3), Thomas should admit that there is continuity between the power that the semen possesses before encountering the female matter and the power that the embryo just conceived possesses. But this conflicts with the fact that the semen and the embryo are

---

9. See QDA, q. 11, ad 1, 101, 276–281: "Posset tamen hoc sustineri [*scil.* quod virtus formativa sit causa operationum quae in embrione apparent] si predictum principium actiuum in embrione pro tanto diceretur uirtus anime, non anima, quia non dum est anima perfecta, sicut nec embrio est animal perfectum. Set tunc eadem difficultas remanebit."

10. See QDA, q. 11, ad 1, 101, 275–276.

11. See QDP, q. 3, a. 9, ad 9, 68a F) and ad 11–12; QDA, a. 11, ad 3, 102, 330–332.

two distinct entities for Thomas. On (1), on the other hand, there would be a substantial discontinuity between the semen and the embryo, but in this case it would be difficult to account for how the semen transmits the form to the embryo. As we have seen before, Thomas accepts the Aristotelian position on the nature of the male semen. Not having been assimilated, the semen is not an organic part of the human being, and so it is not ensouled. But if the semen is not ensouled, it is difficult to understand how concretely the power of the father's soul extends to the semen, unless one takes it as a primitive datum that cannot be further explained, i.e., the fact that the semen possesses a power of the father's soul.[12]

Strictly speaking, given that the semen is not ensouled, the only power that it could have would be to bring about movement, a power itself determined by the movement of detachment from the father, and this would be the only power that the semen could communicate to something else. The semen, that is, could act on the female matter only as an efficient cause "activating," so to speak, the potentiality already contained in that matter. However, that would be equivalent to attributing to the mother an active role of a formal nature in the process of generation. In accordance with the assumption that the semen is not ensouled, Thomas himself is inclined to explain the relation between the father and the semen in terms of a relation between an agent that moves and a body that is moved. In the *Quaestiones de anima,* question 11, for example, Thomas explicitly introduces this analogy, clarifying its meaning in the following way. In one sense, the movement imparted to a moved body by a mover and the power transmitted to the semen by the father are analogous, for as imparted movement does not last forever, so the formative power exercises an action only for a time.[13] In

---

12. Thomas only speaks of a "transfusion" *(transfusio)* of a virtue of the father's soul to the semen. See, e.g., QDP, q. 3, a. 11, ad 6, 75a: "Ad sextum dicendum, quod vis appetitiva animae non habet imperium nisi super corpus unitum; unde pars decisa non obedit animae appetitivae ad votum. Sed semen non movetur ab anima generantis per imperium, sed per cuiusdam virtutis transfusionem, quae in semine manet etiam postquam fuerit decisum." Thomas uses the same term to explain the spiritual transmission of original sin from the father to the child.

13. See QDA, q. 11, ad 2, 102, 325–329: "Set tamen quantum ad aliquid est simile: sicut enim uirtus proicientis, que est finita, mouet motu locali usque ad determinatam distantiam, ita uirtus generantis mouet motu generationis usque ad determinatam formam."

another sense, however, the two cases are different, for while the cause that moves a body is always external to the moving body, the formative power is a permanent force that is internal to the semen.[14] Hence, the semen possesses two types of force: an effective force bringing about movement, which is transmitted from the father as an external cause and which remains internally to the semen, and a formal force (that is, the capacity to impress on the embryo a form similar to that of the father), which the semen possesses of itself. Given how Thomas expresses himself, this is a fact not subject to further explanation.

But even conceding this point, the nature of the formative power has not been entirely clarified by Thomas. Granted that the semen has of itself this formative power, how is it connected to the different forms of ensoulment that the embryo will gradually acquire? And in what way is this formative power, which is not a soul but a virtuality of the father's soul or something material that mimics the powers of the father's soul, responsible for the vital operations of the embryo? In my opinion, the *Quaestiones de anima,* written probably by Thomas in preparation for the corresponding section on the soul in his *Summa theologiae,* evidences tensions that remain unresolved in Thomas's account of the embryological process. More explicitly, it is not entirely clear which of the following two positions he is taking: (1) that before the coming of the rational soul, the embryo has some form of ensoulment, which comes from some type of soul (as vegetative or sensitive), that is responsible for the vital operations of the embryo; or (2), that the embryo has no real ensoulment, since the principle responsible for the embryo's operations is not a soul, but something that only has the power of a soul and that is in fact identical with the formative power, which the semen carries within itself at least from the moment of its detachment from the father. In the first case, the problem that Thomas must then confront is balancing the role of the formative power and that of the different souls that succeed one another in the embryo. In the second case,

---

14. See QDA, q. 11, ad 2, 102, 316–321: "Ad secundum dicendum quod uirtus illa que est in semine a patre est uirtus permanens ex intrinseco, non fluens ab extrinseco, sicut uirtus mouentis que est in proiectis, et ideo quantumcumque pater distet secundum locum, uirtus que est in semine operatur."

the problem is to explain how a corporeal power could account for noncorporeal operations and, more significantly, account for them in a different subject.

As we have seen, in the *Quaestiones de anima,* Thomas seems to lean toward (1). This seems to me to be the sense of the response to the first argument against his position, which, as we have seen, could also be evidence of a rethinking of his earlier position: whether the formative power be understood as a nonensouled principle or as a power of the father's soul, Thomas holds that in neither case is it able to explain the vital *functioning* of the embryo. But there are other passages from the *Quaestiones de anima* where Thomas seems to incline instead toward (2). For example, the objector of the second argument questions whether the vital operations of the embryo depend on a power present in the semen. Thomas's response reaffirms the conviction that they depend on a power of the soul rather than on a soul, and such a power is unequivocally identified with the formative power of the semen.[15] Similarly, the objector of the third argument recalls that Aristotle in the *De generatione animalium* had stated that the embryo is an animal before it becomes a human being *(embryo prius est animal quam homo)*.[16] According to the objector, one way to understand this affirmation is to admit that in the embryo there is a sensitive soul before there is the rational one, setting aside the fact that the rational soul is later simply added to or takes the place of the sensitive soul; if it were otherwise, the embryo could not be called an animal. Once again, Thomas responds that the embryo can be said to be an animal on account of a power that mimics the functions of the soul *(virtus quae habet rationem animae),* without having to posit the existence of a completed sensitive soul, as that of animals.[17]

---

15. See the previous notes, especially note 8.

16. See *De generatione animalium,* II, 3, 736a35–b5. In fact, the Aristotelian text does not state that the embryo is animal *before* it is human, but only that the embryo cannot be *at the same time* animal and human. On this, see Luciano Cova, "Prius animal quam homo: Aspetti dell'embriologia tommasiana," in Chiara Crisciani, Roberto Lambertini, and Romana Martorelli Vico, eds., *Parva Naturalia: Saperi medievali, natura e vita* (Pisa: Istituti Editoriali e Poligrafici Internazionali, 2004), 357–378; in particular, see pp. 370–372.

17. See the text from the *Quaestiones de anima* quoted above, note 8.

Certainly, there are many ways to reconcile these affirmations of the *Quaestiones de anima*. For example, we could assume that here Thomas is rejecting the doctrine of the plurality of forms, and so his purpose is to avoid positing before the rational soul a soul that remains when the rational soul arrives. Thomas would not be denying that the embryo's vital operations are due to a soul, but he would want only to affirm that such a soul disappears when the successive soul arrives. This, for example, is exactly the sense of his response to the eighteenth argument.[18]

Alternatively, we could assume that the expression "power of the soul" *(virtus animae)* does not refer to something that, even if not a soul, nevertheless has the virtuality of a soul, but rather to something that already possesses the virtuality of the rational soul. In other words, one could argue that in light of the response to the first argument against his position, Thomas intends to differentiate the *formative power* that manages the formation of the embryonic body from a *power of the soul* that manages the functioning of the embryo. His aim would be to point out that when one speaks of a sensitive soul of a human embryo before the rational soul, one need not understand there to be in the embryo a true and proper sensitive soul, as that found in an animal, but rather that there be in it a primordial form of human ensoulment limited to the exercise of sensitive functions. Even if these attempts at reconciliation were plausible, it seems to me a certain tension remains in the *Quaestiones de anima*. The main reason is that it does not seem that the expression "power of the soul" *(virtus animae)* can allude in the above-mentioned passages to distinct virtualities in one and the same soul, i.e., the rational soul, but it rather seems to refer to different vital principles that temporally succeed one other in the embryo.

This tension also appears in other texts of Thomas. There are, in fact, passages in which the relation between the formative power and the soul (presumably vegetative), rather than being described as that of mover to moved, is described as that between the form of an artifact in an artisan's mind and the form of the actual artifact.[19] This parallel leads us to think that there is a type of continuity between the

---

18. See QDA, q. 11, ad 18, 103–104, 385–395.

19. See e.g. *Sent.*, II, d. 18, q. 2, a. 3: "Semen in potentia vivit et non actu. Haec autem potentia non est passiva in semine maris, sicut dicimus ligna et lapides esse in potentia domus (sic enim est

formative power of the semen and the soul of the embryo, even if we admit that the formative power and the soul are quite different entities. In the Commentary on the *Sentences,* for example, Thomas does not put particular emphasis on the elements of discontinuity, preferring to talk of one soul, existing potentially in the semen that gradually becomes ever more in act *(magis magis actu).*[20]

But sometimes Thomas revises this parallel by giving more of an instrumental role to the formative virtue. In the *Summa theologiae,* part I, question 118, article 1, Thomas holds that the formative power is either the soul or a part of the soul only virtually *(in virtute),* exactly as the form of a bed is in a saw only virtually. According to this example, as a saw is only virtually a bed, so analogously the formative power is only virtually a soul. As the act of sawing is a movement toward a bed, and so it can be said that the saw is virtually a bed because the saw contributes to constructing a bed, analogously the act of a formative power is a movement toward the soul, and so it can be said that the formative power is virtually a soul because it contributes to generating a body in which a soul will be infused.[21] In the *Summa theologiae,* therefore,

---

potentia in menstruo mulieris), sed est potentia activa, sicut dicimus formam domus in mente artificis esse potentia domum; unde arti comparat eam Philosophus in XVII *De animalibus;* et hanc potentiam Avicenna et Commentator in VII *Metaphysicorum* vocant virtutem formativam; quae quidem virtus quantum ad modum operandi media est inter intellectum et alias vires animae"; QDP, q. 3, a. 11, ad 4; *Exp. Met.,* VII, lec. 8, n. 1451: "Sicut enim artifex non est actu domus, nec habet formam quae sit domus actu, sed potestate; ita sperma non est animal actu, nec habet animam quae est species animalis actu, sed potestate tantum. Est enim in semine virtus formativa: quae hoc modo comparatur ad materiam concepti, sicut comparatur forma domus in mente artificis ad lapides et ligna: nisi quod forma artis est omnino extrinseca a lapidibus et lignis; virtus autem spermatis est intrinseca."

20. See *Sent.,* II, d. 18, q. 2, a. 3: "Illi autem corporali spiritui coniungitur triplex calor, scilicet calor elementaris, qui est sicut instrumentum resolvens et consumens et huiusmodi operans, et calor animae, qui est vivificans, et calor caeli cuius virtute movet ad speciem determinatam. Et virtute huius triplicis caloris, virtus formativa convertit materiam a muliere praeparatam in substantiam membrorum per modum quo est transmutatio corporis in augmente, ut XV *De animalibus* dicitur. Et secundum quod proceditur in perfectione organorum, secundum hoc anima incipit magis ac magis actu esse in semine, quae prius erat in potentia, ita quod conceptum primo participat opera vitae nutritivae, et tunc dicitur vivere vita plantae, et sic deinceps, donec perveniat ad completam similitudinem generantis." See also SCG, II, ch. 86.

21. See ST, I, q. 118, a. 1, ad 3 (the text has been fully quoted in Chapter 3, note 22); also SCG, II, ch. 89, n. 1752. The idea that the formative power is a movement of the father's soul was already present in Aquinas's Commentary on the *Sentences.* We should therefore not insist too much on the change that occurs in the *Summa theologiae.* Nonetheless, the Commentary on the *Sentences* still

Thomas seems to revise the earlier analogy between the formative power and the soul along the lines indicated in the *Quaestiones de anima*. The formative power is a sort of power passed onto the semen by the father in the very act of its detachment from the father, as a splintered stone receives a power of its own that moves it after it has been chipped off by the hand that splinters it.[22] One could conclude, then, that in the *Summa theologiae* Thomas has opted for an analogical reading of the relation between the formative power and the soul: the formative power plays an instrumental role of organizing the matter analogous to the role played by the soul for the function of the whole composite.[23]

If the formative power plays a role that is only instrumental and is limited to the organic formation of the embryonic body, we still have to clarify what happens to this power after the embryo has acquired a vegetative or sensitive soul, and what is its relation to these forms of embryonic ensoulment. As will be recalled, in the *Summa contra Gentiles,* Thomas recognized that the formative power, transmitted from the father so that what is generated is similar in species to what generates it, remains the same for the whole generative process, even if it is not clear what happens after the coming of the rational soul.[24] More explicitly, in the *Quaestiones de potentia,* Thomas observed that such a power and the spirit in which it is immersed remain also after the coming of the rational soul, except that then the power of the semen changes its function, becoming "regulating."[25] In the first part of the *Summa theologiae,* on the other hand, whose drafting was not much

reveals a certain indecision by Thomas, for there he endows the formative power with both efficient and, "in some way" *(aliquo modo),* formal value (see *Sent.,* II, d. 18, q. 2, a. 3; see again Chapter 3, note 22, for the full text).

22. The example recurs in *Sent.,* IV, d. 15, q. 4, a. 2, q.la 3, and QDP, q. 3, a. 11, ad 5.

23. See already in *Sent.,* II, d. 18, q. 2, a. 3, ad 5. There are also places where Thomas endows the expression "power of the soul" *(virtus animae)* with a different meaning (see, e.g., *Sent.,* IV, d. 15, q. 2, a. 2, q.la 2). But it does not seem to me that other meanings are in play here.

24. See SCG, II, ch. 89, n. 1742 (the crucial text has been quoted in Chapter 3, note 22); also QDA, a. 11, ad 2. But see also SCG, IV, ch. 45, n. 3818: "Semen maris, in generatione animalis cuius-cumque, trahit ad se materiam quam mater ministrat, quasi virtus quae est in semine maris intendat sui ipsius complementum ut finem totius generationis; unde et, completa generatione, ipsum semen, immutatum et completum, est proles quae nascitur."

25. See QDP, q. 3, a. 9, ad 16 (for the text, see Chapter 3, note 20). On the continuity of the semen and on its quasi-identification with the spirit, see QDP, q. 3, a. 11, ad 8, 75b: "Ad octavum dicendum,

after the *Quaestiones de potentia,* Thomas seems to revisit his position.[26] In question 118, article 1, ad 4, he rules out that the formative power is the soul of a human being. The formative power cannot be the vegetative nor sensitive soul, as has been said already, since these derive from that power, for otherwise what generates and what is generated would be numerically identical: the formative power, in fact, derives from the father-generating, while the vegetative soul and the sensitive soul belong to the embryo-generated.

Thomas does not examine in detail how the vegetative and sensitive souls derive from the formative power. On the one hand, the vegetative and sensitive souls seem to be a continuation of the formative power of the male semen, but on the other hand, they seem to be potentially present in the material provided by the woman. The general impression that one has from reading the texts of Thomas is, as mentioned earlier, that he wants to keep distinct the formation of the embryo and its functioning. The formative power of the semen, the residual effect in some way of the father's soul, seems to be called upon only to play the role of modifying the material of the mother. It does this by suitably organizing the female's matter so that first there are fully realized the functions of the vegetative soul, and then those of the sensitive soul, both of which are already in the female matter: the first soul in act and the second soul in potency.

Thomas is not completely clear about the moment in which the embryo begins to operate on its own; it could be already with the actualization of the vegetative soul, when the embryo begins to take in food and so begins to grow, or more likely it is with the actualization of the

---

quod virtus praedicta radicatur in spiritu, qui in semine includitur, sicut in subiecto. Fere autem totum semen, ut dicit Avicenna, in spiritum convertitur. Unde licet corpulenta materia, ex qua conceptum formatur, multoties per generationem transmutetur, non tamen virtutis praedictae subiectum destruitur."

26. On this remark and for an overview of Thomas's doctrine of human nature and embryology, see also Bruno Nardi, "L'origine dell'anima umana secondo Dante," *Giornale storico della filosofia italiana* 12 (1931): 433–456, and 13 (1932): 45–56 and 81–102, reprinted in *Studi di filosofia medievale* (Rome: Edizioni di Storia e Letteratura, 1960), 9–68, and Bruno Nardi, "Sull'origine dell'anima umana," *Giornale dantesco* 39 (1938): 15–28, reprinted in *Dante e la cultura medievale* (Rome: Laterza, 1983), 207–224. The point has been recently noted also by Cova, "Prius est animal quam homo," 363, note 22.

sensitive soul, when the embryo begins to move and to act. Nevertheless, Thomas seems to propose in the *Summa theologiae* a noticeably different account of the embryogenesis process. In the *Summa,* in fact, he states that once the sensitive soul is actualized, the formative power disappears along with the disappearance of the semen and the vanishing of the corporeal spirit in which the formative power is found. The series of clarifications *(Nec hoc est inconveniens)* might suggest a rethinking on Thomas's part or, in any case, some caution in the face of criticism he did experience or felt might be directed at him.[27] At first look, this final position of Thomas complicates things unnecessarily. Thomas might have realized that a clear differentiation between the formation of the embryo (guided by the formative power until the coming of the rational soul) and its functioning (regulated by different souls that follow one another) was causing problems concerning the connection between the vegetative and sensitive souls, on the one hand, and the formative power, on the other hand, so that he finally opted for granting that the semen dissolves at the coming of the sensitive soul.[28]

---

27. See ST, I, q. 118, a. 1, ad 4: "Ad quartum dicendum quod in animalibus perfectis, quae generantur ex coitu, virtus activa est in semine maris, secundum Philosophum in libro *De generatione animalium;* materia autem foetus est illud quod ministratur a femina. In qua quidem materia statim a principio est anima vegetabilis, non quidem secundum actum secundum, sed secundum actum primum, sicut anima sensitiva est in dormientibus. Cum autem incipit attrahere alimentum, tunc iam actu operatur. Huiusmodi igitur materia transmutatur a virtute quae est in semine maris, quousque perducatur in actum animae sensitivae, non ita quod ipsamet vis quae erat in semine, fiat anima sensitiva; quia sic idem esset generans et generatum; et hoc magis esset simile nutritioni et augmento, quam generationi, ut Philosophus dicit. Postquam autem per virtutem principii activi quod erat in semine, producta est anima sensitiva in generato quantum ad aliquam partem eius principalem, tunc iam illa anima sensitiva prolis incipit operari ad complementum proprii corporis, per modum nutritionis et augmenti. Virtus autem activa quae erat in semine, esse desinit, dissoluto semine, et evanescente spiritu qui inerat. Nec hoc est inconveniens, quia vis ista non est principale agens, sed instrumentale; motio autem instrumenti cessat, effectu iam producto in esse"; also *Sent.,* II, d. 18, q. 2, a. 3, ad 2.

28. In the *Quaestiones de potentia,* Thomas acknowledges that the vegetative soul and the formative power exert formally the same functions. See QDP, q. 3, a. 11, ad 7, 75a–b: "Ad septimum dicendum, quod anima sensibilis et vegetabilis de potentia materiae educuntur, sicut et formae aliae materiales ad quarum productionem requiritur virtus materiam transmutans. Virtus autem quae est in semine licet deficiat ab aliis actionibus animae hanc tamen habet. Sicut enim per animam materia transmutatur, ut convertatur in totum in actione nutrimenti; ita et per virtutem praedictam transmutatur materia, ut generetur conceptum; unde nihil prohibet quin virtus praedicta operetur quantum ad hoc ad actionem animae sensibilis in virtute ipsius."

If this were the correct reading of this passage of the *Summa,* as some interpreters believe, two problems would remain unresolved. First, if the formative power, which determines the passage of matter from potency to act, disappeared with the coming of the sensitive soul (or even with that of the vegetative soul), generation would come to a conclusion at this point, since from then on the embryo would be able to act on its own and to guide its corporeal development. This conflicts with what Thomas had always held and, what is more, it would go against what is said in the *Summa theologiae,* part I, question 118, article 2, about the necessity of not identifying what generates with what is generated. For in this case, what is generated by the sensitive soul would change its own matter until it receives the rational soul; hence, it would generate itself.

In the second place, as soon as the embryo receives the vegetative soul it is supposed to take in food and begin to operate in act. In fact, the function of the vegetative soul is to feed and increase the matter.[29] But if this is the case, then one does not understand why the formative power must continue to transform the matter when this function can just as well be done by the vegetative soul. If, on the other hand, we hold that increasing the matter and modifying the matter for the formation of organs are distinct operations, then it remains unclear why the vegetative functions are not accomplished by the formative power itself, given that to form organs the matter must be increased. However one interprets the passage from the *Summa,* this second problem captures, in my opinion, a real difficulty unresolved by Thomas's teaching, for the coordination between the vegetative soul and the formative power remains unexplained, while at the same time a careful explanation of their interaction would be called for, given that the functions that they exercise are, at least in part, the same.

While the second problem remains unresolved, the first might have

---

29. See, e.g., ST, I, q. 97, a. 3: "In primo igitur statu anima rationalis communicabat corpori id quod competit ei inquantum est anima, et ideo corpus illud dicebatur animale, inquantum scilicet habebat vitam ab anima. Primum autem principium vitae in istis inferioribus, ut dicitur in libro *de Anima,* est anima vegetabilis, cuius opera sunt alimento uti et generare et augeri"; *Sent. De an.,* II, ch. 3, 80, 193–200. On the functions of the vegetative soul, see also *Sent. De an.,* II, ch. 7, 96, 47 ff.

an explanation. Examined carefully, the response Thomas gives to the fourth argument against his position does not change very much what he said in the *Quaestiones de potentia*. Even though the overall question in which the argument is found asks whether the sensitive soul (i.e., that of a human being) is transmitted with the semen, the fourth argument focuses on the sensitive souls of animals. If the response of Thomas were limited to animals, the change would be less drastic and would concern only the idea, expressed in any case only in the *Quaestiones de potentia,* that the formative power can remain even after the realization of the final form, when the process of generation becomes one of alteration, serving a regulating function. On the other hand, the prohibition against the identity between what generates and what is generated would remain applicable.

In any case, and setting aside all these textual difficulties, there is no doubt that on Thomas's account the formative power cannot be considered as something analogous to today's genetic code, as some interpreters have proposed, much less as something entirely similar to it. There are at least two reasons for this. First, the formative power plays only an instrumental role and only for a time, while the genetic code continues in the embryo. Second, the formative power is only masculine, while the embryonic genetic store is the result of a fusion between the masculine and feminine genetic code.[30] The medieval medical notion of "radical moisture" *(humidum radicale)* turns out to be closer

---

30. Thomas adopts a common idea of Aristotle's theory of generation, namely, the idea that human generation is naturally directed toward the generation of the male. In the wake of Aristotle (see *De gen. an.,* II, 3, 737a27–29), Thomas defines the woman as a "defective male" *(mas occasionatus)* (*Sent.,* IV, d. 36, q. 1, a. 1, ad 2; QDV, q. 5, a. 9, ad 9; ST, I, q. 99, a. 2, ad 1). Thomas explains that the generation of the woman as well as the resemblance of the generated male to the mother is due either to a defect or a weakness of the male formative power or to an excessive resistance or coldness of the female material. Generally speaking, this is a curious aspect of Aristotelian embryogenesis because the generation of the female, described as accidental, is instead necessary to the perpetuity of the species. On the other hand, we have already noted that Thomas does not assign any positive or active role to the woman in the process of human generation, so he rejects the medical theory of the "two seeds" (see *Sent.,* III, d. 3, q. 2, a. 1 and q. 5, a. 1; *Sent.,* III, d. 4, q. 2, a. 1; ST, III, q. 31, a. 5, ad 3). Properly speaking, the female seed is completely inessential to generation. All the same, Thomas concedes that the term "seed" can be used also for the woman, but only to indicate the passive or material principle (see ST, I, q. 115, a. 2, ad 3). For details on the generation of the woman, see *Sent.,* III, d. 11, q. 1, a. 1; d. 15, q. 1, a. 3, ad 2.

to the notion of a genetic code, though the two are called upon to account for completely different aspects of generation. The term "radical moisture," as we will discuss at greater length in the next chapter, indicates that material component received from the parents that constitutes the first organic state of the embryo and that, according to some medieval medical doctors, remains as such for the entire life of the human being. And for Thomas, radical moisture, sometimes explained as a kind of thermal balancing of the destructive action brought about by vital heat, has the task of determining and accounting for the successive forms of organic moisture that lead by degrees to the final form. It might also be mentioned that this notion is rarely discussed by those who talk of the comparability of the formative power and the genetic code.

In conclusion, the vacillations that remain in Thomas's texts indicate at least an uncertainty, or perhaps his deliberately avoiding entering into all the details of the embryogenetic process. For example, we have seen earlier in the Commentary on the *Sentences* that it is the soul existing potentially in the semen that undergoes a process of progressive actualization. Similarly, in the *Quaestiones de anima*, question 11, Thomas asserts that the vegetative soul preexists (likely, in potency) in the male semen.[31] And in some other places, Thomas talks of the semen as the first species of the embryo. In the *Quaestiones de anima*, it is probably his polemic against the thesis of the plurality of souls (for he is responding to an objection that maintains the nonidentity of the different souls from the fact that they appear successively) that leads him to admit that the vegetative soul is the first soul of the semen. More correctly, Thomas should have said that the vegetative soul is the first soul of the embryo, as also the context of the argument would have brought him to conclude.

Nevertheless, this way of speaking leads us to suppose that it is the male semen rather than the female menstrual blood that is the material subject of the biological transformations involved in the different forms

---

31. See QDA, q. 11, ad 1, 102, 310–315: "Et ideo dicendum quod anima uegetabilis prius est in semine, set illa abicitur in processu generationis et succedit alia que non solum est uegetabilis set etiam sensibilis, qua abiecta iterum additur alia que est uegetabilis, sensibilis et rationalis."

of ensoulment. But this would be mistaken, for in no place does Thomas distance himself from the Aristotelian doctrine that denies that the male semen remains in the embryo as a material part of the embryo. This means that the male semen and the female menstrual blood do not mix materially, even though Thomas represents the form of blood as the first form into which the semen is converted.[32] In the *Summa theologiae,* Thomas appears to correct this point, recognizing that the vegetative soul preexists (in act) in the female material.[33] On the one hand, Thomas could not admit that the male semen is the material subject of the process of generation, for otherwise the formative power of the semen would act on itself, determining the passing of souls from potency to act, and in this way, once again, what generates and what is generated would become one. On the other hand, if Thomas admitted that the vegetative soul is already present in the female material, this would imply that the female material is the material subject of the transformations in species of the embryo. Normally Thomas admits

---

32. There are texts (belonging to the early part of Thomas's career) where Thomas appears more disposed to concede that the male semen is part of the generated embryo. See, e.g., *Sent.,* II, d. 18, q. 2, a. 3, ad 4; d. 30, q. 2, a. 2: "Ita hoc semen per virtutem generativam ministratum et praeparatum habet naturam ut ex eo generetur totum cum admixtione eius quod ex matre ministratur, quidquid sit illud. Et huic opinioni consentio, quae rationabilior ceteris videtur"; SCG, IV, ch. 45, n. 3818 (see the text above, note 24). But for an explicit denial of this possibility, see SCG, IV, ch. 45, n. 3821: "Si vero aliquis dicat quod, cum homo naturaliter generatus habeat corpus naturaliter constitutum ex semine maris et eo quod femina subministrat, quicquid sit illud, corpus Christi non fuit eiusdem naturae cum nostro, si non est ex maris semine generatum:—ad hoc manifesta responsio est, secundum Aristotelis positionem, dicentis quod semen maris non intrat materialiter in constitutionem concepti, sed est solum activum principium, materia vero corporis tota ministratur a matre. Et sic, quantum ad materiam corpus Christi non differt a corpore nostro: nam etiam corpora nostra materialiter constituta sunt ex eo quod est sumptum ex matre"; ST, III, q. 28, a. 1, ad 5; ST, III, q. 31, a. 5, ad 3; *Exp. Met.,* V, lec. 21, n. 1090. Already in the Commentary on the *Sentences* Thomas manifested a certain reluctance to consider the male semen as the material element of generation: "Materia enim humani corporis est menstruum, vel etiam semen simul, ut quibusdam placet. Quod autem semen et menstruum causetur in nobis, hoc non est nisi per virtutem naturalem, quae in nos ex parentibus devenit; et ita tota materia corporis humani originem habet ab Adam, non quasi ab eo decisa, sed quasi a virtute quae ab ipso descendit praeparata" (II, d. 30, q. 2, a. 2, *expositio textus*); also II, d. 18, q. 1, a. 1, ad 2: "menstruum materia embrionis dicitur"; d. 31, q. 1, a. 2, ad 4. The Aristotelian source is *De generatione animalium,* I, 20–21, 729a9–b8.

33. See ST, I, q. 118, a. 1, ad 4: "Materia autem foetus est illud quod ministratur a femina. In qua quidem materia statim a principio est anima vegetabilis." For the fact that the female matter, upon which the male semen acts, is already alive, see *Sent. De an.,* II, ch. 7, 96, 61–75.

this point. But if so, the problem remains of reconciling this idea with the idea that the form is introduced only by the father by means of the semen, given that such ensoulments are already contained virtually in the female material. If the male semen and the female matter do not fuse together, Thomas should admit that one form can travel from one subject to another, an admission that Thomas usually is not disposed to make.

3. Natural Generation of the Body versus Creation of the Soul

There are many other problems connected with Thomas's account of embryogenesis, but I would like to call attention to a final aspect that concerns the relation between generation and creation. Some arguments in the *Quaestiones de potentia,* question 3, article 9, criticize the appeal to a creative act of God to account for the existence of the rational soul. It is objected that if the rational soul does not spring from the process of generation and instead is infused by God, the final and defining end of *human* generation is lost. Furthermore, if we think that it is the rational soul that communicates being to the body and we want to maintain the most profound significance of human generation, then we should conclude that the rational soul remotely comes from the semen. More generally, this conclusion can be defended by appeal to the familiar idea that each agent produces something similar to it in form.[34]

Thomas responds to the arguments by specifying that human generation does not have the task of *generating* the rational form (among other things, such a form is incapable of being generated), but rather the task of *disposing* matter for the reception of the rational soul and, in some way, of accounting for the *union* of soul and body, from which union the very body receives being. It is true that the formal reason for generation is the formal resemblance between father and child, but the rational soul is not the factor that ultimately accounts for generation.

---

34. See QDP, q. 3, a. 9, arg. 5–7, 19–20, 64a–b; ST, I, q. 118, a. 2, arg. 3 and 4.

The response of Thomas does not completely resolve the problem raised by the opponents. First, generation does not give to the body a being of its own, different from the being of the soul; second, generation is being demoted to a process of *preparation* for what will become but is not yet a human being. The defining character of what is finally generated becomes in this way external to its generation, and human generation becomes a process that of itself is not attainable on the natural plane. Nevertheless, given the way in which Thomas understands the relations between the final matter and the form and between the final moment of potentiality and the initial moment of actuality, it is true that the final point of the realization of the process of generation and the initial point (that is, at the same time, also final) of the creation of the human soul coincide.[35]

In summary, setting aside difficulties that the teaching of Thomas raises and that are left for the most part without solution as we have seen, it is certain that Thomas admits that from conception the embryo is endowed with a soul, i.e., the vegetative soul.[36] Or, in any case, Thomas endows the embryo with a power of the soul that is responsible for the vital operations the embryo exhibits. In particular, Thomas maintains that it is unsatisfactory to appeal to a material and corporeal formative power to account for ensoulment and the *vital functioning* of the embryo, even though such a power is necessary to account for the process of *organic formation* of the embryonic body, which formative power continues up to the embryonic body's immediate reception of the rational soul. The nature of this power, however, remains largely unclarified, and

---

35. See ST, III, q. 6, a. 4: "Respondeo dicendum quod caro humana est assumptibilis a Verbo secundum ordinem quem habet ad animam rationalem sicut ad propriam formam. Hunc autem ordinem non habet antequam anima rationalis ei adveniat, quia simul dum aliqua materia fit propria alicuius formae, recipit illam formam; unde in eodem instanti terminatur alteratio in quo introducitur forma substantialis."

36. See *Sent.*, III, d. 35, q. 1, a. 1, ad 2: "Ad secundum dicendum quod secundum animam vegetabilem dicitur esse vivere, non quasi in operationibus eius tantum vita consistat, sed quia operationes eius sunt primae operationes vitae in nobis"; *Sup. Gal.*, III, lec. 4, n. 142: "Et sic dicimus, quod in anima prima indicia vitae apparent in operibus animae vegetabilis: quia anima vegetabilis est, quae primo advenit animali generato, ut Philosophus dicit"; ST, I, q. 39, a. 8; QDV, q. 28, a. 1, ad 5. For Thomas, the vegetative soul is something that remains from conception to the end of the life of a human being. See *Sent. De an.*, III, ch. 17.

so a doubt remains whether such a power is a principle immanent to the embryo or only a principle internal to the process of generation but external to the embryo. In any case, since the substantial form is introduced immediately and instantly and only at the end of the process, there is no doubt that for Thomas the rational soul cannot be present in the embryo before the basic vital organs are formed.

CHAPTER FIVE

The Identity of the Embryo

BEFORE DISCUSSING some possible bioethical implications of this account of the process of human generation, we must clarify Thomas's position on what is perhaps the most important philosophical issue involved in these discussions: the identity or continuity of the subject of the embryogenetic process. As we have seen, Thomas's explanation of embryogenesis is reached partly by rejecting the idea that generation is a continuous process. Such a stance becomes necessary once one affirms theses (F1)–(F3), which concern the nature of substantial form, and one affirms the difference between substantial generation on the one hand and quantitative and qualitative alteration on the other (G1). In particular, Thomas rejects the idea that there exists a formal continuant within the generative process, that is, that there is a form that remains numerically the same throughout the whole process.[1]

---

1. See SCG, II, ch. 89, n. 1743: "Species tamen formati non manet eadem: primo habet forma seminis, postea sanguinis, et sic inde quosque veniat ad ultimum complementum"; ST, I, q. 118, a. 2, ad 2; "Non est autem possibile ut una et eadem forma numero sit diversarum specierum." See also *Sent.*, II, d. 18, q. 2, a. 3, ad 4.

Nevertheless, he does admit that the formative power or its subject, the "spirit" *(spiritus)*, which the semen derives from the soul of the father, remains throughout the entire process.[2] If the process of generation is discontinuous, with an alternation of generations and corruptions, how can one defend the identity or continuity of the subject of this process? The identity of the subject of the process, however, must to some degree be admitted, for otherwise one could not even assert that the embryo becomes a human being, nor could one speak of *human* embryos.

1. The Identity and Continuity of the Embryo

In general, the question of the continuity of the embryo in the generative process is to be kept distinct from the question of its identity or unity. In the first case, we are called to demonstrate that the embryo does not completely cease existing at a certain moment of the process for the good of something else. Abstractly, this continuity could be proven in two ways: either (1) by demonstrating that there is something of the embryo (an organic part of it or a portion of its matter) that remains exactly as it is, unmodified from the beginning to the end of the process, or (2) by demonstrating that the process of the embryo's transformation does not include temporary halts or have interruptions. Thomas's conclusion that the process of generation is not continuous, as opposed to the process of alteration, seems to leave little room, however, for defending the embryo's continuity throughout the entire

---

2. See QDP, q. 3, a. 11, ad 8, 75b: "Ad octavum dicendum, quod virtus praedicta radicatur in spiritu, qui in semine includitur, sicut in subiecto. Fere autem totum semen, ut dicit Avicenna, in spiritum convertitur. Unde licet corpulenta materia, ex qua conceptum formatur, multoties per generationem transmutetur, non tamen virtutis praedictae subiectum destruitur." Note that in this chapter, if not indicated otherwise, for the sake of brevity I shall take the terms "identity" and "unity" as equivalent. I shall speak indifferently of numerical unity and numerical identity, identity and unity of subject, and the like. I hope, in this context, no confusion will result. For a recent reconsideration of the issue of the transtemporal identity in Thomas, see Christopher Hughes, "Aquinas on Continuity and Identity," *Medieval Philosophy and Theology* 6 (1997): 93–108; Christina van Dyke, *Metaphysical Amphibians: Aquinas on the Individuation and Identity of Human Beings* (Ph.D. diss., Cornell University, 2000); and Matthew G. McDaniel, *De Anima, DNA: A Modified Stump/Aquinas Hylomorphic Model, the Soul and the Identity of Human Persons, Resurrected* (M.A. thesis, Liberty University, VA, 2010); also available at www.works.bepress.com/matthewgmcdaniel/1 (accessed May 1, 2012), to which I refer for further bibliographical references.

process. A follower of Thomas could admit his conclusion that the process is discontinuous but limit it to the formal plane. The embryo in the very first phases of development can be considered as formally different from the embryo endowed with vital organs. But on the material plane, she/he could be less inclined to concede that the process is totally discontinuous, not only because it seems necessary that there be one and the same matter that gradually becomes organized and grows in quantity but also because there is no observable evidence of any substantial interruption in the process.

The question of the identity or unity of the embryo brings up a different problem: whether we can demonstrate, beyond the transformations that the embryo undergoes and the continuity of these transformations, that the process involves one and the same entity. On closer look, this question includes two different problems. One must first establish when the embryo can be considered an entity distinct from the mother, and second, one must ascertain whether in the generative process one can speak of a transtemporal numerical identity of the embryo so that one can affirm that the baby just born is the same entity as that embryo from which it came when it was first conceived.

Obviously, the questions of identity and continuity are not completely unconnected. If one succeeds in proving that the embryo maintains its identity throughout the process of generation, one has also proven a type of continuity of the process itself and of the subject of that process. Therefore, in what follows, even with this difference in mind, we will talk at times of the identity or continuity of the subject in a way that is substantially equivalent. More particularly, in this chapter we will be concentrating above all on the question of the identity of the embryo.

The difficulty in ascertaining the identity of the embryo is dependent on another difficulty, i.e., that of establishing what exactly happens, according to Thomas, before the coming of the rational soul. It is certain that this difficulty is not encountered with formed embryos, that is, those following the fortieth day. Thomas upholds that these embryos are ensouled and so are entities completely distinct from the mother, although they continue to be materially connected to her in the maternal womb; after the fortieth day, the process of generation is formally ended and the process of growth properly speaking begins. Often Thomas fixes this watershed while discussing whether original sin is transmitted to the one to be born through its conception.[3] At other times it is fixed when he discusses the question of whether by baptizing a pregnant mother the effects of baptism are also passed on to the child in her womb.[4]

But things are different before the coming of the substantial form, for during that time the embryo does not yet have a stable species, as it is incessantly changing form and continuously transforming its matter. The embryogenetic process, which brings the female material inseminated by the male semen to become an embryo at first lacking in form and then endowed with form, seems to encounter problems with both types of continuity, i.e., formal and material. When, then, does the embryo become an entity formally or materially independent? How can one account for the identity that the embryo is supposed to maintain throughout the generative process, from conception to birth?

The impression one has reading Thomas's texts is that there is no one response that he gives to these questions. As just mentioned, after the infusion of the rational soul the embryo is certainly an autonomous entity in all respects.[5] But before that point, Thomas's response is conditioned by the ephemeral status of the embryo, by its unfinished state and potentiality. The principle that Thomas often uses—that if an embryo carries out vital operations, it is necessary that it have an internal principle of ensoulment—does not decide the issue in favor of immediate human ensoulment rather than delayed. As we have said, one could explain the vital principle as a "power of the soul" *(virtus animae)* rather than as a real and proper soul and so concede to the

---

3. See, e.g., *Sent.,* IV, d. 6, q. 1, a. 1, q.la 2, ad 2.

4. See ST, III, q. 68, a. 11; *Sent.,* IV, d. 1, q. 2, a. 6, q.la 2, ad 2: "Ad secundum dicendum quod puer adhuc in utero matris existens, quantum ad humanam cognitionem pertinet, non habet esse distinctum a matre, et ideo per actum hominis consequi non potest nec nunc ut mundetur ab originali per Baptismum nec tunc ut mundaretur per fidem parentum, sed divinitus mundari potest, sicut de sanctificatis in utero apparet"; *Sent.,* IV, d. 6, q. 1, a. 1, q.la 1. On the embryo's material inseparability from the mother, see ST, I, q. 113, a. 5, ad 3; ST, III, q. 68, a. 11, ad 2. The fact that the body of the formed embryo and that of the mother are materially distinct but not separated makes the embryo an ontologically dependent and weak being.

5. See ST, III, q. 27, a. 1, ad 4.

embryo (which is not rationally ensouled) at any rate an improper and imperfect ensoulment. The immanence of a principle of ensoulment, therefore, does not furnish us with a criterion of identity. What is more, in what follows, we shall see that the embryo escapes all the criteria for transtemporal identity that Thomas elaborates in his works.

The vacillation found in Thomas's texts does not help us in answering our two questions. We have seen that at times Thomas concedes that the vegetative soul exists potentially in the semen, while at other times that it exists potentially in the menstrual blood. If we assume that the vegetative and sensitive souls, which characterize the first moments of the embryo's life, are potentially present in the male semen, then the full independence of the embryo could take place only when the formative power of the semen ceases its activity, and so only at the moment of the infusion of the rational soul. But on the other hand, we could assume, following instead Thomas in the *Summa theologiae,* that the vegetative and sensitive souls that the embryo possesses are potentialities of the embryonic matter.[6] In this case, the embryo could be considered as something formally independent from the moment of conception, for right from the first moment the embryo has a soul or a power of the soul, i.e., vegetative, that guides the process of nutrition, growth, and qualitative differentiation of the embryonic matter.[7] Even though Thomas's arguments for rejecting the idea that the ensoulment of the embryo comes from the mother's soul are not completely conclusive as we have seen, it remains true for Thomas that an embryo must have an internal principle of ensoulment. For otherwise we cannot explain why the embryo carries out operations that, if it were truly part of the mother, are not also carried out by her entirely. And so, if the actualization of the potentiality to nourish itself, which the matter of the mother possesses, thanks to the action of the formative power of the male semen, is nothing other than the appearance of the vegetative soul, we have to conclude that the embryo takes on its own identity as an entity formally independent from the mother already with the coming of the vegetative soul.

---

6. See ST, I, q. 118, a. 1, ad 4; also QDA, a. 3, ad 2.
7. See ST, I, q. 118, a. 2, ad 2.

On this problem, I mention in passing that the contrast "immediate ensoulment versus delayed ensoulment" does not entirely capture the core of Thomas's position. On the one hand, there is no doubt that Thomas defends *some* type of immediate ensoulment of the embryo, rejecting both (1) that the soul of the female is the factor responsible for the vital operations of the embryo, and (2) that this factor is exclusively the formative power of the male semen. In both cases, the reason is that the two principles are external to the embryo. As a consequence, Thomas admits that the embryo possesses right from conception at least *vegetative* ensoulment. But on the other hand, he rejects (3) that such ensoulment is from the beginning rational (i.e., human) and (4) that this ensoulment is of itself complete and perfect. More particularly, we have seen that this second denial is reached by his rejecting certain theses. The first thesis is that there are really distinct souls copresent in the human being or in the embryo, for then the souls coming after the first would end up being accidental forms of the body, granted that the soul is the substantial form of the body. The second thesis is that there is in the human being or in the embryo a soul that over time has assumed different degrees and perfections, since then (a) the substantial form would change in intensity, contrary to (F3) that "substantial form does not admit of degrees"; (b) generation would turn out to be indistinguishable from alteration, contrary to (G1) that "natural generation, as opposed to the change of qualities or of quantity (alteration) and that of place (locomotion), is a discontinuous process"; (c) the generation of a human being would not be a true and genuine generation; and (d) the immortality of the rational soul would not be reconciled with the mortality of the vegetative and sensitive souls.[8] What remains after these denials is the idea that there is in the process of generation a continuous substitution of forms. Assuming from now on in our discussion that the *Summa theologiae* expresses Thomas's final position, namely, that the embryo can be considered an entity formally independent from the mother right from conception, since right from the very start the embryo exhibits vital operations that cannot be superimposed on or reduced to

---

8. Ibid.

those of the mother, the problem of the transtemporal identity concerns the embryo right from conception. How then is it possible to safeguard the identity of the embryo from conception up to the formation of the basic vital organs?

The answer that Thomas's interpreters commonly give to this is that the process of human generation is materially continuous and formally discontinuous. This is intuitively clear and makes sense of many of Thomas's claims. But how are we to understand the continuity and identity of matter? Which matter is responsible for the continuity and identity of the subject and how is the identity of the matter to be established if every process of identifying a thing, whether on the metaphysical or cognitive plane, requires a form? Since we are dealing after all with a process of generation, someone could point out how, in an obvious sense, there can be nothing, either on the formal or material plane, that from the start of the process to its end remains exactly as it is. As we have mentioned, Thomas himself holds that one should not be surprised that the process of generation is not continuous. If it were, it would be indistinguishable from a process of nourishment or growth, since if the process were continuous, there would be a subject that is already generated in act from the first moment. But on the other hand, it is undeniable that the process of generation, even if it admits of differentiated subprocesses, is on the whole a process that takes place without interruptions or gaps, and therefore a certain continuity of the process must be guaranteed even if in a rather tenuous way. Thomas's problem is precisely this: how to reconcile the formal discontinuity of the subject with its presumed material continuity. If the criterion for identifying a thing is given by its form, when the form is changed, also the identity of the thing ceases. Consequently, if the criterion for ascertaining the continuity of a thing is given by matter, it seems impossible to set aside the form, since the matter itself is identified with recourse to form. How, then, can we talk of continuity of matter without talking of identity of form?

In what follows, we shall first show how Thomas explains the identity of the subject of a process of generation, and then we shall show how one can speak of identity and continuity with regard to matter.

2. The Identity of the Subject of Generation

When one begins to give an answer to these questions, the first thing to do is to consider what criteria Thomas himself developed for determining the identity of a thing. As it turns out, this task is especially arduous. One reason is that in his works Thomas formulates criteria for establishing the identity of a thing that are quite diverse. In addition, such criteria are not always formulated uniformly and, moreover, one realizes that strictly speaking they are applicable only to entities that *already* exist in act. For example, Thomas often discusses the question of whether someone's body is numerically the same after the human soul is separated from it, and if such a body remains numerically the same at the moment of the final resurrection at the end of time. Evidently, these questions are meaningful since they are asking about an identity between two things that, though at different times, nevertheless exist in act. Similarly, Thomas asks if Socrates and this white thing are the same entity, and again the question makes sense since "Socrates" and "this white thing" refer to things that, at the same time, exist in act. But in the case of an embryo, any criterion of identity seems to fail. For example, when we ask if a given embryo and a given human being are numerically the same thing, the question does not seem germane, since we have seen that Thomas conceives of the embryo as something that does not exist in act, not having a perfect and complete form of its own. Hence, it does not seem that one can say that the embryo is either numerically the same nor numerically different from the human being.

Certainly there is an obvious sense in which an embryo and a human being can be called the same entity, given that a human *comes* from an embryo. But this sense is of little relevance, for a table can also be said to come from the wood of a tree, but the table and tree cannot be called for this reason the same entity. The case of the embryo is more complex. In this case, it is not enough to say that the human comes from the embryo; we must add that the embryo *becomes* a human being, while we cannot say of the tree that it becomes a table. In other words, a simple "principle of traceability," by which it would be possible to determine the identity of a changing subject in whatever phase of the process of change, once the rule of change is known, does not seem sufficient to determine the identity of the subject within a process of generation. Besides admitting a certain order, presumably causal, among the constituents of a process or among the phases that characterize the same subject within a given process, it is also necessary to posit in the case of the embryo that the final form, which is the end or purpose of generation, regulates all the preceding phases in such a way that each one of the preceding phases causally determines and orders the immediately following phase of the process toward the subsequent phases and the final form.[9] It is this teleology that distinguishes the case of the embryo from that of the tree. A tree does not *become* a table because a tree is not oriented naturally toward the table form, but a human embryo is naturally oriented toward the human form. This is the reason why we can say that the embryo *becomes* a human being and that a given embryo is a *human embryo*. In the case of the embryo a principle of traceability also holds, but the rule of transformation is in this case teleological.[10]

A principle of traceability is certainly sufficient for attributing a type of transtemporal identity to an embryo within a process of generation. But when one inquires into the identity of an embryo, one wants to look for something less extrinsic; that is, one wants to know what within the embryo gives rise to this traceability, and, in Aristotelian terms, if this be its form or its matter. At first, someone could attempt to show that the factor responsible for embryonic identity is the form, emphasizing that the exchange of an embryo's species is not arbitrary and chaotic, but rather ordered, since every successive species not only takes the place of the preceding one but also subsumes its functions while adding new ones.

---

9. See, e.g., *Exp. Met.*, VIII, lec. 4, n. 1753: "Quandocumque materia se habet ad diversa secundum ordinem, non potest ex posteriori rediri in id quod praecedit secundum ordinem. Sicut in generatione animalis ex cibo fit sanguis, et ex sanguine semen et menstruum, ex quibus generatur animal. Non potest autem mutari ordo, scilicet ut ex semine fiat sanguis, aut ex sanguine cibus, nisi per resolutionem ad primam materiam, ex eo quod cuiuslibet rei est determinatus modus generationis"; ST, I, q. 118, a. 2, ad 2.

10. On this, see Thomas's explanation of the technical phrase "(to derive) from something" *(ex aliquo)* in *Exp. Met.*, V, lec. 21, nn. 1085–1092.

Earlier we observed that Thomas adopts an explanatory model for the phenomenon of generation that describes the succession of forms as *replacement*. More precisely, we should have said that this model describes the succession of forms as *reabsorption*. Given the way in which Thomas explains the embryogenetic process, the embryo in fact exercises at the beginning of the process only vegetative functions. But right from the start, such functions are oriented toward predisposing the matter so that it can support the exercise of the higher intellective functions. When the embryo's matter becomes much more organized, the embryo begins to exercise also sensitive functions. The principle of its sensitive ensoulment is the same as that of its vegetative ensoulment, such that the functions that the embryo was exercising when it had only a vegetative soul are formally the same that it exercises when it possesses a sensitive soul. The sensitive soul replaces the vegetative soul, reabsorbing its functions, so that the sensitive soul exercises both the vegetative functions that the vegetative soul was exercising and also the sensitive functions. The same happens with the passing from sensitive to rational soul. Even if introduced from outside, the rational soul replaces the sensitive soul, reabsorbing its functions, and so the rational soul continues to exercise the vegetative and sensitive functions once carried out by the sensitive soul and in addition adds the exercise of the intellective functions.[11]

Given this scheme, the passage from embryo to human being implies

---

11. See, e.g., QDA, q. 11, ad 1, 102, 310–315: "Et ideo dicendum quod anima uegetabilis prius est in semine, set illa abicitur in processu generationis et succedit alia que non solum est uegetabilis set etiam sensibilis, qua abiecta iterum additur alia que est uegetabilis, sensibilis et rationalis"; QDSC, a. 3, ad 13, 383a: "Quidam vero dixerunt quod a principio inest anima vegetabilis et illa eadem cum fuerit magis perfecta fit anima sensitiva et tandem fit anima intellectiva, sed per actionem exterioris agentis quod est Deus. Sed hoc est impossibile. Primo, quia sequeretur quod forma substantialis reciperet magis et minus, et quod generatio esset motus continuus. Secundo, quia sequeretur animam rationalem esse corruptibilem, cum vegetabilis et sensibilis corruptibiles sint, dum ponitur fundamentum animae rationalis esse substantia vegetabilis et sensibilis. Non autem dici potest quod sint tres animae in uno homine, ut ostensum est. Relinquitur ergo dicendum quod in generatione hominis vel animalis sunt multae generationes et corruptiones sibi invicem succedentes. Adveniente enim perfectiori forma, deficit imperfectior. Et sic cum in embryone primo sit anima vegetativa tantum, cum perventum fuerit ad maiorem perfectionem, tollitur forma imperfecta, et succedit forma perfectior, quae est anima vegetativa et sensitiva simul; et ultimo cedente, succedit ultima forma completissima, quae est anima rationalis."

that there is one and the same subject that undergoes a process of progressive enrichment of functions. It is true that the embryo's vital functions depend on really distinct souls, but it is also true that each soul that follows, replacing the preceding, reabsorbs into itself the functions exercised by the preceding soul, such that those functions seem to remain exactly as they were in the embryo. From this perspective, beyond an assumed material continuity, the continuity of the embryo could also be safeguarded on the formal plane by the permanence of certain primordial vital functions. The identity of such functions, combined with a certain identity of the matter (which we will examine shortly), could be taken as what allows us to infer the identity of the subject within the process of generation.

This suggestion certainly has plausibility, but on closer look an interpreter may realize that Thomas's reasoning hides certain problems. To bring these to light, we can begin by seeking a deeper understanding of how Thomas characterizes the logical relations between identity and difference.

2.1. Different Kinds of Identity

Aristotle dedicates the ninth chapter of the fifth book of the *Metaphysics* to clarifying the meaning of the terms "identical," "diverse," "similar," and "dissimilar." Commenting on this, Thomas observes that two things can be identical or the same in different ways. (We leave aside identity *per accidens* that, according to Thomas, obtains when either A is an accident of B or B is of A or when A and B are accidents of a third thing C.) Thomas explains four cases in which A and B are *per se* identical or the same: (1) if the matter of A is numerically identical to the matter of B; (2) if the matter of A is specifically identical to the matter of B; (3) if there is a substantial continuity between A and B; (4) if A and B share a single and indivisible definition.[12] Basically, identity expresses a form of unity or union, so that two things can be called

---

12. See *Exp. Met.*, V, lec. 11, n. 911: "Deinde cum dicit 'alia vero' ponit modos eiusdem per se; et dicit, quod aliqua dicuntur eadem secundum se eisdem modis, quibus dicitur unum per se. Omnes enim modi, quibus aliqua unum per se dicuntur, reducuntur ad duos: quorum unus est secundum quod dicuntur unum illa, quorum materia est una, sive accipiamus materiam eandem secundum

"identical" in one sense if, though they each have their own being, they have some property in common or, in a second sense, if, sharing the same being, they can be considered as diverse terms of a relation of identity.[13] An embryo and a human being cannot be said to be identical in this second sense, which is used for the most part when one is speaking of the identity of one thing with itself. Consequently, if we can speak of identity in their case, it must be in the first sense.

Regarding the four-part division above, it is evident that an embryo and a human being cannot be identical in the fourth way (4), for the definition of a human being cannot be given to an embryo. Thomas defines a human being as a mortal rational animal, while an embryo is only a mortal animal. An embryo acquires the property of being rational only with the formation of the basic vital organs, and this occurs, as was said, not before a month and a half of gestation. One might then say that an embryo and a human being are identical in the first sense (1). But an embryo and a human being do not have exactly the same quantity of matter, that is, the same individual matter with the same extension, for the simple fact that after the coming of the vegetative soul, the process of generation becomes a process of bodily growth, of differentiation and formation of vital organs. The argument Thomas uses at times that a human being does not generate a numerically identical human being, since they do not share the numerically same matter, can be used also in the case of an embryo and the generated human being.[14] But we will return to this aspect later.

It is rather reasonable to think that an embryo and a human being do not have exactly the same, numerically identical, individual matter

---

speciem, sive secundum numerum; ad quod pertinet secundus et tertius modus unius. Alio modo dicuntur unum, quorum substantia est una: vel ratione continuitatis, quod pertinet ad primum modum: vel propter unitatem et indivisibilitatem rationis, quod pertinet ad quartum et quintum."

13. See *Exp. Met.,* V, lec. 11, n. 912: "Ex hoc autem ulterius concludit, quod identitas est unitas vel unio; aut ex eo quod illa quae dicuntur idem, sunt plura secundum esse, et tamen dicuntur idem in quantum in aliquo uno conveniunt. Aut quia sunt unum secundum esse, sed intellectus utitur eo ut pluribus ad hoc quod relationem intelligat."

14. See, e.g., *Sent.,* IV, d. 44, q. 1, a. 1, q.la 2, ad 1; ST, III, q. 28, a. 1, ad 5. If the matter that establishes the numerical identity of a thing is that extended by quantity, necessarily an embryo and a man do not amount to the same numerically identical thing. On this, see also *Quodl.* XI, q. 6, ad 2, vol. 1, 161, 69–77: "Ad secundum dicendum quod, licet eadem materia faciat idem numero, non tamen materia nuda, †nec que facit principium in numero†, set una materia, secundum quod est sub

or the same quantity of matter. However there is a passage from an early work, the *Quaestiones de veritate* (belonging to his first Parisian stay in 1256–1259), which we will examine more closely later, where Thomas affirms that an embryo and an animal are not numerically different. Now since for Thomas only the matter is responsible for numerical differentiation, if an embryo and an animal are not numerically different, it follows that they must have the same matter. So this passage could direct us to the second way (2), i.e., that the matter of A is *specifically* identical to the matter of B. But also this way encounters a difficulty, for the matter of a human being is a (perfectly) organic matter, while the embryo has a matter that is nonorganic (or in any case not yet perfectly organic), and hence the matters seem to be not *specifically* identical. At a certain moment later on, when flesh and bones are formed, this criterion might work, but at the start of the generative process it cannot give an account of identity between an embryo and a human being. The problem is that flesh and bones are formed only with the coming of the rational soul, when the embryo is no longer an embryo but has become by then a human being.[15]

---

dimensionibus terminantibus ipsam, facit idem numero; unde, licet multe forme reiterentur in materia corporis resurgentis, tamen resurget corpus sub eisdem dimensionibus et cum eisdem principiis essencialibus." If, as the above text shows, for the numerical identity of a thing the (numerical) identity of its essential principles is required, then no numerical identity can hold between an embryo and a man because of the embryo's lack of rationality. On the link between (numerical) identity of a thing's essential principles and identity of the thing with respect to the subject, see also *Quodl.* XI, q. 6, vol. 1, 160–161, 34–44: "Dicendum quod, ad hoc quod aliquid sit idem numero, requiritur ydemptitas principiorum essencialium; unde, quodcunque principiorum essencialium etiam in ipso indiuiduo uariatur, necesse est etiam ydemptitatem uariari. Illud autem est essenciale cuiuslibet indiuidui quod est de ratione ipsius indiuidui, sicut cuiuslibet rei sunt essencialia materia et forma; unde, si accidencia uarientur et mutentur, remanentibus principiis essencialibus indiuidui, ipsum indiuiduum remanet idem"; and QDA, q. 19, ad 5. In the CT, I, ch. 153 and, especially, ch. 154, Thomas explicitly relates the identity with respect to the subject to the (numerical) identity of a thing's essential principles, while he distinguishes the identity with respect to the subject from the numerical identity provided by individual matter: "Vnde licet [*supple:* trina dimensio] non eadem numero redeat, idemptitas subiecti non impeditur ad quam sufficit unitas essentialium principiorum" (ch. 154, 141, 113–115). This criterion was already formulated in the early DPN, § 6, 47, 63–64: "Eorum igitur que sunt idem numero, forma et materia sunt idem numero, ut Tullii et Ciceronis," and in *Sent.*, IV, d. 44, q. 1, a. 1, q.la 3.

15. Thomas seems to assume that it is the *type* of matter rather than the *quantity* of matter on which the extension determining the individuality of a given body depends that establishes the numerical identity of a formed human body across time. See the following text from the SCG:

Hence, there remains only the third way (3) of accounting for a supposed identity, and the substantial continuity between an embryo and a human being might restore the sense of identity that we are seeking. As a first approximation, two things A and B can be said to be substantially continuous if and only if there is a continuity of a subject that from A becomes B. This characterization, however, is rather opaque, since what is meant by the continuity of a subject remains unclear. Most of all, it is vitiated by circularity, for it explains identity in terms of continuity, but it is clear that the continuity of a subject presupposes that the subject already has an identity of its own. Moreover, the continuity should not even be taken in too strict a sense, for as we have said, the embryo does not possess its own being in act and so neither its own being one; as a consequence, if the embryo cannot be counted as one, it can neither be said to be numerically identical to or numerically different from the human being to which the embryo will gives rise. If an embryo and a human being were numerically different, there would be a name of a single species for them. If so, both could be called human beings, and so there would be no difference between two human beings

---

"Quod etiam quarto obiicitur, resurgentis unitatem non tollit. Quod enim non impedit unitatem secundum numerum in homine dum continue vivit, manifestum est quod non potest impedire unitatem resurgentis. In corpore autem hominis, quandiu vivit, non semper sunt eaedem partes secundum materiam, sed solum secundum speciem; secundum vero materiam partes fluunt et refluunt: nec propter hoc impeditur quin homo sit unus numero a principio vitae usque in finem. Cuius exemplum accipi potest ex igne, qui, dum continue ardet, unus numero dicitur, propter hoc quod species eius manet, licet ligna consumantur et de novo apponantur. Sic etiam est in humano corpore. Nam forma et species singularium partium eius continue manet per totam vitam: sed materia partium et resolvitur per actionem caloris naturalis, et de novo adgeneratur per alimentum. Non est igitur alius numero homo secundum diversas aetates, quamvis non quicquid materialiter est in homine secundum unum statum sit in eo secundum alium. Sic igitur non requiritur ad hoc quod resurgat homo numero idem, quod quicquid fuit materialiter in eo secundum totum tempus vitae suae resumatur: sed tantum ex eo quantum sufficit ad complementum debitae quantitatis; et praecipue illud resumendum videtur quod perfectius fuit sub forma et specie humanitatis consistens. Si quid vero defuit ad complementum debitae quantitatis, vel quia aliquis praeventus est morte antequam natura ipsum ad perfectam quantitatem deduceret, vel quia forte aliquis mutilatus est membro; aliunde hoc divina supplebit potentia. Nec tamen hoc impediet resurgentis corporis unitatem: quia etiam opere naturae super id quod puer habet, aliquid additur aliunde, ut ad perfectam perveniat quantitatem, nec talis additio facit alium numero; idem enim numero est homo et puer et adultus" (SCG, IV, ch. 81, n. 4157, see also nn. 4151–4152; and *Sent.*, IV, d. 44, q. 1, a. 2, q.la 4; *Sup. De Trin.*, q. 4, a. 2 and ad 1). We shall return to this point later.

and between a human being and a human embryo. In principle, nothing stops one from working with such an expanded ontology, but it is evident, that for Thomas a human being and a human embryo *appear* different and it is of such empirical diversity that a philosophical explanation must give an account.

Given these complications, an interpreter could refine the concept of substantial continuity and hold that in the case of an embryo and a human being Thomas assumes that substantial continuity is given by the fact that A and B share one and the same being. To share one and the same being can be understood synchronically or diachronically, and it is clear that an embryo and a human being can only be said to share one and the same being in the second way. The sharing of one and the same being could guarantee that beyond the formal and material modifications of a subject, one has always to do with one and the same subject.

This refinement of the condition for substantial continuity, however, is not able to resolve completely the question of the identity of the embryo, and this for two reasons. In the first place, the being of a thing depends on its form, and so if a thing changes form (as happens in the case of the embryo), it then also changes its own being. In the second place, the simple appeal to the continuation and existential story of a thing seems to be a condition that is too vague in that it does not explain precisely and adequately the identity of a thing: a thing could be modified so radically as to be no longer recognizable, to the point that no one would say that it is the same thing, even though that thing never ceased to exist. Sharing one and the same being, therefore, is a condition still too extrinsic to A and B, and again, it does not explain the identity between A and B but presupposes it. One senses that even the criterion of substantial continuity is inadequate to account for the identity of an embryo. So, where do we go from here?

As we shall see later, the presupposition of the identity of subject of the embryo will be to a certain extent inevitable given the way that Thomas sets up the problem of the identity of a thing. The identity of the subject of the generative process is, in the end, presupposed by Thomas, and this depends on the fact that in general the notion of identity seems to be for Thomas a primitive notion, not explainable by more fundamental notions. In a certain sense, some type of identity must be presupposed in explaining the identity of some other thing. It is evident that if we explain the transtemporal identity of a thing in terms of the identity of form or of matter, we can once again bring up the question of identity with regard to the form or the matter, such that there is no end to the posing of the question. If the identity of an embryo, as we shall see, is metaphysically unexplainable, since it can be guaranteed neither by the matter nor the form, it is unavoidable that such an identity be assumed by Thomas as a basic given, which can be inferred from extrinsic data. If this is the case, we could say that what Thomas is really seeking is only a condition that would allow us to ascertain such an identity.

From this point of view, the condition of sharing one and the same being may be after all a good condition from which the identity could be inferred. In particular, in the case of an embryo A and a human being B, substantial continuity tells us that A does not have its own being but is something in potency to being B, which expresses the authentic being of A. Thomas systematically explains the relation between A and B by using the contrasting notions of imperfect/perfect, incomplete/complete. That A has an imperfect or incomplete form means that the form attributable to A when A is not yet B is not the genuine form of A. More explicitly, to be an embryo does not express the complete or perfect form of an embryo, but only expresses an incomplete or imperfect form of being a human being, which is the genuine form of the embryo. Hence, the being of A is exhausted in its being in potency to B, and being B expresses the perfect and complete being of A, a being that A does not yet possess, insofar as it is A, except in an imperfect and incomplete way. In my view, in the case of the embryo, substantial continuity between A and B can be restored precisely by the metaphysical *incompleteness* of the embryo with respect to the human being.

2.2. Incomplete versus Complete Identity

We can see how this substantial continuity manifests itself from another point of view. Commenting on the fifth book of the *Metaphysics,*

Thomas distinguished different senses of continuity and explained that in one sense "the continuous" is that which has only a single movement and cannot be otherwise, while a movement is single or continuous if it is indivisible from the viewpoint of time, and also if, more fundamentally, it regards a single subject.[16] In the case of movement, the singleness of the subject is evidently presupposed, but nevertheless it still can be deduced from the continuity or temporal indivisibility of the movement itself. As Thomas explains at length, commenting on the fifth book of the *Physics* of Aristotle (V, lec. 6 ff.), this happens in ordinary movements of local motion, but it also takes place in the process of generation: since generation, even if proceeding by jumps in species, does not have interruptions or gaps, the subject of generation has to be single, for the movement of generation is single and indivisible from the viewpoint of time. The singleness of a subject is the basis of the singleness of a movement, while the singleness and temporal indivisibility of a movement is that from which the singleness of the subject in motion may be inferred.

As we have noted, when in his writings Thomas characterizes substantial unity and identity, he is always attempting to define some subject that is already in act with respect to its parts or with respect to one of its states that will follow, and for this reason his characterizations can be applied only indirectly to the case of the embryo. In fact, all of them have difficulty capturing the identity or unity holding between an embryo and a human being. For example, the embryo cannot be said to be a subject that is indifferent in form according to the species (the second sense of *unum per se* discussed by Thomas in his commentary on the *Metaphysics,* book V, chapter 6), for the embryo changes species and until it reaches a complete specific form, it is not a true and proper subject.

Nevertheless, Thomas recognizes that an embryo and a human being are numerically the same subject. How can the notion of the identity of subject be sharpened? What are the metaphysical conditions that determine it? The numerical nondifference between an embryo and a human

---

16. See *Exp. Met.,* V, lec. 7, nn. 852–855.

being, affirmed by Thomas at least in the *Quaestiones de veritate,* implies their numerical identity and this implies the numerical unity of the subject. Now, Thomas usually relates numerical nondifference to non-difference of matter and this latter to nondifference of continuity.[17] If we assume this connection, we can conclude that the numerical unity of a subject, which can be deduced from the unity of its movement, implies some form of unity of matter.[18] And this implies in turn, at a more abstract level, a kind of unity of genus.

Thomas often links matter and genus. When a human being is defined as a rational animal, for example, Thomas maintains that the genus and the difference of the definition ("animal" and "rational" respectively) are in some way connected to the matter and to the form of the human being that is defined. But Thomas rejects any literal interpretation of this parallel. The genus "animal" cannot be taken only from the matter of a human being, nor the difference "rational" only from the form. Both the genus and the difference designate the entire composed substance: the genus designates the composed substance in an indeterminate way (or as something indeterminate), while the difference designates it in a determining way (or as something that determines the genus), and the species designates the same composed substance in a determinate way (or as something completely determinate). Hence, the

---

17. See *Exp. Met.,* V, lec. 12, n. 913: "*Quaedam* vero dicuntur diversa numero, quia differunt secundum materiam, sicut duo individua unius speciei. [. . .] Contingit enim quaedam esse idem numero, scilicet subiecti, sed diversa ratione, sicut Socrates hoc album," and n. 915: "Et tamen alii modi unius, vel eius quod est idem, possunt reduci ad istos hic tactos. Diversitas enim generis in diversitate speciei. Diversitas vero continuitatis in diversitate materiae."

18. See *Exp. Phys.,* VII, lec. 2, n. 892: "*Numero* quidem est idem motus, qui est ex eodem termino a quo in idem numero sicut in terminum ad quem; ita tamen quod sit etiam in eodem numero tempore; et cum hoc oportet quod sit eiusdem mobilis numero. Et ad exponendum quod dixerat, subiungit quod motus numero unus est ex eodem in idem, sicut ex *hoc albo,* quod significat unum numero, in *hoc nigrum,* quod etiam nominat aliquid idem numero, et secundum *hoc tempus* deter-minatum, quod etiam est unum numero: quia si esset motus secundum aliud tempus, licet aequale, non esset numero unus, sed specie tantum"; and lec. 8, n. 952: "Et ideo ad comparandum tam loci mutationes quam alterationes, considerandum est quot sint species alterationis vel loci mutationis, utrum scilicet eadem vel plures. Et hoc quidem potest considerari ex rebus in quibus est motus: quia si illa *quae moventur,* idest secundum quae est motus per se et non secundum accidens, differunt specie, et motus specie differunt; si vero differunt genere, et motus differunt genere; et si numero, et motus differunt numero, ut in quinto dictum est."

genus designates the entire composed substance in a *material* way with respect to the difference that designates it in a *formal* way. The different semantic comportments of the terms of genus, difference, and species do not reveal analogously different ontological comportments of their referents.[19]

If we apply these considerations to the case of living organisms of different species, we see that the genus designates a common and shared material structure that can be described in terms of the vital functions exercised by such a structure, functions that can be posited as matter or potency with respect to the higher, more specific vital functions. Furthermore, the specific difference indicates a more sophisticated material structure that can be described in terms of vital functions that can be posited as form or act with respect to the lower vital functions. Of itself, the genus does not exist outside the species, for there does not exist a material structure capable of supporting vital functions that are not perfected. That is, there cannot be an animal apart from one of the animal species that specify, in one way or another, the generic vital functions.[20]

In this schema, the unity of genus that is found, not between two complete species, but between what does not yet have a species and that which finally has one, could only be a potential unity, in the sense that the genus stands to the species as what is undetermined stands to what is determined. In this way, the identity of the subject can be explained in terms of the identity of matter, and this, given that we are dealing with living organisms, in terms of the identity of the vital functions exercised by such organisms. Rather than being fixed and determined once and for all, the unity between an embryo and a human being turns out to be, after all, variable and gradual. As the process is realized, the degree of unity becomes continually less generic and continually more specific, just as in the reverse case when a substantial form ceases, the same functions could be thought to maintain a degree of unity that becomes more and more generic. The unity of matter between

---

19. On the imperfect parallelism between language and reality, see, e.g., *Exp. Met.*, VII, lec. 1, n. 1252 ff.

20. On the nonexistence of the genus beyond the species, see *Exp. Met.*, VII, lec. 12, n. 1544 ff.

an embryo and a human being is conditioned by the same gradualness. The embryo just conceived does not have a properly human matter, since the embryonic matter is nothing but human matter in a yet incomplete and imperfect form. As the embryo is perfected, however, the embryonic matter becomes an ever more human matter, until the embryonic matter and the matter of a human being fully coincide. In this way, the unity between an embryo and a human being passes from partial to total, from indeterminate to determinate.

The connection between matter and genus brings us back once again to the problem of the identity of functions. The notion of the identity of generic functions that gradually become more specific seems to account rather well for the identity between an embryo and a human being. Unfortunately, however, Thomas devotes little space to explaining concretely the workings of the mechanism of replacement of forms and of absorption of functions that a successive form carries out on the preceding form, nor does he discuss problems that possibly could arise from his account. On the other hand, he does say more about the reverse process of the separation of the form from the body and the gradual ceasing of vital functions. In light of how Thomas treats this inverse case, however, it turns out to be difficult to preserve the numerical unity of the subject within the process of generation, given that in the process of a substance's corruption the unity of the subject is not maintained. In the various places where Thomas discusses substantial corruption, in fact, he observes that when the substantial form ceases in a human being, the subject not only does not maintain a numerical identity but the identity of the genus is also not numerically the same. In other words, once the property "being rational" is lost, it is not only true that the human body that still lives is not numerically the same body. In addition, it is not the same *living* body *numerically* as before when it was rational, but it is a living body that is identical *only in genus*.[21] That is, Thomas seems to differentiate between generic identity

---

21. See ST, I–II, q. 67, a. 5, ad 1: "Ad primum ergo dicendum quod, remoto rationali, non remanet vivum idem numero, sed idem genere"; QDP, q. 8, a. 4, ad 5, 223b: "Ad quintum dicendum, quod alius est modus quo definiuntur accidentia, et quo definiuntur substantiae. Substantiae enim non definiuntur per aliquid quod sit extra essentiam eorum: unde id quod primo ponitur in definitione

and numerical generic identity: a living body that is no longer rational is generically the same as the rational living body (insofar as they are both living), but numerically there is a different living being. At the biological level, this implies that the animal functions exercised by a rationally ensouled living body cannot be numerically the same animal functions exercised by the same living body lacking rationality, although at the generic level they are exactly the same functions.

If we apply this analysis to the case of the embryo, the hope of preserving a numerical identity of the generic functions, as an expression of the numerical identity of the matter, vanishes. The animal functions carried out by an embryo before the arrival of the rational soul and the same animal functions carried out by a human being after the arrival of the rational soul are not only not numerically the same but they are also not numerically generically the same. They are identical only in genus, which is to say very little, for there is no such thing as perfect generic vital functions, as if they could be isolated in themselves, nor is the type of functioning or the degree of perfecting of such functions numerically the same before and after the coming of the rational soul.

Even with this negative conclusion, the case of the separation of the human soul from the body allows us to say that in the case of something that is becoming a certain species, the degrees of lesser generic unity ought to be described as degrees of greater determination and specification of the functions carried out by one and the same subject.[22]

---

substantiae est genus, quod praedicatur in eo quod quid de definito. Accidens vero definitur per aliquid quod est extra essentiam eius, scilicet per subiectum, a quo secundum suum esse dependet. Unde id quod ponitur in definitione eius, loco generis, est subiectum; sicut cum dicitur: simum est nasus curvus. Sicut ergo in definitionibus substantiarum, remotis differentiis, remanet genus; ita in definitione accidentium, remoto accidente, quod ponitur loco differentiae, remanet subiectum; aliter tamen et aliter. Remota enim differentia remanet genus, sed non idem numero: remoto enim rationali, non remanet idem numero animal, quod est animal rationale; sed remoto eo quod ponitur loco differentiae in definitionibus accidentium, remanet idem subiectum numero: remoto enim curvo vel concavo, remanet idem nasus numero"; ad 8, 224a: "Ad octavum dicendum quod, remota differentia constitutiva, remanet genus in communi, non in eodem secundum speciem vel numerum"; QDM, q. 2, a. 9, ad 18. On the permanence of the identity of the genus once the differences are subtracted, see also *Sent. De an.,* II, ch. 28, 189, 108–113: "Deinde cum dicit: *Omnes enim hii intelligere* etc. ostendit causam predicte positionis. Manifestum est autem quod, remota differencia qua aliqua ad inuicem differunt, remanent idem, sicut si rationale auferatur ab homine remanebit de numero irrationabilium animalium."

22. See *Exp. Met.,* V, lec. 7, n. 861: "Et sic patet quod propinquissimo modo dicuntur aliqua esse unum genere, et similiter sicut aliqua dicuntur esse unum materia. Nam illa etiam quae dicuntur

Hence, the identity and unity of the embryo is not demonstrated by Thomas, but is only deduced from the fact that the substitution of functions can be suitably described in terms of perfecting the ensoulment possessed by a given matter. Such an identity or unity, however, remains substantially a vague or generic identity, an identity of a subject that does not maintain any property or part, material or formal, throughout its entire history. This is true for an embryo with respect to a human being, and also for a human being with respect to every phase of its existence.

Working from what Thomas offers us in his texts, we can conclude that there is not a solid biological basis for defining the generic unity between an embryo and a human being. In fact, the only tool that Thomas uses to account for the identity of the subject within the process of generation is metaphysical rather than biological, namely, the abstract and metaphysical notions of potency and act. We can look upon the embryo as that which is in potency a human being and upon a human being as that which the embryo is, but in act, because once the process of generation is set in motion the embryo is that which naturally and of itself becomes a human being, and the human form is that which, as the goal toward which the process tends, retrospectively directs the entire process of generation. As a consequence, the unity of the subject is drawn from the simple stipulation that what is in potency and what is in act must be numerically identical, although what is in potency, insofar as it is potency, and what is in act, insofar as it is in act, express, with respect to the final form, only a proportional or analogous unity.[23] Potency and act, therefore, require one and the same subject simply because it is presupposed that what is in potency is the same as

esse unum materia, distinguntuur per formas. Genus enim, licet non sit materia, quia non praedicaretur de specie, cum materia sit pars, tamen ratio generi sumitur ab eo quod est materiale in re; sicut ratio differentiae ab eo quod est formale. Non enim anima rationalis est differentia hominis, cum de homine non praedicetur; sed habens animam rationalem, quod significat hoc nomen rationale. Et similiter natura sensitiva non est genus hominis, sed pars. Habens etiam naturam sensitivam, quod nomine animalis significatur, est hominis genus. Similiter ergo et propinquus modus est quo aliqua sunt unum materia et unum genere." On the gradualism of the generic unity in a human being, see *Exp. Met.*, V, lec. 7, n. 862. See also ST, III, q. 50, a. 5, ad 2, and for emphasis on the connection between numerical unity and unity of subject, QDSC, a. 3, ad 19; QDM, q. 2, a. 9, ad 18; and *Sent.*, III, d. 5, q. 1, a. 3, ad 4.

23. See, e.g., *Sent.*, III, d. 1, q. 2, a. 1; *Exp. Met.*, VII, lec. 8, nn. 876 and 879 and lec. 12, n. 916.

what is in act.[24] Such seems to be, in the end, the only unity or identity that can be acknowledged between an embryo and a human being.[25]

2.3. Some Difficulties

This result of our investigation seems to resolve the question of the identity of the embryo. However, an interpreter could object that it does not, since the identity between potency and act is had only in the final moment of the realization of a thing's potency. For example, in the process of the construction of a house, the moment when the final brick is put in place, fully realizing the potentiality of the bricks arranged in a suitable way to be a house, coincides with the moment in which there is a house in act, but the house in act only with difficulty

---

24. See for instance the following text: "Dicit ergo primo, quod actus est prior tempore potentia; ita tamen quod idem specie, est prius agens, vel ens actu quam ens in potentia; sed idem numero est prius tempore in potentia quam in actu. Quod sic manifestatur. Si enim accipiamus hunc hominem qui est iam actu homo, fuit prius secundum tempus materia, quae erat potentia homo. Et similiter prius tempore fuit semen quod potentia est frumentum, quam frumentum actu, *et visivum,* idest habens potentiam videndi, quam videns in actu. Sed tamen quaedam existentia in actu fuerunt priora secundum tempus in his existentibus in potentia, scilicet agentia, a quibus reducta sunt in actum. Semper enim oportet quod id quod est in potentia ens, sit actu ens ab agente, quod est actu ens. Unde homo in potentia fit homo in actu ab homine generante, qui est in actu. Et similiter musicum in potentia respicit musicum in actu, discendo a doctore qui est musicus actu. Et ita semper eo quod est in potentia, est aliquid prius quod movet, et movens est in actu. Unde relinquitur, quod licet idem numero prius tempore sit in potentia quam in actu, tamen aliquod ens in actu secundum idem specie, est etiam prius tempore, quam ens in potentia" (*Exp. Met.,* IX, lec. 7, nn. 1847–1848). Obviously, this does not entail that there cannot be a negative sense of numerical unity (numerical unity as indivision) according to which the embryo as well can be said to be, of itself, something numerically one. See, e.g., DUI, ch. 5, 310, 40–49: "Nec est dicendum quod aliqua substantia separata sit unum tantum specie uel genere, quia hoc non est esse simpliciter unum: relinquitur quod quelibet substantia separata sit unum numero. Nec dicitur aliquid unum numero quia sit unum de numero—non enim numerus est causa unius sed e converso—, sed quia in numerando non diuiditur; unum enim est id quod non dividitur."

25. See *Sent.,* IV, d. 44, q. 1, a. 1, q.la 2 and ad 2 (for the link between the numerical identity of a subject and the continuity or lack of interruption of the being it exhibits). For an interesting explanation of the numerical identity of a subject in terms of its properties of origin, see *Quodl.* V, q. 5, a. 1, vol. 2, 373, 42–55: "Responsio. Dicendum quod, cum in generatione hominis sicut et aliorum animalium semen patris sit agens, materia uero a matre ministrata sit sicut paciens ex quo corpus humanum formatur, inpossibile est eundem filium nasci siue sit alius pater siue sit alia mater; sicut etiam non est idem numero sigillum siue sit alia cera siue sit aliud corpus sigilli ex cuius impressione cera sigillatur."

could be considered numerically identical with the bricks still scattered in the work yard. Therefore, she/he could argue that, on our reconstruction, we can conclude only that the embryo in its final phase and the human being in its initial phase are in some sense numerically the same, but this does not allow us to say that the human being and the embryo just conceived are numerically the same entity.

We could nonetheless escape this difficulty, arguing that the relation between the embryo in its final phase and the human being in its initial phase is exactly the same as that between the embryo in whatever other phase and the embryo in the state of actuality immediately following. Generalizing, then, we could insist that the embryo just conceived and the human being are numerically the same subject because the whole process of generation can be described in its entirety as a process of passing from potency to act. Looked at in this way, the imperfection of form that characterizes the first phases of the embryo's life manifests not so much the possession of some one form of a lower metaphysical rank, of itself imperfect, as the imperfect and incomplete possession of the final form, an imperfection that is such only because its activity is confined to certain lower functions. The process of generation, though it implies changes of species in the embryo, does not imply changes of *perfect* species. It is a matter of potential changes, describable in terms of the perfecting of one final form that, retroactively, regulates and directs the entire process. A proof of this seems to be given by the fact that Thomas describes the various phases of the embryo's actualization and ensoulment as each in potency with respect to the following phase.[26] There is, evidently, a relation of strong potentiality, in the sense that

---

26. See, e.g., SCG, III, ch. 22, n. 2030: "In actibus autem formarum gradus quidam inveniuntur. Nam materia prima est in potentia primo ad formam elementi. Sub forma vero elementi existens est in potentia ad formam mixti: propter quod elementa sunt materia mixti. Sub forma autem mixti considerata, est in potentia ad animam vegetabilem: nam talis corporis anima actus est. Itemque anima vegetabilis est potentia ad sensitivam; sensitiva vero ad intellectivam. Quod processus generationis ostendit: primo enim in generatione est fetus vivens vita plantae, postmodum vero vita animalis, demum vero vita hominis. Post hanc autem formam non invenitur in generabilibus et corruptibilibus posterior forma et dignior. Ultimus igitur finis generationis totius est anima humana, et in hanc tendit materia sicut in ultimam formam. Sunt ergo elementa propter corpora mixta; haec vero propter viventia; in quibus plantae sunt propter animalia; animalia vero propter hominem. Homo igitur est finis totius generationis."

each soul actualizes, through substitution, the potentiality of the preceding soul instead of being a simple perfecting of the preceding soul. The embryonic actualities and forms are, therefore, imperfect because they are in potency to other actualities and forms that follow.[27]

Numerous texts of Thomas tend to confirm our reading. For example, in the *Quaestiones de virtutibus,* which dates from the final years of his life (1271–1272), Thomas describes the process of the passage from an imperfect form to a perfect form as a process of gradual actualization of one and the same subject.[28] The degrees of actualization are defined according to the way in which each degree is in potency to some other. To say of an act that it is in potency to another act is to say that such an act is not perfect. In his early *Quaestiones de veritate,* Thomas compared an imperfect act to becoming, that is, to an act that is, by definition, incomplete, intermediate between pure potentiality and pure actuality.[29] And he argued in this way even when discussing local motion in various places in his Commentary on the *Physics.*[30] While discussing a quite different question (namely, the conversion of bread into the body of Christ in the Eucharist) already in his Commentary on the *Sentences,* Thomas noted how the subject involved in an imperfect act and in a perfect act must be the same.[31] There are also more explicit places where Thomas takes the property of "being in perfect act" as coextensive with "being in act" and the property of "being in imperfect act" as coextensive with "being in potency."[32] On

---

27. See, e.g., QDA, q. 11, 103, 335–337: "Ad nonum dicendum quod sicut anima in embrione est in actu, set imperfecto, ita operatur, set operationes imperfectas." On the different degrees of souls' perfection, see also *Sup. Isaiam,* ch. 1, I, 8, 52–61.

28. See *De virt.,* q. 1, a. 11, 740a: "Moveri autem de forma imperfecta ad perfectam, nihil est aliud quam subiectum magis reduci in actum: nam forma actus est; unde subiectum magis percipere [*fortasse pro* recipere] formam, nihil aliud est quam ipsum reduci magis in actum illius formae. Et sicut ab agente reducitur aliquid de pura potentia in actum formae; ita etiam per actionem agentis reducitur de actu imperfecto in actum perfectum."

29. See QDV, q. 8, a. 14; q. 27, a. 4, ad 4. See also ST, III, q. 63, a. 4, ad 2.

30. See, e.g., *Exp. Phys.,* III, lec. 1–3.

31. See *Sent.,* IV, d. 11, q. 1, a. 3, q.la 1, ad 3: "Ad tertium dicendum quod transmutatio naturalis panis ponit actum imperfectum, ut patet in V *Physicorum,* et quia idem est subiectum actus perfecti et imperfecti, ideo oportet quod subiectum transmutationis naturalis sit id quod est subiectum postmodum actus perfecti, scilicet formae, ad quem tendit motus, et non ipsum iam perfectum."

32. See CT, I, ch. 216, 171, 167–169: "Est autem imperfectum omne quod in potentia existit antequam reducatur in actum."

the basis of such identifications, an interpreter can conclude that the unity of potency and act implies the unity between what is in imperfect act and what is in perfect act. Such an implication allows us to extend to the embryo from conception numerical identity with the generated human being. Such an extension is supported, in addition, by the metaphysical principle that the preexistent matter must be part of what is generated, since the preexistent matter is in what is generated insofar as it is the matter that becomes what is generated in the very act in which such matter perfectly and completely actualizes its own potentiality.[33]

The identity of subject that is presupposed by the unity between potency and act seems, then, to resolve the problem of the identity of the embryo.[34] However, our hypothetical opponent could still object to the upshot of our inquiry and note that, as already mentioned, the infusion of the rational soul brings about a radical substitution of the preceding form, such that the vegetative and sensitive functions carried out by the rational soul cannot be numerically the same as those carried out by the preceding sensitive soul. For the simple fact is that the sensitive activity of the rational soul is introduced from outside along with the rational soul, while the sensitive activity carried out by the sensitive soul is derived from the matter by virtue of the action of the male semen.[35]

---

33. See, e.g., *Exp. Met.,* VII, lec. 6, n. 1412.

34. See *Exp. Met.,* VIII, lec. 5, n. 1767: "Ultima materia, quae scilicet est appropriata ad formam, et ipsa forma sunt idem. Aliud enim eorum est sicut potentia, aliud sicut actus. Unde simile est quaerere quae est causa alicuius rei, et quae est causa quod illa res sit una; quia unumquodque inquantum est, unum est, et potentia et actus quodammodo unum sunt."

35. For a clear formulation of this radical discontinuity, see the following texts, from the start and the end of Thomas's career, that is, *Sent.,* II, d. 18, q. 2, a. 3, ad 4: "Anima autem sensibilis in homine per essentiam coniungitur animae rationali, et ideo totum est per creationem. Sed tamen modus traductionis seminis est similis in homine et in aliis animalibus, quia in semine hominis est etiam virtus formativa sicut in animalibus; sed quia actio illius virtutis est materialis, ut dictum est, non potest actio eius pertingere ad essentiam immaterialem; sed tamen per actionem huius virtutis primo consequitur conceptus vitam nutritivam et postea vitam sensitivam. Sed quia, ut Avicenna dicit, in hoc processu sunt plurimae generationes et corruptiones, sicut quod semen convertitur in sanguinem et sic deinceps, quando venitur ad secundam perfectionem, prima perfectio *non manet eadem numero,* sed acquiritur simul cum acquisitione secundae. Et sic patet quod in infusione animae rationalis homo simul consequitur in una essentia animae animam sensitivam et vegetativam, et *priores perfectiones non manent eaedem numero*" (my emphasis), and ST, I, q. 118, a. 2: "Sic

I believe that this last objection does not weaken very much our proposed reading. The objection suggests that according to Thomas's texts a certain organic structure that is in near potency to becoming a human being is not numerically the same as the human being in act. It suggests that the introduction of the final material part, and so also of the ultimate form, numerically changes the function carried out by the preceding material parts, while still recognizing that this function continues to be specifically the same.

In reply, we could say that although Thomas maintains that in a human being the sensitive soul is immortal according to its substance *(secundum substantiam)*, not insofar as it is sensitive but insofar as it is a rational soul (even if it is corruptible as to the exercise of concrete sensitive acts),[36] nevertheless in the various places where Thomas discusses the question "whether the vegetative and sensitive souls exist by creation," he continues to hold that the sensitive activity of the rational soul is drawn from the potency of the matter. Even if the derivation of the vegetative and sensitive souls from the potency of matter does not imply that the vegetative and sensitive souls are caused by matter (the reason being that their actions transcend the material properties of the bodily organs tasked with the exercise of the corresponding faculties),[37] nevertheless the vegetative and sensitive souls manifest organic activities that are carried out by the rational soul. In one sense, it is obvious that Thomas cannot understand the sensitive ensoulment that is not yet perfected by the rational soul and the sensitive ensoulment that is perfected by its coming as numerically the same sensitive ensoulment, for the

---

igitur dicendum est quod anima intellectiva creatur a Deo in fine generationis humanae, quae simul est et sensitiva et nutritiva, corruptis formis praexistentibus." For a denial that the human sensitive soul is extracted from the matter's potentiality, see also *Quodl.* XI, q. 5, ad 1, 159, 86–90: "Ad primum ergo dicendum quod anima sensitiua educitur de potencia materie in brutis, in nobis uero non, set est per creationem, cum eius essencia sit essencia anime rationalis, que est per creationem"; but also *Sent.,* II, d. 18, q. 2, a. 3, ad 4. As has been noted in Chapter 1 (note 18), one could deduce the opposite conclusion from the fact that Thomas tends to present the actualization of the matter's potentiality as a matter's state, that is, its being in actuality. See also ST, I, q. 90, a. 2, ad 2: "Ad secundum dicendum quod actum extrahi de potentia materiae, nihil aliud est quam aliquid fieri actu, quod prius erat in potentia"; and especially QDP, q. 3, a. 9.

36. See QDA, q. 11, ad 13; ST, I, q. 76, a. 3, ad 1; CT, I, ch. 92.

37. See QDP, q. 3, a. 11; QDSC, q. 2; *Quodl.* IX, q. 5; CT, I, ch. 91.

simple fact that otherwise, with the coming of rational ensoulment there would not be any perfecting and therefore no substitution of form. But in another sense, we can concede that for Thomas such sensitive ensoulments are numerically the same ensoulment insofar as they are sensitive ensoulments *of one and the same subject*. And this for at least two reasons: both because the perfecting concerns the ensoulment of one and the same matter, and also because, in an obvious sense, the perfecting concerns the same ensoulment that before being perfected was not perfected. If it were otherwise, one could not in any way speak of perfecting, nor could one consider the matter that was perfected by an imperfect form as the characteristic matter of the ultimate perfecting.

Thomas tends to confirm this conclusion, often reiterating that the sensitive activity carried out by the human rational soul is specifically more sophisticated than the sensitive activity carried out by the sensitive soul of the most complex other type of animal. But as far as I know, he never says that in one human being the sensitive activity carried out by the rational soul is specifically more sophisticated than the sensitive activity carried out by the sensitive soul. Moreover, just as it would be too much to hold that the sensitive activity carried out by the rational soul is *numerically* the same as that carried out by the sensitive soul, so it would be too little to hold that the sensitive activity carried out by the rational soul is only *specifically* the same as that carried out by the sensitive soul. For in this latter case, we would have a series of difficulties in distinguishing the relation that holds between a half-formed human being and a formed human being, on the one hand, from the relation that holds between any two human beings.

As we will better see in what follows, the principal problem in determining the identity of the embryo comes from the fact that there is a sense of identity midway between strict numerical identity or unity and specific identity or unity that Thomas himself tries to express, but which turns out to be difficult to capture. Strict numerical identity implies that there is one single subject that remains exactly as it is throughout whatever process of change; specific identity implies that there are two numerically different subjects. Socrates who from sitting stands is an example of being one in number in the strict sense, while Socrates and Plato are one in species. But young Socrates and old

Socrates are neither one in species nor one in number in the strict sense as characterized above. Certainly, young Socrates and old Socrates are one in number; nobody could deny that they are indeed the same Socrates. But Socrates does not remain exactly as he is throughout his life because he again and again changes his matter. For this reason, young Socrates and old Socrates could not be said to be one in number in the strictest sense of numerical unity. All that suggests that sometimes there are objects that, although not remaining exactly the same in the course of their history, continue to be seen as the same object.

To make this important point clearer, we can consider one of the examples that Thomas himself discusses, namely, the relation between a river and its water. This, of course, is a classic philosophical example often used (together with those of fire and the sea, also found in Thomas) to raise the problem of the permanence and metaphysical consistency of the objects of our ordinary experience. In the example of the river, its water continually flows, so that the river never contains the same water. If the identity of the water were responsible for the identity of the river, the river would have to be considered as continually numerically different: there would not be a single river, but an infinite succession of numerically different rivers. We could avoid this counterintuitive conclusion by maintaining that the river, even if it never has the same water, still always contains the same amount of water. But this response can also be questioned, since the river continually increases and decreases its capacity, and so it never retains the same amount of water. In ascertaining the identity of an object, it seems that neither the identity of the matter (or of the material parts) nor that of the amount of the matter is strictly speaking necessary. However when we look at the river, we continue to think that we are standing before the same river and not an infinite succession of rivers. In the case of the river, it seems to be the form of the river that guarantees the identity of subject, but it is not any generic form of river, but that *particular form* of river that allows us to identify every new material part and new amount of water as a part or amount of that river.[38]

---

38. See, e.g., *Exp. Meteor.*, II, lec. 6, n. 170: "Secundum est, quod movet dubitationem, de qua oportet primo videre veritatem, antequam propositum manifestet. Et est ista quaestio: utrum partes

The same could be said in the case of the embryo with respect to its functions and to its matter. Although the functions that succeed one another over time cannot be numerically the same, and as there is not numerically the same matter in the embryo, still the subject of these functions and of this matter remains the same. This can be deduced from the fact that the new functions that are introduced are formally the same as those preceding functions; that is, they are not only the same functions by species but also the same functions because they are functions of the one and the same subject.[39]

Taking stock of this extensive discussion of the identity of the subject of generation, the conclusion we can draw is that Thomas seems to see the embryo's pure sensitive activity, even if perfected, as in potency to the sensitive activity exercised by the rational soul, just as the matter actualized by some imperfect form remains in potency, as the material element *(ut materiale),* to a perfect form, which constitutes its formal element.[40] Thomas seems to grant that the two sensitive activities are numerically the same activity.[41] We can affirm this on the basis of Thomas's recourse to the Aristotelian example of *De anima,* II, 3,

---

maris semper maneant eaedem numero; aut permutentur secundum numerum, et maneant eaedem secundum quantitatem, sicut accidit in aere et in aqua potabili fluminum et in igne. In his enim omnibus partes fiunt aliae et aliae numero, sed species vel forma multitudinis harum partium manet eadem: et hoc apparet maxime in aquis fluentibus et in fluxu flammae, quae per successionem fumi semper innovatur, ut supra dictum est, et tamen flamma semper manet eadem in numero."

39. See *Sent.,* IV, d. 44, q. 3, a. 3, q.la I, ad 6; QDA, q. 19, arg. 13 and ad 13, 163, 84–91 and 167, 327–337: "Preterea. Quod cedit in nichil non resumitur idem numero. Set si potentie sensitiue non manent in anima separata, oportet quod cedant in nichilum. Ergo in resurrectione non erunt eedem numero; et sic, cum potentie sensitive sint actus organorum, neque organa erunt eadem numero, neque totus homo erit idem numero; quod est inconueniens. [. . .] Ad tertium decimum dicendum quod sicut sensus, prout nominat potentiam, non est forma totius corporis, set anima sensitiua (sensus autem est proprietas compositi), ita etiam potentia uisiua non est actus oculi, set anima, secundum quod est principium talis potentie; quasi ita dicatur quod anima uisiua est actus oculi, sicut anima sensitiua est actus totius corporis (potentia autem uisiua est proprietas consequens). Vnde non oportet quod sit alius oculus resurgentis, licet alia potentia sensitiua."

40. See ST, I, q. 66, a. 2: "Nec hoc excluditur, si una illarum formarum sit perfectior et continens in se virtute alias. Quia potentia, quantum est de se, indifferenter se habet ad perfectum et imperfectum, unde sicut quando est sub forma imperfecta, est in potentia ad formam perfectam"; SCG, III, ch. 22 (see the long text quoted above, note 26). On the unity between what is *ut materiale* and what is *ut formale,* see *Sent.,* IV, d. 14, q. 1, a. 4, q.la 2.

41. See, e.g., QDSC, a. 3, ad 2, 382a: "Ad secundum dicendum quod cum forma perfectissima det omnia quae dant formae imperfectiores, et adhuc amplius; materia, prout ab ea perficitur eo

414b20 ff., i.e., that of the pentagon and the square potentially contained in it that are said to be the same figure.[42] Thus, the embryo can be described as what is material with respect to the human being, which human being comes to express the perfect and formal state of the embryo. As Thomas explains, commenting on the sixteenth chapter of the fifth book of the *Metaphysics*, i.e., the chapter Aristotle dedicates to the term "perfect," for a thing a perfect state P is the final end of that thing, and the final end is not only what is last for that thing but also that by virtue of which that thing can exist and become P.[43] Applied to the embryo, this implies that for an embryo to be a human being is the final end of the embryo, and such an end is not just the terminal phase of the embryonic development but it is also that by virtue of which the embryo can exist and become a human being.

---

modo perfectionis quo perficitur a formis imperfectioribus, consideratur ut materia propria, etiam illiusmodi perfectionis quam addit perfectior forma super alias; ita tamen quod non intelligatur haec distinctio in formis secundum essentiam, sed solum secundum intelligibilem rationem. Sic ergo ipsa materia secundum quod intelligitur ut perfecta in esse corporeo susceptivo vitae, est proprium subiectum animae."

42. See, for example, *Quodl.* IX, q. 5, a. 1, *ad alia;* QDA, q. 9 *passim;* q. 11, 100, 252–253: "Forma perfectior dat materie quicquid dabat forma inferior, et adhuc amplius"; QDA, q. 11, ad 18, 103–104, 385–395: "Ad octauum decimum dicendum quod, sicut ex superioribus questionibus patet, ab una et eadem forma materia recipit diuersos gradus perfectionis; et secundum quod materia perficitur inferiori gradu perfectionis, remanet adhuc materialis ad altioris perfectionis gradum. Et sic secundum quod corpus perficitur in esse sensibili ab anima humana, remanet adhuc ut materiale respectu ulterioris perfectionis. Et secundum hoc animal, quod est genus, sumitur a materia; et rationale, quod est differentia, sumitur a forma"; ST, I, q. 76, a. 3, ad 4; ST, I, q. 118, a. 2, 548a: "Tam in homine quam in animalibus aliis, quando perfectior forma advenit, fit corruptio prioris: ita tamen quod sequens forma habet quidquid habet prima, et adhuc amplius"; ST, I–II, q. 57, a. 2, ad 2; QDA, q. 2, ad 8, 20, 411–421: "Ad octauum dicendum quod similitudo Philosophi de figuris ad partes anime attenditur quantum ad hoc quod, sicut tetragonum habet quicquid habet trigonum et adhuc amplius, et pentagonum quicquid habet tetragonum, ita sensitiua anima habet quicquid habet nutritiua, et intellectiua quicquid habet sensitiua, et adhuc amplius. Non ergo per hoc ostenditur quod nutritiuum et sensitiuum essentialiter differant ab intellectiuo, set magis quod unum illorum includat alterum"; also QDA, q. 7. This example also recurs in other works: see DEE, ch. 5; QDSC, a. 1, ad 24; a. 3; *Quodl.* I, q. 4, a. 1; CT, I, ch. 92; *Sent. De an.*, II, ch. 1. I take the relative pronoun *quicquid* in the dictum *forma perfectior habet quicquid habet imperfecta et adhuc amplius* (i.e., the more perfect form has whatever has the imperfect form, and something more) to designate not only something that is specifically identical but also something that, in one sense or another, remains numerically the same through the process of generation.

43. See *Exp. Met.*, V, lec. 18, n. 1039: "Finis non solum habet quod sit ultimum, sed etiam quod sit cuius causa fit aliquid."

The teleology that governs the entire process of generation and the principle of the identity of subject between what is in potency and what is in act allow us to say that Thomas would not be against affirming that the human being that someone is now is numerically identical (even though in a broad sense of numerical identity) with that embryo that earlier was in potency the human being that now is in act.

3. The Identity of the Embryo and the Succession of Souls

That the not-yet-formed embryo has an imperfect or incomplete form has another important consequence, and this can be brought out by considering the question from another point of view. There is a phase in which the embryo is only in a vegetative state and another phase in which there is added to this state a sensitive state. Thomas is cautious in characterizing these states. In his works, he says that in a certain phase the embryo possesses a vegetative soul and therefore lives a plant life;[44] he does not say that the embryo has the form or species of a plant, although there are passages from which one could easily infer this. In fact, his terminology is not new, but rather common in the embryological debates of his time, and so we should not read into it any particular significance. Still, if we wish to explore the possible implications of these affirmations, the difference reveals an important point, insofar as Thomas is affirming two things: (1) that there is a phase in

---

44. See, e.g., *Sent.*, II, d. 18, q. 2, a. 3 (the text has been quoted at length in Chapter 4, note 20); SCG, II, ch. 89, n. 1745; SCG, III, ch. 22, n. 2030; CT, I, ch. 92, 114, 100–121: "Nam omnis motus naturalis paulatim ex imperfecto ad perfectum procedit, quod tamen aliter accidit in alteratione et generatione. Nam eadem qualitas suscipit magis et minus; et ideo alteratio que est motus in qualitate, una et continua existens, de potentia ad actum procedit de imperfecto ad perfectum. Forma uero substantialis non recipit magis et minus, quia esse substantiale unicuique est unum et indivisibiliter se habens; unde una generatio non procedit continue per multa media de imperfecto ad perfectum, sed oportet esse ad singulos gradus perfectionis nouam generationem et corruptionem. Sic igitur in generatione hominis conceptum quidem primo uiuit uita plante per animam uegetabilem; deinde remota hac forma per corruptionem, acquirit quadam alia generatione animam sensibilem et uiuit uita animalis; deinde remota hac anima per corruptionem, introducitur forma ultima et completa que est anima rationalis, comprehendens in se quicquid perfectionis in precedentibus formis erat."

embryonic development in which the embryo appears indistinguishable from a plant,[45] and (2) that, nevertheless, the human embryo is not a plant.

The second point of this affirmation is understandable. Something receives the form of a plant and can be said therefore to be a plant only at the end of the process of vegetative formation. As mentioned earlier, in the first phases the embryo does not have a complete form: not only a human form but also that of a plant. Still, a human embryo in the phase in which it lives a plant life is functionally indistinguishable from a plant that is already formed. But, if it lives a plant life and carries out the identical functions that a plant does, why is the human embryo not a plant? We can ask the same question about an embryo-human being that lives an animal life and an embryo-horse. In an obvious sense, we can reply that they are different because the embryo-human being is part of a process of human generation, and the embryo-horse is part of a process of equine generation; of themselves, neither a human embryo can bring forth a horse or an equine embryo a human being.[46] This criterion could be proposed, but it presupposes that we are already able to know how to distinguish between the two processes.

If, on the other hand, we abstract from the processes in which the two embryos are found, how could we tell the difference between the two, supposing it is possible to differentiate them? At first glance, a formal criterion of a functional kind is not enough to distinguish one from the other. Generically, the two embryos carry out the same functions: nutrition and growth at the vegetative level, movement and sensation at the sensitive level. Sometimes Thomas says that the two embryos are specifically different. This is understandable, since Thomas illustrates the difference while having in mind the sensitive functions carried out by an animal, as a horse, and those carried out by an actual human being. In this case, we can speak of a greater structural and

---

45. See ST, I, q. 119, a. 1: "Cum homo non differat ab animalibus et plantis secundum animam vegetabilem, sequeretur quod etiam corpora animalium et plantarum non multiplicarentur per conversionem alimenti in corpus nutritum."

46. See, e.g., SCG, II, ch. 22, n. 986a: "Virtus quae est in semine hominis non potest producere brutum vel plantam."

functional complexity (what Aquinas calls a greater "nobility") of the human being over the horse.[47] But how do we distinguish an embryo-human being in the animal phase from an embryo-horse in its animal phase?

Thomas is rather elusive on this point in his writings. But based on the explanation that he offers of the embryogenetic process as we have reconstructed it, we can state that a horse embryo or a plant are distinguished from a human being embryo that lives an animal life or that lives a plant life by the *type* of functioning. This criterion could be what allows us to identify a subject within a given process, distinguishing it from subjects involved in processes specifically different. In general, the process of differentiation takes place *a posteriori,* since the vegetative and sensitive souls do not exist apart from a body involved in a given process. So, for example, if we had to explain why the human embryo that lives an animal life cannot be identified with the embryo of another animal species, we could argue that by genus the two lives are identical, but by species they are different.[48] (Not only that, but if the sensitive soul that is in animals and the sensitive soul that is in a human being could be placed of themselves in a genus or in a species, the conclusion would be that they are not of the same genus or the same species.)[49] In this case, although the argument is purely conjectural, Thomas could grant that an embryo-human being that lives an animal life and an embryo-horse are distinguished rather by the different *degree of perfection* in the exercise of one and the same type of generic functions, which implies the presence of material parts, organized and differentiated in different ways.[50]

This is nothing more than a hypothesis since, as we have seen, Thomas is of the opinion that genera do not exist as genera apart from species, and that there do not exist vital animal functions that are not at the same time also human or equine animal functions. If being an animal does not exist prior to or apart from individual animal species, it follows

---

47. See, e.g., QDP, q. 3, a. 10, ad 1–2; QDA, q. 11, ad 12.
48. See QDP, q. 3, a. 11, ad 1–2.
49. See QDA, q. 11, ad 14; *Exp. Gen.,* I, lec. 10.
50. See, e.g., *Sent.,* III, d. 4, q. 1, a. 2, q.la 1.

that an embryo-human being that lives an animal life is not, strictly speaking, an *animal,* for it is no species of animal. Nor, strictly speaking, can we affirm that the embryo lives an authentic *animal* life. Until the rational soul is added, which carries out at the same time also the vegetative and sensitive functions, the embryo only manifests rough outlines of vital vegetative and sensitive operations typical of a human being. It is above all the soul of the father that works in the embryo, by means of the formative power, and guarantees a formal continuity to the entire process. If we assume, therefore, that the alternation of generations and corruptions in the process of human generation concerns rough outlines or virtualities of the soul rather than true and proper souls, the authentic ensoulment of the embryo takes place only at the moment of the infusion of the rational soul. In this case, the differentiation among the vegetative soul, the sensitive soul, and the rational soul is possible, properly speaking, only through an act of mental abstraction.[51] In other words, for Thomas, in an ensouled embryo there can be only one soul. Nevertheless, we can speak of different souls insofar as within the single soul there can be isolated different powers or faculties that can be described as capacities for exercising vegetative, sensitive, or rational functions.[52] Viewed in this way, the forms of vegetative and sensitive ensoulment that exist before the coming of the rational soul would be nothing other

---

51. See *Sent.,* II, d. 18, q. 2, a. 3, ad 2 and ad 4. As we have seen, many texts bear witness to granting a real vegetative ensoulment to the embryo right from conception. Sensitive ensoulment and finally rational ensoulment follow upon the vegetative ensoulment. When Thomas must explain the ordering of the soul's potencies, he mentions a temporal order in their formation: see, e.g., ST, I, q. 77, a. 4. There are, however, texts where the opposition is between nonensouled (or imperfectly ensouled) embryos, on the one hand, and ensouled (or perfectly ensouled) embryos, on the other hand, and so the distinction between the different souls is presented as a result of an act of mental abstraction. See, e.g., *Sent.,* IV, d. 38, q. 1, a. 2, q.la 2, ad 3: "Ad tertium dicendum quod naturalis est ordo quo fit progressus de imperfecto ad perfectum; unde et in totis potestativis fit progressus ab una parte in aliam, sicut embryo prius habet animam vegetabilem *aliquo modo* quam sensibilem, et sensibilem quam rationalem" (my emphasis); QDP, q. 3, a. 9, ad 9, 68a; a. 12; *Exp. Gen.,* I, lec. 10, n. 80; QDA, q. 11, ad 18; QDSC, a. 3, ad 3, 382a; *Quodl.* I, q. 4, a. 1. All these texts, however, can be harmonized if we assume that Thomas wants to discuss the order of souls from different perspectives: diachronically, by clarifying how the soul's different potencies can be distinguished according to the process of their formation, and synchronically, namely, by clarifying how they can be distinguished when, at the end of the process, they are exercised by one and the same soul.

52. For Thomas, the potencies can be distinguished according to the acts they exercise and the objects they are directed toward. On this point, see ST, I, q. 77, a. 3.

than rough and preparatory outlines of the authentic vegetative and sensitive ensoulment that is carried out by the rational soul.

4. Identity of Subject and Identity of Matter

As we have seen earlier, Thomas assumes that the subject of the process of generation must be the same from beginning to end. Rather than demonstrating this identity, he presupposes it, limiting himself to providing some arguments that enable him to affirm it. Still, this is an identity that is quite uncertain. When a substantial form ceases, the material subject of the form not only does not keep a numerical identity but the identity of genus is also not numerically the same, as was said. Applied to a human being, the case of a corpse raises serious doubts about whether any attempt to safeguard the numerical identity and numerical unity between an embryo and a human being can be successful, for reflection on substantial corruption has led us to portray the identity between an embryo and a human being as an identity or unity that is rather weak. There does not seem to be anything in the embryo that remains exactly as it is in the formed human being, and so our conclusion was that in the case of an embryo and a human being the only identity or unity possible is a unity or identity of subject *(idem subiecto)*. As we have seen, the embryo's identity of subject can be determined indirectly by reflection on the fact that the process of generation can be described as a passage from potency to act, from what is imperfect and incomplete to what is perfect and complete, and such a passage requires that the subject must be the same. It is, in fact, an extrinsic identity and, so to speak, established negatively, that is, drawn from the observation that over the course of generation there are not many embryos, but always only one embryo, which does not undergo any process of division or multiplication. Since it is not divided into more embryos, we can say that the embryo is only one: being an undivided entity, it is numerically one, and so one in number.[53] If the embryo is

---

53. While Thomas normally relates numerical multiplicity to matter, he does not always connect numerical unity or identity to it. In the case of beings lacking matter, for example, numerical unity or identity depends on form. See, e.g., DUI, ch. 5, 310, 50–74: "Nec iterum hoc uerum est, quod

only one in number, it is only one subject. We can accord to the embryo, then, a certain although broad numerical unity.

Now for Thomas, it is the form that plays the role of imparting being and being one to a thing (since to be and to be one are conceived by Thomas as logically convertible properties).[54] It remains a fact, however, that there is no form, not even a generic form, that stays numerically the same in the process of human generation. This should lead us to correct our taking that conclusion (regarding form and identity) in a very restrictive sense; that is, we should abandon the idea that it could be the form that, by some claim, plays the role of criterion for identifying the embryo. In fact, numerical unity or identity understood positively, as unity or identity of form or of matter, does not seem to be in any way applicable to the embryo.[55] The embryo is indivisible according to subject, but it is not indivisible according to quantity or according to substance:[56] not according to quantity, for its quantity can be divided and is continually modified, and not according to substance, for the embryo does not remain uniform in species, a condition that can be found only by the first or last subject of a given process.[57]

---

omnis numerus causetur ex materia. [. . .] Non enim materia est principium indiuiduationis in rebus materialibus, nisi in quantum materia non est participabilis a pluribus, cum sit primum subiectum non existens in alio; unde et de ydea Aristotiles dicit quod, si ydea esset separata 'esset quedam, id est indiuidua, quam impossibile esset praedicari de multis.' Indiuidue ergo sunt substantie separate et singulares; non autem indiuiduantur ex materia, sed ex hoc ipso quod non sunt nate in alio esse, et per consequens nec participari a multis." For more details on the relationship between "numerical unity" *(unum numero)* and "unity by number" *(unum de numero),* see also the text from the *De unitate intellectus* quoted above, note 24. The description of the predicate "being one" (as well as sometimes of the predicate "being individual") as "being something undivided in itself and divided from something else" often recurs in Aquinas's writings. See, for example, the following texts: *Sent.,* I, d. 19, q. 4, a. 1, ad 2; QDV, q. 1, a. 1; *Sup. De Trin.,* q. 4, a. 2, ad 3, 125, 258–260: "De ratione indiuidui est quod sit in se indiuisum et ab aliis ultima diuisione diuisum"; QDP, q. 9, a. 7; ST, I, q. 11, a. 1; *Exp. Met.,* III, lec. 8 and lec. 10; *Exp. Met.,* IV, lec. 2.

54. The principle that the form is cause of both a thing's being and its being one recurs in many places. Among others, see ST, I, q. 76, a. 3: "Nihil enim est simpliciter unum nisi per formam unam, per quam habet res esse, ab eodem enim habet res quod sit ens et quod sit una"; *Exp. Met.,* VIII, lec. 5, n. 1767 and especially QDP, q. 9, a. 7, ad 15. On the convertibility of being and being one, see *Sent.,* I, d. 24, q. 1, a. 3.

55. For a twofold way of understanding numerical unity or identity, discussed by Thomas with respect to prime matter, see DPN, § 2, 41, 99–106.

56. See *Exp. Met.,* V, lec. 8, n. 867.

57. See *Exp. Met.,* V, lec. 7, nn. 859–860.

This being the case, our hypothetical opponent could be deeply unsatisfied with our conclusion, maintaining that to speak of unity, identity, and continuity of the subject is too abstract and hardly informative. Concretely, what do an embryo and a human being have in common? What allows us to say, concretely, that an embryo and a human being are not only *one single* subject but also the *same* subject?

In the *Summa theologiae,* Thomas discusses the case of the identity between the living and the dead body of Christ, agreeing with criticisms leveled by the Augustinian theologian Giles of Rome.[58] Thomas argues that the change of form implies a change of species, and this is a numerical change since numerical unity depends on a species that allows that thing to be counted as *one* thing of that species. If a thing loses its form, then, it cannot be called in any way the same thing, for it can no longer be counted as *one* thing of that species. A few questions earlier, while discussing the question "whether the relics of the saints are in some way to be adored," Thomas explains that "the dead body of a saint is not numerically identical with what it was before when it was living on account of the diversity of form, which is the soul; nevertheless it is identical by an identity of matter, which is once again to be united to its form."[59]

Comparing this with what Thomas says in other places, the distinction between numerical identity of the body and identity of matter turns out to be problematic, for numerical identity or unity of a thing normally is made to depend on matter, while in this passage Thomas distinguishes numerical identity, tied to the identity of form, from identity of matter. The fact that a thing is no longer numerically the same if it is changed by species is rather plausible, but within a species, numerical identity seems able to be determined only by reference to

---

58. See ST, III, q. 50, a. 5.

59. See ST, III, q. 25, a. 6, ad 3: "Ad tertium dicendum quod corpus mortuum alicuius sancti non est idem numero quod primo fuerit dum viveret, propter diversitatem formae, quae est anima: est tamen idem identitate materiae, quae est iterum suae formae unienda." The phrase "identity of matter" *(identitas materiae)* appears only twice in Thomas's writings: for the second occurrence, see ST, I, q. 119, a. 1, arg. 5 and ad 5, in the context of the discussion of the material identity of man across his life. On the other hand, the idea that a change in species entails a numerical change is expressed by Thomas in many places. See, e.g., ST, I–II, q. 67, a. 3 and a. 5 (see the following note).

matter. Thomas's distinction only seems to shift the problem. Let us look again at the case of the dead body of the saint. To say that the dead body of the saint and the body of the saint in life are not numerically the same body, even if the matter of the body remains the same, seems to help little. Our hypothetical opponent could point out that the matter of the body of the saint can be said to be the same only if it remains the same *in number,* and the matter can remain the same in number only if it is the matter of the same body *in number.* It turns out, then, that it is inconsistent for Thomas to say that the body of the saint does not remain the same in number, even while the matter of the body remains the same in number.

But even with this difficulty, the distinction that Thomas makes seems to have its own plausibility. If the matter of a human body, for example, were to take on the appearance of a horse, probably no one would be inclined to say that the thing we have now in front of us is numerically the same as the first; but if in this passage there has not been either a loss or a transformation of matter, one could concede that the matter or the amount of matter has stayed the same. In a change of species, numerical identity of a thing is given strictly by the form and this determines its identity as subject.[60] Within the species of human being, it is still true that Socrates and Plato are each numerically one through the form, but the matter still plays a role in differentiating Socrates and Plato, allowing them to be counted as *two* human beings. In the case of a human being that becomes a horse, though, the identity of matter does not appear so relevant for establishing numerical identity and the identity of subject.

The distinction between numerical identity and identity of matter, in any case, seems to break the connection between identity and continuity of a thing that we have presupposed at the beginning of our discussion in this chapter. It is evident that the identity of matter guarantees only the continuity of a certain thing, while it cannot safeguard its

---

60. See ST, I–II, q. 67, a. 3: "Unum et idem numero manens non potest transferri de una specie in aliam."

identity. Similarly, numerical identity guarantees only that there is one and the same thing, but it tells us nothing about the continuity or lack thereof of the history of that thing. For example, if we were able to substitute all the material parts of a human being, replacing them with other material parts in every respect similar, and we put the substituted material parts together, giving life to a second human being completely similar to the first, the first human would continue to be the same subject (probably the same body), while the second, that is, the one newly constituted, would be a different subject, though having the same matter as the one who had been taken apart. In any case, the distinction between the numerical identity of the body of the saint and the identity of matter makes it clear that there is at work another criterion of identity. That is, one can speak of identity with regard to matter without regard to whether it is the matter of the one and the same subject.

It is quite difficult to handle the case of the embryo within this theoretical framework. On the one hand, the embryo has no form, identical in number, that allows us to establish an identity of subject (as does happen in the case of the river with respect to the continuous change of its material parts, as we have seen), even if it does seem implausible to treat the embryogenetic process as a process that passes something from one species to another in the way one can imagine a human being becoming a horse. Even taking into account the emphasis that Thomas places on the sequence of specific forms that the embryo assumes in the course of generation, the case of the embryo is not analogous to the case of the human being that could be transformed into a horse, for throughout its history the embryo never really presents any complete species. It should be remembered that for Thomas embryos are "entities on the way toward a species" *(entia in via ad speciem),* and therefore do not have at any of their phases a definite species. On the other hand, it seems that neither continuity nor identity of matter holds for the embryo, since the embryo continually modifies its matter and, we could hypothesize, constantly renews it.

Nevertheless, in order to avoid giving in completely to the idea that there is no link, except a purely causal link, between an embryo and a human being, we could hypothesize that there is a portion of matter that remains exactly as it is in the passage from embryo to human being. What could be the conditions that allow us to fix the numerical identity of this portion of matter?

Thomas seems to provide a response to this difficulty when he discusses two different questions: first, whether the male semen or the female blood perdures in the embryo, and second, what metaphysical factor is primarily responsible for the transtemporal numerical identity of an object, whether matter, quantity, or extension? As a rule, Thomas confronts the first question in the theological context of the discussion of the bodily transmission of original sin and the restoration of the mortal body at the moment of the final resurrection. It is in this context that Thomas discusses the notion, attributed explicitly to the medical doctors, of "radical moisture" *(humidum radicale)* that, as we suggested in the last chapter, could be compared with extreme caution to the modern notion of genetic code. In fact, we shall now see that not even this notion plays a theoretical role analogous to that of genetic code. The second question, on the other hand, is discussed in the philosophical context of the inquiry into the principle of individuation of a material substance.

4.1. The Material Continuity of the Human Body

Thomas discusses the problem of the restoration of the mortal body at the moment of the final resurrection and specifically how to guarantee that the resurrected body is the same as the earthly body. He does this by investigating above all the manner in which food is converted into the matter of the body. There are three main places in his works where this problem is discussed: the Commentary on the *Sentences,* II, d. 30, q. 2, and IV, d. 44, q. 1, a. 2, q.1a 4, and finally the *Summa theologiae,* I, q. 119, a. 1. It is, above all, in the first passage that Thomas notes that in his day there were two opinions concerning the material continuity of a human being. The first held that all the matter of a human being is already contained in the very first embryonic matter (just as all the matter of the universe was contained in the embryonic matter of the first human being), and this to such an extent that what rises at the final judgment has exactly that amount of matter and no other. This opinion assumed that the matter introduced through food only serves to maintain, by means of heat, the amount of primordial matter, but does not add any other matter.[61] The second position, while admitting with the first that the matter of a human being is already all contained in the embryonic primordial matter, differed from it by holding that such an amount of matter is increased, thanks to the matter that is introduced through food, although the "added" matter does not remain exactly as it is throughout the whole life of a human being.[62] Both positions shared the idea that there is a primitive nucleus of matter that remains stable for the whole duration of the human's life and guarantees one's bodily continuity at the final resurrection. In his reply, Thomas attacks precisely this belief, so that our suggestion to cautiously liken the genetic code to "radical moisture" must inexorably be given up.

The reason to reject the first opinion is quickly explained. That something increases implies that it modifies its dimensions. There are then only two possible cases: either the quantity of matter that changes dimensions is the same or greater. If it is the same (putting aside whether the extension of matter comes about naturally or through divine intervention),

---

61. See *Sent.,* II, d. 30, q. 2, a. 1: "Quidam posuerunt, ut in littera Magister sentire videtur, quod illud quod ex parentibus decisum est est illud solum in quo veritas hominis nati consistit. Hoc autem in maiorem quantitatem excrescit omnino salvatum, ita quod nihil sibi additur ut maiorem quantitatem recipiat; sed tota quantitas hominis completi per multiplicationem illius materiae efficitur; et hoc tantum esse dicunt quod in resurrectione resurget, reliquum autem quasi superfluum deponetur. Ponunt etiam alimenti sumptionem necessariam esse non quidem ad augmentum ut nutritiva augmentativae deserviat, neque iterum ad restaurationem deperditi, sed solum in fomentum caloris naturalis."

62. See *Sent.,* II, d. 30, q. 2, a. 1: "Et ideo aliorum positio est concedentium quidem cum primis quod aliquid est in humano corpore et similiter in aliis corporibus quae nutriuntur quod quidem semper manet fixum toto tempore vitae, secundum determinatam partem materiae (in quo principaliter veritatem humanae naturae consistere dicunt); aliquid autem est aliud quod superfluit et refluit, id est advenit et consumitur: hoc autem est quod ex cibo generatum est. Differunt tamen a primis in hoc quod dicunt, sumptionem alimenti non solum in fomentum caloris naturalis necessariam esse, sed etiam in augmentum quantitatis. [. . .] Et secundum hoc ponunt isti quod illud quod est ex alimento generatum non est omnino alienum a veritate humanae naturae, sicut primi dicebant, sed est secundario ad ipsam pertinens, secundum quod est necessarium ad debitae quantitatis complementum; unde non totum hoc in resurrectione deponitur quod ex alimento conversum est, sed reservabitur tantum quantum expedit ad perfectionem quantitatis. Et huiusmodi positionis primus auctor invenitur Alexander Commentator, ut Averroes in *libro de Gener.* dicit."

the process of increase becomes a process of rarefaction, and this evidently cannot be admitted for the case in question. If instead, the quantity of matter is greater, then either the added matter is created from nothing or there is a different matter that is added. The first possibility is excluded, for what can be accounted for naturally should not be explained by recourse to miracles, and also because God has created the matter of all things all at once. Hence it follows that the added matter comes from the introduction of food.[63]

The opponent's idea that some given matter could be so extended to obtain a substance (an idea founded on the belief that prime matter, being deprived of form, is in potency to all possible forms) clashes with two facts, according to Thomas. First, matter does not give rise to a substance thanks to extension, but thanks rather to quantity on which extension ultimately depends. Second, prime matter can in principle acquire all forms, but when it begins to acquire a form, that form requires a sequence of accidental determinations such that each member in the series determines the next in order for the form to be realized.[64]

---

63. See *Sent.*, II, d. 30, q. 2, a. 1: "Haec autem positio irrationalis videtur ex duobus, scilicet ex parte eius quod augetur et ex parte alimenti quod advenit. Non enim potest fieri augmentum, nisi secundum hoc quod materia quae primo est terminata sub parvis dimensionibus postmodum ad maiores dimensiones perducitur. Hoc autem non potest fieri nisi dupliciter, vel ita quod de materia sit tantum sub magnis dimensionibus quantum sub parvis, et talis mutatio de parvo in magnum necessario fit per rarefactionem [. . .]; vel ita quod plus de materia sit sub magnis quam sub parvis. Hoc autem non potest contingere nisi vel quia est materia de novo creata vel per hoc quod illud quod erat materia alterius corporis efficitur materia huius, in hoc illo corpore transmutato. [. . .] Augmentum autem corporis humani constat quod per rarefactionem non fit. Nec iterum per additionem materiae de novo creatae, quia materiam omnium simul creavit Deus, ut sancti dicunt. Restat ergo ut fiat augmentum humani corporis per hoc quod additur materia quae suberat formae alterius corporis, illo corpore in corpus humanum secundum veritatem converso, et hoc est nutrimentum."

64. See *Sent.*, II, d. 30, q. 2, a. 1: "Alii vero alium modum adinveniunt: dicunt enim quod materia prima, quantum in se est, caret omni quantitate et forma; ergo aequaliter se habet ad recipiendum omnes quantitates sicut ad recipiendum omnes formas. Unde quantumcumque parum sit de materia prima in quovis parvo corpore, potest recipere quantamlibet quantitatem; adeo quod ex grano milii totus mundus fieri potest. Nec mirum cum ex materia punctali totus mundus sit factus: cum enim materia quantitate careat, indivisibilis est, et ad modum puncti se habens. Iste autem modus multipliciter deficit. Primo, quia imaginatur indivisibilitatem materiae ad modum puncti, ut sic ex materia mundus sit factus per quamdam quasi extensionem, sicut si res parva in magnam extendatur. Hoc autem non est verum. Materia enim dicitur indivisibilis per negationem totius generis quantitatis. Punctus autem est indivisibilis sicut quantitatis principium, situm determinatum

It does not seem possible, therefore, that there is some one portion of primordial matter that remains exactly as it is for the whole lifetime of a human being. But still, these arguments against the first position do not completely exclude the possibility that the primordial matter, albeit modified, could remain for the entire duration of the human's life.

The reply given to the second opinion, however, excludes this possibility also. Thomas in fact argues that the activity of nutrition consists not only in the increase of matter but also in the replacement of organic parts corrupted by the vital heat associated with digestive activity. Hence, it is unthinkable that there could remain unaltered a primitive nucleus of matter endowed with radical moisture. This latter notion was introduced by the medical doctors for the purpose of counterbalancing the destructive activity of heat. Thomas is of the opinion that the organic state of the radical moisture cannot remain exactly as it is in the human being, but it can remain only as appropriately modified and combined with more complex forms of moisture. Hence, again, it is unintelligible that there could remain unaltered a primitive nucleus of matter endowed with radical moisture.[65] Thomas's conclusion does

---

habens. Unde ex materia res quanta efficitur, non per extensionem (loquendo de materia prima) cum extensio non sit nisi eius quod alicuius quantitatis erat, sed per quantitatis susceptionem. Secundo, etsi prima materia, prout in se consideratur, nullam quantitatem habeat, non tamen sequitur quod sit in potentia respectu cuiuslibet quantitatis imaginabilis. Cum enim quantitates determinatae et omnia alia accidentia secundum exigentiam formae materiam recipiant, eo quod subiecta materia cum forma est causa eorum quae insunt, ut in *1 Physic.* dicitur, oportet quod materia prima ad nullam quantitatem sit in potentia, nisi quae competat formae naturali, quae in materia esse potest. Materia vero prima non est in potentia ad alias formas nisi ad illas quae sunt in rerum natura, vel per principia naturalia educi possunt. [. . .] Quarto, quia quando loquimur de materia existente in hac re, iam dimittimus considerationem materiae absolute: non enim potest accipi illud materiae quod est in hac re nisi secundum quod est divisum ab illa parte materiae quae est in re alia. Divisio autem non accidit materiae nisi secundum quod consideratur sub dimensionibus saltem interminatis: quia remota quantitate, ut in *1 Physic.* dicitur, substantia erit indivisibile. Unde consideratio materiae huius rei est consideratio non materiae absolute, sed materiae sub dimensione existentis."

65. See *Sent.,* II, d. 30, q. 2, a. 1: "Sed istud non videtur veritatem habere. Cum enim de natura caloris sit ut humorem consumat (caloris dico ignei), oportet quod calor ignis, qui est instrumentum animae vegetabilis, ut in *2 de Anim.* dicitur, indifferenter quantum in se est omne humidum consumat; unde non potest efficax ratio inveniri quare aliquod humidum signatum permaneat in tota vita. [. . .] Assumunt etiam in assertionem suae opinionis distinctionem Philosophi de carne secundum speciem et secundum materiam, et medicorum de humido nutrimentali et radicali. Sed quod neutra earum pro eis faciat, in responsione ad argumenta patebit." On the correct way of

not leave room for doubt: there is nothing of the matter, as taken with some quantitative determination, that remains exactly as it is throughout the entire process of human generation.[66]

4.2. Identity of Matter, Quantity, and Extension

A little earlier we observed that there is a second way of investigating the problem of the numerical continuity of an object, namely, the question of the principle of individuation of a material substance. We cannot here reconstruct Thomas's position on this subject, but we would like to examine how certain changes in his thinking on the role to be accorded quantity in the individuation of material substances have

---

understanding, according to Thomas, radical moisture see the answer to the third argument: "Ad tertium dicendum quod, secundum medicos, humidum quod ex primis generantibus trahitur, non oportet ut dicatur radicale quia semper remanet distinctum secundum materiam et proprietatem ab humido ex alimento aggenerato, sed quia calor naturalis in illo humido prius extitit, et illud quod permiscetur non participat speciem nisi ex virtute illius humidi cui permiscetur; unde est quasi radix totius illius quod postmodum ex alimento convertitur. Non autem ita quod utrumque humidum post finem digestionis ultimae distinctum remaneat, sed totum permixtum accipit unam proprietatem; et utraque materia, scilicet quae prius suberat primo humido et secundo advenienti, aequaliter se habet ad hoc quod transeat et ad hoc quod virtutem speciei participet. Nec dicitur consumi humidum radicale propter discessum talis materiae, sed propter hoc quod non permanet proprietas quam totum mixtum habebat ex virtute primi humidi; tunc enim non potest fieri restauratio, quia virtus speciei non manet." On the notion of "radical moisture" and for other bibliographical references, see Philip L. Reynolds, *Food and the Body: Some Peculiar Questions in High Medieval Theology* (Leiden: Brill, 1999), esp. 105–119, and Chiara Crisciani, "Aspetti del dibattito sull'umido radicale nella cultura del tardo Medioevo (secoli XIII–XV)," in Josep Perarnau, ed., *Arxiu de Textos Catalans Antics 23/24: Actes de la II Trobada Internacional d'Estudis sobre Arnau de Vilanova* (Barcelona: Institut d'Estudis Catalans, 2005), 333–380. On the problem of the numerical identity of the human body, see also Guido Alliney, "L'identità del corpo mortale e del corpo glorioso nei dibattiti duecenteschi," *Esercizi filosofici* 3 (1996): 187–197.

66. See *Sent.*, II, d. 30, q. 2, a. 1: "Tertia positio est quam ponit Averroes in *1 de Generat.*, dicens quod nihil materiae potest accipi in corpore signatum quod sit fixum et permanens, sed totum quidquid est in corpore, potest dupliciter considerari: vel ex parte materiae, et sic non est permanens; vel ex parte formae et speciei, et sic est permanens. Comparat enim Aristoteles in *1 de Generat.*, transmutationem cibi in carnem adustioni lignorum. Videmus enim quod si ignis accendatur et continue ligna addantur, secundum quod alia consumuntur, forma ignis semper manebit in lignis, sed tamen materia quaelibet consumitur, alia materia sibi succedente, in qua species ignis salvabitur; et secundum hoc, etiam illud quod pertinet ad speciem et formam carnis semper manebit, quamvis illud quod recipit hanc formam, continue consumatur et restauretur. [. . .] Et huic positioni inter omnes magis consentio sine praeiudicio aliarum."

repercussions on the problem at hand, namely, the material identity-continuity of the embryo.

In the *Summa theologiae,* while discussing the numerical identity of the body of Christ as it passes through death, Thomas notes that whenever the subject subsists in a single nature, it is necessary that if the identity of the form ceases, so does numerical identity. But this does not hold of Christ, being a subject subsisting in *two* natures, human and divine. Hence, the body of Christ is an exception; thus, in his case, one can say that the body remains simply *(simpliciter)* the same. Thomas, however, clarifies that the adverb "simply" can be understood in two ways. If it is taken as a synonym for "absolutely" *(absolute),* then one can say that the living body and dead body of Christ are simply the same, for they are absolutely the same; that is, they share the same subject *(idem supposito).* If "simply" is taken instead as a synonym for "entirely" *(omnino)* or "totally" *(totaliter),* then the living body and dead body of Christ are not simply the same. On the other hand, the body of a dead human being is not simply the same (either absolutely or entirely and totally) as that of the living human being, but only in a certain respect *(secundum quid),* that is, according to matter.[67] If there is an identity of number, there must be an identity of subject *(idem numero dicitur aliquid secundum suppositum).*[68] But since there is not an identity of subject between a living body and a dead body of a human being, there is no identity of number.

But how can Thomas speak of identity of number as to matter but not identity of number as to subject? When we examine the case of a living body that becomes a dead body, in fact, the matter of which we speak does not seem to be some organic part or other of the subject, but the subject itself considered in its entirety as something distinct from its formal properties. If we assume that when Thomas speaks of the identity of matter in the case of the passing from a living to a dead body, or from the latter to the risen body, Thomas is speaking of identity of material subject, then it seems that the identity of matter can only with difficulty be distinguished from the identity of subject.

67. See ST, III, q. 50, a. 5; see also *Quodl.* II, q. 1, a. 1.
68. See, e.g., QDSC, q. 3, ad 19, 383b.

Nevertheless, Thomas seems to think that there can be a criterion to fix the identity of matter without being at the same time constrained to assume that such a criterion is able to fix the identity of the subject of which it is the matter. Let us look at this more closely.

According to the tradition and Thomas himself at the start of his career, the identity of matter can be made to depend on what was known in the Middle Ages as the "form of corporeity" *(forma corporeitatis)*. This expression indicates the extension of a material substrate that supports the different forms: in other words, the material substrate's three-dimensionality or formal configuration.[69] Especially at the beginning of his career, Thomas admitted that matter could have of itself a form of corporeity, that is, an extended bodily configuration that ontologically precedes the coming of substantial form and is responsible for the identity of the matter. Among other quandaries, various problems connected to the difficulty of having an accidental form (i.e., extension or quantity, on which extension depends) ontologically prior to a substantial form forced him to revise this position.[70] At the start of his career, however, he seemed to have accepted this position. In particular, whether commenting on the *Sentences* or in his *De ente et essentia*, Thomas characterized being a body as that in which can be mapped out the three dimensions, being at the same time in potency for further perfecting.[71] In the course of his career, Thomas showed

---

69. See CT, I, ch. 154, 140, 29–45: "Ex hoc autem quod resurrectionem ponimus diuina uirtute futuram, de facili uideri potest quomodo corpus idem numero reparetur. Cum enim supra ostensum sit quod omnia etiam minima sub diuina prouidentia continentur, manifestum est quod materia huius humani corporis, quamcumque formam post mortem hominis accipiat, non effugit neque uirtutem neque cognitionem divinam. Que quidem materia eadem numero manet, in quantum intelligitur sub dimensionibus existens secundum quas hec materia dici potest et est indiuiduationis principium. Hac igitur materia eadem manente, et ex ea virtute divina corpore reparato humano, nec non et anima rationali, que cum sit incorruptibilis eadem manet, eidem corpori coniuncta, consequens fit ut homo idem numero reparetur."

70. This is not the place to dwell on this issue. For details, see Silvia Donati, "La dottrina delle dimensioni indeterminate in Egidio Romano," *Medioevo* 14 (1988): 149–233; Joseph Owens, "Thomas Aquinas: Dimensive Quantity as Individuating Principle," *Mediaeval Studies* 50 (1988): 279–310. On the notion of "form of corporeity" *(forma corporeitatis)*, see *Sent.*, I, d. 8, q. 5, a. 2; *Sent.*, II, d. 3, q. 1, a. 1; *Sup. De Trin.*, q. 4, a. 2; ST, I, q. 66, a. 2.

71. See, e.g., *Sent.*, I, d. 25, q. 1, a. 1, ad 2: "Ratio corporis in hoc consistat quod sit talis naturae ut in eo possint designari tres dimensiones. Si nomine corporis significetur res huiusmodi, ut in ea

some hesitation concerning the role of three-dimensional extension in determining the individual identity of matter; in particular, he showed uncertainty concerning the following point: whether to consider a defined and determinate three-dimensional extension or a generic and indeterminate three-dimensionality as the principal factor in the individuation of matter.

At least at the start of his career, Thomas seemed to have been greatly inclined toward the solution of Avicenna favoring "determinate dimensions" *(dimensiones terminatae)* as the principle responsible for the individuation and numerical unity of a thing.[72] For example, what makes the body of young Socrates and the body of old Socrates numerically the same body is not so much that they have the same matter, as that they maintain the same three-dimensional extension. An interpreter could identify such three-dimensional extension with the quantity of the matter or bodily mass. In a certain sense this is true, but this identification is not entirely correct, for the substitution of material parts could also produce a total substitution of the quantity of matter that, therefore, could not remain one in number.

Thomas explained this intuition better while commenting especially on the *De Trinitate* of Boethius (1256–59), by observing that what allows us to say that a body has the same quantity of matter is at the end of the day a sort of "formal" element. In that work, Thomas identified this as "site" *(situs),* understood not spatially, as the placement of a thing in a place or as the reciprocal spatial disposition of the parts in a whole, but

---

possint designari tres dimensiones sub hac conditione, ut superveniat alia perfectio quae compleat ipsam in ratione nobiliori sicut est anima, sic est corpus pars animalis"; DEE, ch. 3. This characterization also recurs in SCG, IV, ch. 81, and ST, I, q. 18, a. 2.

72. On the distinction between determinate dimensions and indeterminate dimensions, see *Sup. De Trin.*, q. 4, a. 2, 125, 214–231: "Dimensiones autem iste possunt dupliciter considerari. Vno modo secundum earum terminationem;—et dico eas terminari secundum determinatam mensuram et figuram, et sic ut entia perfecta collocantur in genere quantitatis—; et sic non possunt esse principium indiuiduationis; quia cum talis terminatio dimensionum uarietur frequenter circa indiuiduum, sequeretur quod indiuiduum non remaneret semper idem numero. Alio modo possunt considerari sine ista determinatione, in natura dimensionis tantum, quamvis numquam sine aliqua determinatione esse possint, sicut nec natura coloris sine determinatione albi et nigri; et sic collocantur in genere quantitatis ut imperfectum, et ex his dimensionibus interminatis materia efficitur hec materia signata, et sic indiuiduat formam. Et sic ex materia causatur diuersitas secundum numerum in eadem specie."

rather understood formally, as a difference in the category of quantity. Site should be understood, namely, as the final limit of the three-dimensionality or bodily extension.[73] The site of a body certainly presupposes the quantity of that body.[74] But site is what allows us to infer and to determine such quantity and therefore the matter that supports such quantity.[75] Understood in this sense, site establishes the formal delimitation of a three-dimensional extension, and as such, gives rise to the configuration of the body.[76] Being a body, understood with respect to its formal aspect of having site (which, as we have said, constitutes the intrinsic formal principle of the material delimitation of a subject and the intrinsic formal principle that allows the individuation of three-dimensionality itself),[77] could be proposed as what determines the numerical identity of a matter in continual change (or of a subject as material support of the different and successive forms). By determining the numerical identity of matter, site determines also the numerical identity of the subject, even though the alteration of the site of the parts does not take away from the numerical identity of the subject.[78]

Actually, however much at first plausible, we could have difficulty in assigning to site the role of being the factor responsible for the individuation of matter. First, this attempted solution assigns to the matter of a thing an intrinsic three-dimensional extension that determines the identity of that thing apart from the substantial form that informs

---

73. See *Sup. De Trin.*, q. 4, a. 2, ad 3, 125–126, 260–277: "Nullum autem accidens habet ex se propriam rationem diuisionis nisi quantitas; unde dimensiones ex se ipsis habent quandam rationem indiuiduationis secundum determinatum situm, prout situs est differentia quantitatis. Et sic dimensio habet duplicem rationem indiuiduationis, unam ex subiecto sicut et quodlibet aliud accidens, et aliam ex se ipsa, in quantum habet situm; ratione cuius etiam abstraendo a materia sensibili ymaginamur hanc lineam et hunc circulum. Et ideo recte materie conuenit indiuiduare omnes alias formas, ex hoc quod subditur illi forme que ex se ipsa habet indiuiduationis rationem, ita quod etiam ipse dimensiones terminate, que fundantur in subiecto iam completo, indiuiduantur quodammodo ex materia indiuiduata per dimensiones interminatas preintellectas in materia."

74. See *Sent.*, IV, d. 10, q. 1, a. 2, q.la 4, ad 3.

75. See *Sent.*, IV, d. 44, q. 2, a. 2, q.la 2; *Sup. De Trin.*, q. 4, a. 3, 129, 192–203.

76. On the notion of figure as termination of three-dimensionally extended quantity, see *Sent.*, III, d. 16, q. 2, a. 1, ad 1; *Sent.*, IV, d. 4, q. 1, a. 1; ST, I, q. 78, a. 3, ad 2; ST, III, q. 63, a. 2, ad 1.

77. See *Sup. De Trin.*, q. 4, a. 3. See also *Sent.*, IV, d. 12, q. 1, a. 1, q.la 3, ad 3, and IV, d. 44, q. 2, a. 2, q.la 2.

78. See *Sent.*, IV, d. 44, q. 1, a. 1, q.la 3, ad 2; q. 1, a. 2, q.la 5, ad 3; q. 2, a. 2, q.la 3.

matter. It is well known that Thomas changed his mind on the role of extension in the process of substantial individuation precisely by reflecting on this difficulty. Second, sometimes Thomas separates the numerical identity of the subject from three-dimensional numerical identity.[79] On the one hand, Thomas realizes that it is not possible to account for a form being found in different matters without admitting something in matter itself (a predisposition or some formal characteristic) that accounts for the different ways in which the form is received in such matters. This task, at the beginning of his career, was given precisely to three-dimensional determinate extension. But on the other hand, Thomas, almost immediately, comes to reject this Avicennian solution and adopts that of Averroes, making "indeterminate dimensions" *(dimensiones interminatae)* the real factor responsible for material individuation and the numerical unity of a thing. In making this shift in position, however, Thomas rethinks the relation existing between substantial form and accidental form, and in the end, he also does not find this Averroist solution totally satisfactory.

Thomas sees that the principal philosophical problem in the Avicennian solution is that determinate dimensions are not able to give an account of the numerical identity of a thing given hypothetical or real quantitative variation in its matter. Taking up again our earlier example, it is evident that the body of young Socrates and the body of old Socrates are not exactly the same body, for they cannot have the same matter or the same dimensions; they are nevertheless the body of one and the same human being. What allows this logical passage (from one and the same body to the body of one and the same human being) is precisely the notion of indeterminate dimensions. At the same time, however, Thomas realizes that his conception of substantial form stops him from admitting the actual existence of a nonsubstantial element (whether indeterminate or determinate dimensions) ontologically prior to the coming of substantial form. To avoid conflicts between the Aristotelian ontology that he has chosen and an inescapable theoretical demand, he

---

79. See, e.g., CT, I, ch. 154, 141, 113–115: "Vnde licet [*supple:* trina dimensio] non eadem numero redeat, idemptitas subiecti non impeditur ad quam sufficit unitas essentialium principiorum."

will introduce an asymmetry between the ontological order and the logical order in the account of the formation of a thing. He assumes that ontologically three-dimensional extension does not precede the substantial form, but nevertheless such extension must be conceptually presupposed *(praeintellecta)* to give an account of the coming of substantial form.[80] At the start of his career, in the Commentary on the *Sentences* to be exact, Thomas identified this element that must be conceptually presupposed as what remains also after the separation of the human soul, hence giving continuity and identity to bodily matter.[81]

It is true that Thomas does vacillate about the role to be assigned to dimensions in the process of substantial individuation, and it is also true that he is not completely clear (1) how a generic and indeterminate three-dimensional extension, as such, can guarantee the numerical identity of a thing, and not just be the condition of possibility for the numerical identity of a thing, nor (2) what the conceptual presupposition of an indeterminate three-dimensional extension implies ontologically. Nevertheless, Thomas remained firm on the point that the material identity of an object is given by its matter considered *with site* and *with dimensions*.[82] One should not be surprised, then, if at times Thomas ties the material identity of an object to that determinate object's being very clearly visible, a result of direct observation. With

---

80. On the conceptual presupposition *(praeintellectio)* of indeterminate dimensions to substantial form, see *Sent.,* IV, d. 11, q. 1, a. 1, q.la 3, ad 4, and d. 12, q. 1, a. 3, q.la 1, ad 3; *Sent.,* II, d. 3, q. 1, aa. 1 and 4; QDV, q. 5, a. 9, ad 6; *Sup. De Trin.,* q. 4, a. 2, ad 3 and ad 5; QDA, a. 9 and ad 17; ST, I, q. 76, a. 6, ad 1.

81. See *Sent.,* IV, d. 44, q. 1, a. 1, q.la 1, ad 3: "Ad tertium dicendum quod illud quod intelligitur in materia ante formam remanet in materia post corruptionem, quia remoto posteriori, remanere adhuc potest prius. Oportet autem, ut Commentator dicit in I *Physicorum* et in *libro De substantia orbis,* in materia generabilium et corruptibilium ante formam substantialem intelligere dimensiones non terminatas, secundum quas attendatur divisio materiae, ut diversas formas in diversis partibus recipere possit; unde et post separationem formae substantialis a materia, adhuc dimensiones illae manent eadem; et sic materia sub illis dimensionibus existens, quamcumque formam accipiat, habet maiorem identitatem ad illud quod ex ea generatum fuerat quam aliqua pars alia materiae sub quacumque forma existens; et sic eadem materia ad corpus humanum reparandum reducetur quae prius eius materia fuit."

82. For an introduction to the principle of individuation in Aquinas, see John F. Wippel, *The Metaphysical Thought of Thomas Aquinas: From Finite Being to Uncreated Being* (Washington, DC: Catholic University of America Press, 2000), 351 ff. See there for further references.

respect to any object of our common experience, what at the microscopic level of observation or knowledge would not be able to guarantee the continuity of that object could provide such a guarantee at a more general or macroscopic level of observation or knowledge. In particular, the identification of some thing as one object in number seems to take place by the conceptual classification of all and only those properties, both descriptive and spatiotemporal, that can be associated with the object to which we are making reference when we use a demonstrative pronoun with a noun.[83] In a certain sense, this cognitive and referential-linguistic criterion is a counterpart to the metaphysical criterion, i.e., site, that Thomas identified and discussed at length, especially in his Commentary on the *De Trinitate* of Boethius composed a short time after his Commentary on the *Sentences*. Site does not absolutely precede every substantial form, but reveals a precondition, to some degree formal, that the prime matter must have, even if in a completely potential way—and that a matter already informed by a lower or imperfect form must have in an actual way—to be able to receive the perfect substantial form.

Metaphysically, site follows the substantial form and it is what formally puts an end to the three-dimensional extension of the matter, so giving to the matter and to each of its parts a precise bodily configuration. On the other hand, logically, site precedes the substantial form, so allowing for one and the same form to be found in different individual matters. The role played by site in determining the material configuration of a subject is important for understanding how one can speak, in the case of a matter, of a species or a type of matter. In brief, Thomas seems to think that what accounts for the body of young Socrates being the same as the body of old Socrates is not the quantity of matter or matter determinate in its dimensions, but rather it is matter that is

---

83. See *Sent.*, III, d. 21, q. 2, a. 4, q.la 1: "Respondeo dicendum ad primam quaestionem quod ad veritatem resurrectionis exigitur quod idem numero resurgat. Individuatio autem, secundum quam est aliquid unum numero, ex diversis accidentibus manifestatur, quorum collectio in alio non invenitur; et quia visus, ut dicit Philosophus in principio *Metaphysicorum*, plures nobis rerum differentias ostendit, ideo quod sit idem numero nunquam melius quam per visum manifestatur, et ideo visibilis apparitio fuit unum de argumentis resurrectionis"; also ad 1: "apparitio visibilis non inducebatur ad probandum veritatem carnis [. . .], sed ad probandum identitatem suppositi."

indeterminate extensionally which gives rise gradually to determinate identities of the parts and of the organic components. The matter of the two bodies is not the same, even though the body of young Socrates and the body of old Socrates have the same type of matter; that is, they possess the same organs which maintain, even if in a variable way, the same site or formal configuration and so the same capacity to exercise vital functions. Although the quantity of matter and the single portions of matter of the body of young Socrates are not to be found in the body of the old Socrates, nevertheless the two bodies continue to be composed of human organs, flesh, and bones, and more particularly of organs, flesh, and bones that keep one and the same numerical site or formal configuration.

Many times in the course of his career Thomas returns to the Aristotelian distinction between flesh according to species and flesh according to matter. Discussing the passage from *De generatione animalium* where Aristotle introduces this distinction, Thomas denies that by this distinction Aristotle intended to refer to two really distinct fleshes.[84] This was the interpretation of certain theologians according to which the embryo would acquire flesh according to species from the one generating, and this remains in the individual as long as he/she lives, while flesh according to matter would be obtained through assimilation by nutrition, and this changes continually.[85] For various theological reasons that we need not enter into here, Thomas maintains that this distinction concerns different ways of considering one and the same flesh: the flesh understood as a portion of matter (i.e., the flesh according to matter) and the flesh understood as a type exhibited by that portion of matter (i.e., the flesh according to species) are not really distinct things, if they are considered with respect to that portion. Instead, the first refers to a portion of matter apart from its formal configuration, while the second refers to the same portion with a given formal configuration. The upshot is that even if one portion of matter cannot remain the same from the beginning to the end of a human's

---

84. The passage from the *De generatione animalium* discussed by Aquinas is I, 5, 321b20.

85. See, for example, Bonaventure, *Commentaria in quattuor libros Sententiarum,* II, d. 30, a. 3, q. 2, 735.

life, still the formal configuration of the matter can remain the same, just as, taking up another example of Thomas, a fire remains the same even if the wood that feeds it is consumed and changes continually.[86]

With respect to what we are saying here, it can be noted that to safeguard the numerical identity of an object, Thomas does not seem to posit any particular restrictive condition on the substitution of material parts: as long as there continues the function connected with such parts, which function depends remotely on their formal configuration, the material parts can be freely substituted. The substitution of basic and homogeneous material parts, as flesh and bones, comes about naturally by nutrition, while the substitution of complex organic parts, as the hands, an eye, or whatever other organ, can take place only by some external intervention. The examples of fire and water, which exemplify this situation well, occur often in Thomas's texts.

In particular, it is worth noting the distinction that Thomas makes when dealing with matter between the material and the formal-functional aspects, a distinction he connects to the Aristotelian distinction between flesh according to matter and flesh according to species. This distinction allows Thomas to speak of the identity of matter even when the single parts or portions of matter are, in whole or in part, changed. So, again following Thomas's example, if we described a city or the body of citizens *(civitas)* as the totality of all the citizens that carry out determinate functions, then if all the citizens of a city were substituted, that city could not be said to be materially the same. Still, it could continue to be considered formally the same city, as long as the citizens

---

86. See, e.g., ST, I, q. 119, a. 1, ad 2: "Ad secundum dicendum quod aliqui per carnem secundum speciem intellexerunt id quod primo accipit speciem humanam, quod sumitur a generante: et hoc dicunt semper manere, quousque individuum durat. Carnem vero secundum materiam dicunt esse quae generatur ex alimento: et hanc dicunt non semper permanere, sed quod sicut advenit, ita abscedit. Sed hoc est contra intentionem Aristotelis. [. . .] Et ideo aliter dicendum est, quod haec distinctio Philosophi non est secundum diversas carnes, sed est eiusdem carnis secundum diversam considerationem. Si enim consideretur caro secundum speciem, idest secundum id quod est formale in ipsa, sic semper manet: quia semper manet natura carnis, et dispositio naturalis ipsius. Sed si consideretur caro secundum materiam, sic non manet, sed paulatim consumitur et restauratur, sicut patet in igne fornacis, cuius forma manet, sed materia paulatim consumitur, et alia in locum eius substituitur." This distinction is also discussed in *Sent.*, II, d. 30, q. 2, a. 1, ad 2; *Quodl.* VIII, q. 3 and ad 1; *Exp. Gen.*, I, lec. 15.

that had taken the place of the earlier ones continued to exercise the same identical functions that the previous citizens had exercised.[87]

This example is interesting, for it shows how for Thomas one can speak of a threefold identity of an object: material identity, formal identity, and material formal identity. An object can lose its material identity but still continue to be the same object if its material formal identity is preserved, an identity on which depends the identity of its functions. As long as there is preserved the transtemporal identity of an object, Thomas seems to posit only two limitations on the substitution of material parts. In the first place, the substitution of parts must guarantee that the functions carried out by such parts are maintained, and for this reason a genuine substitution of parts can take place only using matter that is functionally appropriate and homogeneous. (One could hypothesize that this should place very strict limits on the type of matter that could be used in replacing or repairing human matter.) In the second place, the substitution of parts ought to take place in succession and not simultaneously.[88] For example, a city could continue to be

---

87. See, e.g., *Sent.*, IV, d. 44, q. 1, a. 2, q.la 4: "Tertia autem opinio quantum ad aliquid differt a secunda et quantum ad aliquid convenit cum ea. Differt quidem quantum ad hoc quod ponit totum quod est sub forma carnis et ossis eadem ratione ad veritatem humanae naturae pertinere, quia non distinguit aliquid materiale signatum permanens in homine toto tempore vitae eius quod per se pertineat ad veritatem humanae naturae et primo, et aliquid fluens et refluens quod pertineat ad veritatem humanae naturae solum propter quantitatis perfectionem, non propter primum esse speciei, sicut secunda opinio dicebat; sed ponit omnes partes quae non sunt praeter intentionem naturae aggeneratae pertinere ad veritatem humanae naturae quantum ad id quod habent de specie, quia sic manent, non autem quantum ad id quod habent de materia, quia sic fluunt et refluunt indifferenter. Ut ita etiam intelligamus contingere in partibus hominis unius sicut contingit in tota multitudine civitatis, quia singuli subtrahuntur a multitudine per mortem, aliis in locum eorum succedentibus; unde partes multitudinis fluunt et refluunt materialiter, sed formaliter manent, quia ad eadem officia et ordines substituuntur alii, a quibus priores subtrahebantur; unde respublica una numero manere dicitur. Et similiter etiam dum quibusdam partibus fluentibus aliae reparantur in eadem figura et in eodem situ, omnes partes fluunt et refluunt secundum materiam, sed manent secundum speciem; manet nihilominus unus homo numero."

88. See, e.g., ST, I, q. 119, a. 1, ad 5: "Ad quintum dicendum quod, sicut Philosophus dicit in I *de Generat.*, quando aliqua materia per se convertitur in ignem, tunc dicitur ignis de novo generari: quando vero aliqua materia convertitur in ignem praeexistentem, dicitur ignis nutriri. Unde si tota materia simul amittat speciem ignis, et alia materia convertatur in ignem, erit alius ignis numero. Si vero, paulatim combusto uno ligno, aliud substituatur, et sic deinceps quousque omnia prima consumantur, semper remanet idem ignis numero: quia semper quod additur, transit in praeexistens. Et similiter est intelligendum in corporibus viventibus, in quibus ex nutrimento restauratur id quod

called the same if all its citizens were replaced successively with other citizens. But if the citizens were substituted all at once, it would not be the numerically same city, for in this case, one could plausibly argue, there would be an interruption in the existential story or continuity of that city.

In the final analysis, it is the identity of the formal configuration of the matter that is the explanatory factor regarding the identity of an object. Such an identity is the result of an interaction between the matter and the functions that, with respect to the form, such matter is called upon to carry out. The formal identity of the matter is founded remotely on the identity of the three-dimensional extension of the material parts, on which depends the functional specificity of such parts with respect to the whole into which they are inserted. This final observation takes us back to the distinction between indeterminate dimensions and determinate dimensions of an object, which we introduced at the beginning of this chapter. How can we employ this distinction in the case of the embryo?

The notion of determinate dimensions does not seem applicable to the case of the embryo, for one is dealing with a subject that is continually changing its own matter and therefore its own formal configuration. But the notion of indeterminate dimensions could give us that sense of identity of matter that guarantees continuity to the embryogenetic process. The indeterminate dimensions of the embryonic matter seem to be the same throughout the process insofar as they are dimensions of one and the same subject. What allows us to say this could be that the embryonic matter, once it becomes independent from the mother (i.e., right from conception), or the embryo itself considered as material subject of the forms that it gradually assumes, acquires a three-dimensional extension that perdures, even if modified in its particular

---

per calorem naturalem consumitur." Some contemporary philosophers also hold that these limitations are necessary to assure some form of an object's identity across time. For an introduction to contemporary debates concerning the metaphysical constitution and identity of objects with respect to the change of their parts, see E. Jonathan Lowe, *A Survey of Metaphysics* (Oxford: Oxford University Press, 2002), ch. 2, and Michael J. Loux, *Metaphysics: A Contemporary Introduction* (London: Routledge, 2006), ch. 8, to which I refer the reader for further bibliographical references.

quantitative determinations, throughout the whole process. And so we could conjecture that if we could follow over time the spatiotemporal history of an embryo, we would realize that it is one and one and the same entity that becomes a human being; that is, there is no interruption in the existential story or continuity of that embryo. This would be the guarantee that between an embryo and a human being, apart from the continual substitution of parts, there is some numerical identity given by the matter, an identity that is reflected in the identity of the material functions that the embryo and later the human being is able to carry out.[89]

It is probably from this perspective that Thomas tries to disassociate the generic identity between two things from their material identity. For example, in *Summa theologiae,* I-II, q. 67, a. 5, one reads:

> When you remove the [substantial] difference of a species, the substance of the genus does not remain numerically identical. Thus if you remove the difference constituting whiteness, the substance of color does not remain numerically identical, for then the numerically same color would be at one time whiteness and at another blackness. The reason is that genus is not related to difference as matter is to form, as if the substance of the genus would remain numerically identical when the difference is removed, as the substance of matter remains numerically identical when the form is removed. For genus and difference are not parts of the species, for then they would not be predicated of the species.[90]

---

89. See *Sup. De Trin.,* q. 4, a. 2, 125, 231–242: "Vnde patet quod materia secundum se accepta nec est principium diuersitatis secundum speciem nec secundum numerum; set sicut est principium diuersitatis secundum genus prout subest forme communi, ita est principium diversitatis secundum numerum prout subest dimensionibus interminatis. Et ideo, cum hee dimensiones sint de genere accidentium, quandoque diuersitas secundum numerum reducitur in diuersitatem materie, quandoque in diuersitatem accidentis, et hoc ratione dimensionum predictarum."

90. See ST, I–II, q. 67, a. 5: "Non enim, remota differentia alicuius speciei, remanet substantia generis eadem numero, sicut, remota differentia constitutiva albedinis, non remanet eadem substantia coloris numero, ut sic idem numero color sit quandoque albedo, quandoque vero nigredo. Non enim comparatur genus ad differentiam sicut materia ad formam, ut remaneat substantia generis eadem numero, differentia remota; sicut remanet eadem numero substantia materiae, remota forma. Genus enim et differentia non sunt partes speciei, alioquin non praedicarentur de specie. Sed

While the identity of genus, which is an identity that is above all of the "logical" type, is not preserved when the specific difference ceases to exist, the identity of matter, which expresses a more real identity, seems to be preserved when the substantial form ceases to exist.[91]

In particular, and this is what is of interest for the case of the embryo, Thomas seems to assume that this identity of matter is preserved not only during the passage from something that is already formed to something no longer formed but also during the passage from something not yet formed to something that is formed. Given how Thomas expresses himself, every time there is a change from what is imperfect to what is perfect and the imperfect thing's being is not part of the nature of what changes, one can admit identity of matter in what changes. So, Thomas illustrates, one can say that being a baby is not part of the essence of a human being, and so the same entity that is now a baby will later be an adult human being. This condition, obviously, is not to be understood as a sufficient condition, for then we would have to admit (which Thomas rejects) that the same entity that now is a human being could later become a horse, for being a human being is not part of the essence of a horse.[92] Rather, what Thomas intends to say is that a baby and an adult human being share the same specific difference, and so all the properties that are characteristic of a baby as a baby or of an adult as an adult do not prevent a baby and an adult human

---

sicut species significat totum, idest compositum ex materia et forma in rebus materialibus, ita differentia significat totum, et similiter genus, sed genus denominat totum ab eo quod est sicut materia; differentia vero ab eo quod est sicut forma; species vero ab utroque. Sicut in homine sensitiva natura materialiter se habet ad intellectivam, animal autem dicitur quod habet naturam sensitivam; rationale quod habet intellectivam; homo vero quod habet utrumque. Et sic idem totum significatur per haec tria, sed non ab eodem. Unde patet quod, cum differentia non sit nisi designativa generis, remota differentia, non potest substantia generis eadem remanere, non enim remanet eadem animalitas, si sit alia anima constituens animal."

91. On the "logical" character of generic, specific, and numerical identity-unity, see *Exp. Met.*, V, lec. 8, n. 876.

92. See ST, I–II, q. 67, a. 3: "Est autem considerandum quod imperfectio quidem quandoque est de ratione rei, et pertinet ad speciem ipsius, sicut defectus rationis pertinet ad rationem speciei equi vel bovis. Et quia unum et idem numero manens non potest transferri de una specie in aliam, inde est quod, tali imperfectione sublata, tollitur species rei, sicut iam non esset bos vel equus, si esset rationalis. Quandoque vero imperfectio non pertinet ad rationem speciei, sed accidit individuo secundum aliquid aliud, sicut alicui homini quandoque accidit defectus rationis, inquantum impeditur in eo

being from being numerically identical, which is not true of a human being and a horse. In the same way, we could conjecture, one can say that being an embryo is not part of the essence of a human being, and so the same entity that is now an embryo will later be a human being. More precisely, as the properties that belong to an embryo as embryo are not logically incompatible with the properties that belong to a human being as human being, once it is assumed that an embryo as a human being and a human being as a human being share, or better, *are able* to share, the same specific difference, the conclusion then follows that the same entity that is now an embryo will be, or better, *is able to be,* a human being later.

What conclusions can we draw from the preceding discussion? As is clear, the line of reasoning that we have taken until now—generalizing from statements present in works coming from very different periods in Thomas's career in order to sketch a position that is, when all is said and done, rather coherent—is purely conjectural. Not only does one encounter in the texts of the Dominican master revisions and conflicting statements concerning the numerical identity of a thing, as was seen, but Thomas spends little time explaining the numerical identity that holds between an embryo and a human being. And there are texts that seem to deny that one can really speak of numerical identity between an embryo and a human being. For example, while it is rather common to read in Thomas that the semen and the living organism that arises from it are numerically one and the same thing since one is in potency to the other, there are also passages (as in the text from his early Commentary on the *Sentences*) in which Thomas denies that the sown wheat and the grown wheat are numerically the same thing.[93]

---

rationis usus, propter somnum vel ebrietatem vel aliquid huiusmodi. Patet autem quod, tali imperfectione remota, nihilominus substantia rei manet"; ST, II–II, q. 4, a. 4, ad 1: "Tunc enim oportet quod, adveniente perfecto, imperfectum excludatur. [. . .] Sed quando imperfectio non est de ratione imperfectae, tunc illud numero idem quod erat imperfectum fit perfectum: sicut pueritia non est de ratione hominis, et ideo idem numero qui erat puer fit vir"; also *Sent.,* III, d. 31, q. 2, a. 1, q.la 3.

93. See *Sent.,* IV, d. 44, q. 1, a. 1, q.la 1, ad 1: "In seminatione grani granum seminatum et natum non est idem numero, nec eodem modo se habens, cum primum seminatum fuerit absque folliculis cum quibus nascitur. Corpus autem resurgens erit idem, sed alio modo se habens, quia fuit mortale et surget in immortalitate."

And Thomas goes further in *Quodlibet* I, a text from the final period of his career (1268–1272). In discussing the question "Once the soul is added to the body, are all the forms that once inhered in it, both substantial and accidental, corrupted?" he seems to revise his earlier position about the accidental forms conceptually presupposed to the substantial form *(praeintellectae)* surviving after the corruption of the substantial form. He argues that the indeterminate dimensions of a body, after the corruption of a substantial form, remain only specifically, and not numerically, identical in the body that is no longer ensouled.[94] Perhaps what happened here is that Thomas came to see in an acute way the difficulty of reconciling (1) the radical primacy of substantial form (along with the presupposition, at least conceptual, of accidental predispositions in matter that prepare for the coming of substantial form) with (2) the possibility of defining the numerical identity of dimensions independently of the subject of which they are the

---

94. See *Quodl.* I, q. 4, a. 1 *(Utrum anima adueniente corpori corrumpantur omnes forme que prius inerant, et substanciales et accidentales)*, vol. 2, 183–184, 47–94: "Responsio. Dicendum quod inpossibile est in uno et eodem esse plures formas substanciales. Et hoc ideo quia ab eodem habet res esse et unitatem; manifestum est autem quod res habet esse per formam, unde et per formam res habet unitatem; et propter hoc, ubicunque est multitudo formarum, non est unum simpliciter. Sicut *homo albus* non est unum simpliciter, nec *animal bipes* esset unum simpliciter si ab alio esset animal et ab alio bipes, ut Philosophus dicit. Set sciendum est quod forme substanciales se habent ad inuicem sicut numeri, ut dicitur in VIII Methaphisice, uel etiam sicut figure, ut de partibus anime dicit Philosophus in II De anima: semper enim maior numerus uel figura uirtute continet in se minorem, sicut quinarius quaternarium et pentagonus tetragonum; et similiter perfectior forma uirtute continet in se inperfectiorem, ut maxime in animalibus patet: anima enim intellectiua habet uirtutem ut conferat corpori humano quicquid confert sensitiua in brutis, et similiter sensitiua facit in animalibus quicquid nutritiua in plantis, et adhuc amplius. Frustra igitur esset in homine alia anima sensitiua preter intellectiuam, ex quo anima intellectiua uirtute continet sensitiuam, et adhuc amplius; sicut frustra adderetur quaternarius posito quinario; et eadem ratio est de omnibus formis substancialibus usque ad materiam primam. Ita quod non est in homine diuersas formas substanciales inuenire, set solum secundum rationem, sicut consideramus eum ut uiuentem per animam nutritiuam et ut sentientem per animam sensitiuam et sic de aliis. Manifestum est autem quod semper, adueniente forma perfecta, tollitur forma inperfecta, sicut et adueniente figura pentagoni, tollitur figura quadrati. Vnde dico quod, adueniente anima humana, tollitur forma substancialis que prius inerat, alioquin generatio esset sine corruptione alterius, quod est inpossibile. *Forme uero accidentales que prius inerant disponentes ad animam, corrumpuntur quidem non per se, set per accidens ad corruptionem subiecti, unde manent eedem specie, set non eedem numero*, sicut etiam contingit circa dispositiones formarum elementarium, que primitus materie aduenire apparent" (last emphasis is mine). See also QDSC, a. 3, ad 12, 382b–383a.

dimensions. In this case, Thomas seems to acknowledge that one cannot prescind from substantial form in defining the numerical identity of a thing or of any part and aspect of that thing. By determining the being and being one of a thing, substantial form drives a mechanism of redefinition, both numeric and specific, of all the components of that thing, whether they are essential or accidental. Hence, dimensions can be said to be numerically identical only because they are dimensions of a numerically identical subject. Since once the form ceases, the numerical identity of the subject ceases, it follows that, once the form ceases, the numerical identity of the dimensions ceases also.

In the case of the embryo, this analysis takes away much of the strength of the hypothesis, suggested above, that considers indeterminate dimensions as the material continuant of the embryo. There does not seem to be any function, dependent on the formal configuration of the matter, that remains numerically identical during the passage from embryo to human being. At the end of the day, only the existential continuity of the embryo seems to guarantee and enable us to ascertain the identity of subject of the embryo.

The conjectural nature of our analysis and the difficulty in applying it to the case of the embryo come, as we have noted a number of times, from the fact that Thomas dedicates little space to discussing the problem of the identity of the embryo and from the fact that all characterizations of numerical identity found in his works provide a criterion for the numerical identity of a matter or of a subject that is already in act. The transtemporal identity of embryos can be settled only with difficulty by these characterizations since for Thomas embryos are not entities existing in act (or at least not completely and perfectly existing in act), inasmuch as they are constantly changing entities, and so it seems that any criterion of numerical identity that is rigid cannot be applied to them. As we have seen, the numerical identity between an embryo and a human being can only be presupposed and argued for on bases that are very extrinsic, inferring it, for example, from the identity of the subject of a process that involves something that from being in potentiality becomes being in actuality. Concretely, however, there seems to be little room to clarify this identity better, i.e., in a way that fits with modern-day analyses of the transtemporal identity of objects.

In the end, the conclusion that we can draw from this discussion is decidedly negative. The embryo and the human being cannot be said to be identical because of the substantial form or because of the matter, whether this be individual or specific, or because of three-dimensional extension or because of the quantity of the matter. Nevertheless, it remains true that they are the same subject. This can be derived from the fact that, metaphysically, the embryo is in potency to a human being so that a human being is what an embryo is in act, as well as from the fact that the process of generation is indivisible over time, and so if we had at hand a procedure that allowed us to follow, step by step, the history of the embryo, we would realize that what is involved is always *one and one and the same* subject.

CHAPTER SIX

Bioethical Implications

THE CONCLUSION of the last chapter was that Thomas Aquinas seems to accord to the embryo a transtemporal identity as subject of the process of generation, even if he has significant difficulties in stating precisely what type of identity holds between an embryo and a human being. Since the subject of the generative process is matter, understood as what is in potency to form, Thomas also accords to the embryo the status of matter with respect to the form of human being.[1] While the human being to be generated is the final end of the process, the embryo is the subject of that process and is what gives real continuity to the process leading from prime matter to the human being. The embryo is the authentic subject of the process of generation, and it is the embryo that is in potency to the form of human being. In particular, it is the *same* embryo that undergoes the progressive substitution of forms, reentering into different species and living different lives.

---

1. See, e.g., SCG, II, ch. 30; *Exp. Phys.*, V, lec. 3; *Exp. Met.*, VIII, lec. 1; *Exp. Met.*, XII, lec. 2.

If the vital functions exercised by the embryo cannot be considered as numerically identical to the functions exercised by the human being, they nevertheless are the same functions because they are functions of one and the same subject. Hence, the embryo and the human being to which it will give rise can be considered the same subject.[2]

Furthermore, I suggested in the last chapter that we should keep distinct the problem of the identity of the embryo from that of its continuity. What gives formal continuity to the process of a human being's generation is the presence of a formative power that continually transforms a matter that, as a result of this action, is continually modified to the point of taking on different species. The material continuant of the process, on the other hand, is given by the mother's matter, specifically by the menstrual blood, into which the semen also seems to be converted.[3] (Incidentally, this is also what permits us to speak, as Thomas notes, of consanguinity between parents and children.)[4] On the other hand, the identity of the embryo can be established only extrinsically. The embryo does not possess a form that it maintains for the entire process and for the whole duration of the process, and so the embryo does not possess an identity that is given once and for all. Its identity can only be established diachronically, by reflecting on the fact that it is the subject of one and *the same* process that in its turn is, therefore, a process that concerns one and *the same* subject. Since the process in its entirety is uninterrupted and temporally indivisible, even if characterized by an alternation of generations and corruptions, the presupposed identity of the subject allows us to develop a cognitive procedure that permits us, at every moment of that process, to establish the identity of the subject and to reconstruct its path. As was seen, Thomas establishes a strict correlation between the identity of a movement and the identity of its subject: each can be inferred from the other.

---

2. See *Sent.,* IV, d. 38, q. 1, a. 2, q.la 2, ad 3; SCG, II, ch. 89, nn. 1743–1745; QDSC, a. 3, ad 13.

3. See *Sent.,* III, d. 3, q. 5, a. 1; ST, III, q. 31, a. 5, ad 3; *Sup. Ioan.,* ch. 1, lec. 6.

4. It is due, more precisely, to the fact that both the semen and the female menstrual matter are derived from blood. See *Sent.,* IV, d. 40, q. 1, a. 1, ad 4.

1. The Origin of Human Life and the Affirmation That the Embryo Is a Human Being in Potency

Although the rational soul appears for males only around the sixth or seventh week, embryos before that time are, for Thomas, certainly ensouled (by a principle internal to the process, even if, as we have seen, it is not always clear if this principle is also internal to the embryo), but they do not have human ensoulment. In an embryological account such as Thomas develops, which views the introduction of the substantial form as a defining moment in the process, it is one thing to call something *human* and another to call something a *human being* or a *man*. Something can be called a human being only when it has the form of a human being, but something can be called human if it has some relation to the form of human being. Obviously, not every relation is pertinent here: even an animal can have some relation to the form of human being, but this is no reason to call whatever animal "human." Rather it is necessary that something have a significant relation to the form of human being, as the relation of being a part or principle of what in fact exhibits that form or the relation of being involved for some reason in the process of the generation of what exemplifies that form.

On Thomas's account of human generation, one can say that an embryo is human, but not that it is a human being except potentially. To lessen the status of an embryo from that of a human being to that of being human does not have of itself specific bioethical consequences with regard to abortion, since a restrictive bioethical theory could assume that the decisive property for rejecting an act of abortion is that of being human rather than being a human being. Such a theory, however, could be too restrictive, since the property of "being human" has such an extension as to encompass also entities that do not possess any particular bioethical value. For example, the corpse of a human being can also be called "human," but it is evident that someone could accord to the corpse little or no bioethical value or at least one different from that accorded to the embryo. Also a human being's actions or feelings are "human," but someone could readily exclude such entities from the field of a bioethical theory. A supporter of a restrictive bioethical theory could undoubtedly reply that "being human" is not to be understood as referring to whatever depends upon or is related, directly or by extension, to a human being, but rather is to be understood as referring to what exhibits some degrees of being a human being. The term "human," that is, refers to that of which one can predicate denominatively the form of human being, either (1) insofar as it is an essential part of a human being or (2) insofar as it is what can be a human being. While matter and form are an example of (1), an embryo is an example of (2), for an embryo is a human being in potency. But what does it mean to say that an embryo is a human being in potency?

The way in which an embryological account such as we have reconstructed can be put in dialogue with the contemporary bioethical debate on abortion depends on two factors: first, on the way in which one attempts to harmonize the formal discontinuity of the process of generation with the assumed identity of the subject of this process; second, on the value one places on the potentiality of the embryo to be a human being. As is well known, there is considerable discussion in contemporary bioethics about the so-called Potentiality Argument.[5] Here I do not want to take a stance in such a debate. My point, as I stated in the preface, is more limited. I mean to show that, in the abstract, however the factors mentioned above are developed, an account such as Thomas's is fully compatible both with a position in

---

5. For opposing positions, see, for example, Patrick Lee, *Abortion: The Unborn Human Life* (Washington, DC: Catholic University of America Press, 1996) and "The Pro-Life Argument from Substantial Identity: A Defense," *Bioethics* 18 (2004): 249–263; Dean Stretton, "Essential Properties and the Right to Life: A Response to Lee," *Bioethics* 18.3 (2004): 264–282; Patrick Lee, "Substantial Identity and the Right to Life: A Rejoinder to Dean Stretton," *Bioethics* 21 (2007): 93–97. For further discussion about this argument, also see Francis C. Wade, "Potentiality in the Abortion Discussions," *Review of Metaphysics* 29 (1975): 239–255; Enrico Berti, "Quando esiste l'uomo in potenza? La tesi di Aristotele," in Maurizio Mori, ed., *Quale statuto per l'embrione umano? Problemi e prospettive* (Milan: Bibliotechne, 1992), 52–58; Maurizio Mori, "Il feto ha diritto alla vita? Un'analisi filosofica dei vari argomenti in materia, con particolare riguardo a quello di potenzialità," in Luigi Lombardi-Vallauri, ed., *Il meritevole di tutela* (Milan: Giuffré, 1990), 735–839; Massimo Reichlin, "The Argument from Potential: A Reappraisal," *Bioethics* 11 (1997): 1–23. For a recent reconsideration of the Potentiality Argument and further bibliographical references, see John P. Lizza, "Potentiality and Human Embryos," *Bioethics* 21.7 (2007): 379–385; Bertha A. Manninen, "Revisiting the Argument from Fetal Potential," *Philosophy, Ethics, and Humanities in Medicine* 2.7 (2007), www.peh-med.com/content/2/1/7 (accessed May 1, 2012); and John P. Lizza, *Potentiality: Metaphysical and Bioethical Dimensions* (Baltimore, MD: Johns Hopkins University Press, forthcoming).

favor of and against abortion. Concretely, however, as we will argue, Thomas's account provides certain philosophical reasons for taking up a position that is generally against abortion, even setting aside the question of when the hominization of the embryo takes place.

The way in which the second point is developed, however, is relevant for determining the ethical value to be assigned to the act of abortion. If one holds that the embryo *is not* a human being *precisely because* it is a human being in potency (based on the argument that what is able to be F is not yet F), one can conclude that it is irrational to make an act of abortion and an act of voluntary homicide morally equivalent. But on the other hand, if one holds that the embryo *is* a human being *precisely because* it is a human being in potency (based on the argument that what has a full and genuine potentiality to become F, that is, what is becoming F, ought already to be considered somehow F), one can conclude that it is irrational not to make an act of abortion and an act of voluntary homicide morally equivalent. We come back, then, to the question with which we started: what does it mean that an embryo is a human being in potency?

As we have said many times, Thomas takes as the point of departure for his embryological account the Aristotelian characterization of the soul as the form of an organic, physical body that has life potentially. Following Aristotle, Thomas distinguishes two different cases of something having life potentially, that of semen and that of the embryo of a human being. In the light of this distinction, if "to be potentially a human being" is understood in the sense of having life potentially that Aristotle ascribes to semen, the conclusion would be that for Thomas embryos are absolutely lacking in human life. For as semen is in potency to life in the sense that it can have life even if it does not yet have it, so the embryo would be said to be in potency to human life in the sense that it does not yet possess it.[6] This, however, does not seem to be the

---

6. Unlike other organic materials, the semen is in proximate potency to life, although it is still deprived of it: "Non enim quandocumque, et qualitercumque dispositum, aliquid potest dici esse in potentia, etiam ad id quod fit ex eo. Nunquam enim poterit dici, quod terra sit in potentia homo. Manifestum est enim quod non; sed magis tunc dicitur esse in potentia homo, quando ex praecedenti materia iam factum est sperma. Et forte neque adhuc est in potentia homo, ut infra patebit" (*Exp. Met.*, IX, lec. 6, n. 1832).

correct interpretation of Thomas's position. Semen and the embryonic body manifest different potentialities for life in general and human life in particular. As we have seen, Thomas has no doubt that the male semen is completely deprived of life, not only rational, but also vegetative and sensitive. But Thomas also seems to have no doubt that embryos possess something that acts as a soul, i.e., a power or an intrinsic principle of ensoulment, which is able to explain the elementary vital operations (vegetative and sensitive) that embryos exhibit. If we put aside the problem of how to understand the statement of Thomas that the first embryonic species is that of the semen (a statement that seems to collapse two different cases), there is no doubt that Thomas keeps the embryo and semen quite distinct.

Metaphysically, the embryo is constituted immediately after the male semen has actualized the potentiality for life that the female menstrual blood possesses of itself. The embryo is born with the very first actualization of the potentiality of the female matter to be ensouled. The semen, therefore, is in potency to every form of ensoulment, while the embryo is born already with some form of ensoulment, i.e., vegetative ensoulment. Nevertheless, the semen and the embryo seem to be in the same situation with respect to the rational ensoulment. In fact, Thomas is clear that the explanatory principle of embryonic vital operations is not and cannot be the rational soul, and so embryos cannot be said to have a human soul from the moment of their conception.[7] This can be easily supported by comparing what happens to the embryo before the arrival of the rational soul and what happens to a human being after the separation of the rational soul. In the *Summa theologiae,* for example, Thomas affirms the principle that a thing maintains its species as long as it is able to exercise the operations characteristic of that species.[8] Applied to the case of the embryo, this principle tells us that the embryo is not a human being as long as it is not able to exercise the operations characteristic of the human species, which are rational

---

7. On the essential role played by the soul in making each organic part of a human body a human organic part, see SCG, II, ch. 89, n. 1752 (the text is quoted in full in Chapter 8, note 4). See also the following notes.

8. See ST, I, q. 76, a. 8: "Nulla pars corporis habet proprium opus, anima recedente: cum tamen omne quod retinet speciem, retineat operationem speciei."

activities, such that embryonic matter is not properly a human matter as long as it is not perfected by the rational soul.

These statements should lead us to correct what was said earlier about the possibility of extending to the embryo the property of "being human." From Thomas's point of view, the adjective "human" seems applicable, strictly speaking, only to the matter and to the form of a human being. Still, someone could defend such an extension pointing out that although neither the embryonic matter nor form can be said to be human, this still does not prevent the embryo in its entirety from being called human. This reply, however, has a less than satisfactory ring, because once it is admitted that neither the embryo's matter nor its form are human, to say that the embryo has the property of "being human" is to say only that the embryo is part of a process of human generation, and this is clearly a condition that is too weak for extending to the embryo the property of "being human." In reality, it is hard to misunderstand Thomas in his holding that the embryonic matter and form are not yet human but are only a *disposition* for human matter and form.⁹

Nevertheless, the interpretation that makes the potentiality for the rational soul of the semen equivalent to that of the embryo also turns out to be inadequate, and this for two reasons. First, properly speaking the semen does not have a passive potency to be ensouled, but only an active potency to ensoul, and so the semen *qua* semen cannot become rationally ensouled, while the embryo *qua* embryo can naturally do this.¹⁰ Second, the semen in any case would be in remote potency with respect to rational ensoulment, in the sense that nothing prevents the

---

9. See, e.g., ST, III, q. 5, a. 3: "Caro enim et ceterae partes hominis per animam speciem sortiuntur"; a. 4: "Cum enim corpus proportionetur animae sicut materia propriae formae, non est vera caro humana quae non est perfecta anima humana, scilicet rationali"; q. 6, a. 4, ad 1: "Caro humana sortitur esse per animam. Et ideo ante adventum animae non est caro humana: sed potest esse dispositio ad carnem humanam"; *Sup. Ioan.*, ch. 1, lec. 7.

10. Thomas rejects the view that the semen possesses some passive potency in *Sent.*, II, d. 18, q. 2, a. 3: "Semen autem decisum nondum est actu simile toti, sed in potentia propinqua, et ideo non remanet post divisionem animae in actu, sed in potentia; propter quod dicitur II *De anima* quod semen in potentia vivit et non actu. Haec autem potentia non est passiva in semine maris, sicut dicimus ligna et lapides esse in potentia domus (sic enim est potentia in menstruo mulieris), sed est potentia activa, sicut dicimus formam domus in mente artificis esse potentia domum."

semen from being able to be or to give rise to a rationally ensouled organism, but of itself the semen is indifferent with respect to being able to be or not to be rationally ensouled, nor is it able to self-determine itself one way or another. On the other hand, an embryo right from the start is in near potency with respect to rational ensoulment, in the sense of being inserted into a process that, if suitably supported and not interrupted, will lead it of itself to being rationally ensouled: the embryo can become a human being because it is becoming a human being. It is no longer indifferent with respect to alternatives, but is oriented toward being rationally ensouled.

But even with these clarifications in mind, the statement that the embryo, as the male semen, is a human being in potency is still a source of difficulties, and how one interprets this statement depends on how one interprets the notion of potency. This is a delicate point in the teaching of Thomas, at times badly understood. If we examine it more closely, we can note that the difficulty that an interpreter confronts (and which Thomas himself probably confronted) is to ascertain an intermediate state between that of the semen, which is a human being in remote potency because it has not yet begun the process of perfecting toward the final form, and that of the embryo that is completely ensouled and is now a human being in act and is in potency only with respect to its operations. Certainly the property of "being a human being," which coincides with the property of "being rationally ensouled," cannot be attributed to the semen at all, but it can be attributed to the formed embryo. But what happens in the case of embryos that are not yet formed, to embryos before the fortieth day?

The property of "being in potency to F" can be understood in at least two ways:

(1) If that which can be called "F" is that which is F in act, then that which is in potency to F cannot be called "F";
(2) If that which is F is that which can be F, then that which is in potency to F can be called "F."

The semen clearly falls under (1), while an embryo that is not yet formed could fall under (2). But if so, the term "potency" would be used equivocally, since the term would not have the same meaning in (1) and in (2). When the first interpretation (1) is formulated, in fact, one is assuming that "being in potency to F" is simply equivalent to "being able to be or being able to become F."[11] Given this sense, on (1) also embryos cannot be called human beings. On the other hand, it is evident that "being able to be or being able to become F" cannot be taken as a defining characteristic of F: one cannot say that there is a table when there exists something that simply can be or become a table. Analogously, one cannot say that for there to be a human being it is sufficient to have something that can be or become a human being. If it were, we could not distinguish the condition of being able to be a human being from the condition of being a human being, for in this case being able to be a human being is equivalent to being a human being—which is absurd.

The meaning of "potency" in (2), instead, is different. When this interpretation is formulated, one is assuming that "being in potency to F" is equivalent to "being in the process of becoming F." What is in potency to F is already F, although it is not yet F in a complete and perfect way. In this sense, the embryos could be called human beings, since they are inserted into a process of being perfected, which, once it is triggered, of itself will lead to their being human beings, while the semen cannot yet be called a human being in potency. So also one cannot say that there is a table when there exists something that simply can be or become a table, but you can say this when there exists something that has started to become a table. Both the piece of wood barely worked on and the table almost finished are both in potency to being a table. On interpretation (1), an embryo is a human being still in potency; on interpretation (2), an embryo is already in potency to being a human being.

---

11. Obviously, it is required that a thing *x* can become F *insofar as x,* for otherwise one could say that the earth as well is potentially a man—a conclusion that Thomas, following Aristotle, rejects. The reason for Thomas's refusal is precisely that earth *insofar as earth* is not naturally predisposed to become a man. What Thomas requires is that *x* must have of itself, *qua x,* the potentiality of becoming F (see *Exp. Met.,* IX, lec. 6).

Evidently, to opt for (1) or (2) is a question of preference. Someone could consider reasonable the idea that a table in formation is not exactly the same thing as a finished table, and so conclude that the two cases must be treated in different ways theoretically. But someone could consider it more reasonable to distinguish the case of the table in formation from that of the piece of wood that has not yet been worked upon, rather than distinguish it from the case of the finished table, since it is reasonable to think that a table in formation and a finished table are already the same table. The idea that the table in formation and the finished table manifest two phases of the perfecting of one and the same entity, and above all of one and the same form, might go well with the adversaries of Thomas who, as mentioned, took up a position very close to the present position of the Roman Catholic Church in granting human ensoulment to the embryo just conceived.[12] As we have seen, however, Thomas denies that there can be a perfecting of the form, while he seems to admit that one can speak of the perfecting of one and the same subject.

The difficulty in arguing for a preference for Thomas depends fundamentally on the fact that at times Thomas seems to present not-formed embryos as entities completely lacking species, since they are entities lacking a complete species, while at other times he seems to present them only as entities lacking a complete species. On the one hand, the fact that embryos are transitory entities, impossible to define in themselves, has us lean toward the first interpretation.[13] Thomas emphasizes this fact at times, recalling that some fundamental properties can be attributed to a subject only at the end of the process of

---

12. See Chapter 3, position B1.

13. See SCG, II, ch. 89, nn. 1756–1757; but already *Sent.,* IV, d. 11, q. 2, a. 3, q.la 3: "Ad tertiam quaestionem dicendum quod nihil recipit speciem nisi in termino generationis; agresta autem adhuc est in via generationis ad vinum, sicut sanguis quando coagulari incipit, est in via generationis ad animal; unde sicut ille sanguis non est animal, ita agresta non est vinum." See also *Sent. Ethic.,* I, ch. 9, 31, 61–71: "Ad hoc autem quod aliquid sit ultimus terminus motus naturalis, duo requiruntur. Primo quidem quod sit habens speciem, non autem in via ad speciem habendam, sicut generatio ignis non terminatur ad dispositionem formae, sed ad ipsam formam. [. . .] Secundo autem requiritur quod id quod est terminus motus naturalis sit integrum."

generation. For example, an embryo can be said to be in a relation of filiation with the generating father only at the completion of generation since, properly speaking, not-formed embryos cannot yet be called children of the father who generated them.[14] On the other hand, the fact that embryos are entities "on the way toward the species," leads us to assume at the same time that embryos already have something of the species toward which they are tending. Someone could take this fact as a good reason for extending to the embryo, however weakly, the status of being a member of the human species. As a matter of fact, in the case of an embryo that gives rise to a human being, we speak of a *human* embryo. Viewed in this way, one may assume that to say embryos have an incomplete and imperfect form is not to say that embryos, not having a perfect and complete form, have absolutely no form; it is rather to say that embryos have a form *all the same,* even if incomplete and imperfect.

Commenting toward the end of his career on the first book of *De generatione et corruptione,* Thomas seems to argue in this direction, observing that not-formed embryos necessarily have a form and that, therefore, as such they are entities in act, for otherwise one could not even admit that there is an alternation of generations and corruptions in the process of animal generation. Their form, however, is imperfect and incomplete.[15] Based on passages like that just referred to, one cannot avoid thinking that for Thomas (1) an embryo not yet formed ought to be considered as the same subject that will later become the formed embryo, that is, the human being; in addition, (2) that the form

---

14. See QDP, q. 3, a. 3, 43b.

15. See *Exp. Gen.,* I, lec. 8, n. 60: "Dicendum est ergo quod non ens simpliciter intelligitur hic materia cum privatione adiuncta alicui formae. Sed duplex est forma: una quidem perfecta, quae complet speciem alicuius rei naturalis, sicut forma ignis vel aquae aut hominis aut plantae; alia autem est forma incompleta, quae neque perficit aliquam speciem naturalem, neque est finis intentionis naturae, sed se habet in via generationis vel corruptionis. Manifestum est enim in generatione compositorum, puta animalis, quod inter principium generationis, quod est semen, et ultimam formam animalis completi, sunt multae generationes mediae, ut Avicenna dicit in sua *Sufficientia;* quas necesse est terminari ad aliquas formas, quarum nulla facit ens completum secundum speciem, sed ens incompletum, quod est via ad speciem aliquam." See also QDSC, a. 3, ad 13; *Quodl.* IX, q. 5, a. 1, *ad sed contra;* and especially *Quodl.* I, q. 4, a. 1 (this text has been quoted at length in Chapter 5, note 94).

of an embryo not yet formed is imperfect in that it manifests a preparatory phase or degree of the perfect and perfected form; but nevertheless
(3) there is not any continuity and numerical identity between such
forms because the succeeding one substitutes in a radical way for the
preceding one. From this point of view, the move from an embryo not
yet formed to a formed embryo is a move that can be described in terms
of a perfecting, occurring by the substitution of forms, of one and the
same subject.[16]

In light of what has been said, I believe one can safely say that for
Thomas an embryo can be described as something that right from its
conception is "in the process of becoming a human being." However,
in light of the detailed clarifications that Thomas introduces, I maintain that an embryo ought more properly be described as something
that is in the process of becoming a human being but is not yet a
human being, rather than be described as something that already is a
human being and is being perfected and completed. Using the terminology of Thomas, we can say that while the semen is something that
is in potency to that which is a first act, the embryo already possesses a
first act and is in potency both to a more perfect first act and to an
imperfect second act with respect to the imperfect first act that it
possesses.[17]

---

16. See, e.g., *Exp. Met.,* IX, lec. 7, n. 1848: "Si enim accipiamus hunc hominem qui est iam actu
homo, fuit prius secundum tempus materia, quae erat potentia homo. Et similiter prius tempore fuit
semen quod potentia est frumentum, quam frumentum actu, *et visivum,* idest habens potentiam
videndi, quam videns in actu. Sed tamen quaedam existentia in actu fuerunt priora secundum
tempus in his existentibus in potentia, scilicet agentia, a quibus reducta sunt in actum. Semper enim
oportet quod id quod est in potentia ens, sit actu ens ab agente, quod est actu ens. Unde homo in
potentia fit homo in actu ab homine generante, qui est in actu. Et similiter musicum in potentia
respicit musicum in actu, discendo a doctore qui est musicus actu. Et ita semper eo quod est in
potentia, est aliquid prius quod movet, et movens est in actu. Unde relinquitur, quod *licet idem
numero prius tempore sit in potentia quam in actu,* tamen aliquod ens in actu secundum idem specie,
est etiam prius tempore, quam ens in potentia" (my emphasis); also *De virt.,* q. 1, a. 11 (see the text
in Chapter 5, note 28); QDV, q. 13, a. 1, ad 10, vol. 2, 418, 274–279: "Ad decimum dicendum quod
illud quod est prius in intentione naturae quandoque est posterius tempore, sicut se habet actus ad
potentiam in eodem susceptibili quia esse in actu est per prius a natura quamvis *una et eadem res
prius tempore sit in potentia quam in actu*" (emphasis mine).

17. See *Sup. Ioan.,* ch. 1, lec. 17, and *Sup. Eph.,* lec. 3, for a discussion of the different senses of
being in potency to "the vital operations" *(opera vitae).*

2. The Elusive Human Nature of the Embryo

In summary, Thomas seems to admit that the embryo maintains its identity during the entire process, becoming perfected through a substitution of forms.[18] As we have already noted, in a passage from his early *Quaestiones de veritate* Thomas had observed that there cannot be a numerical difference between what is at first imperfect and later perfect.[19] In the *Quaestiones de potentia,* which follows these questions on truth by some years, Thomas had clarified this observation by recalling that the numerical identity between what is at first imperfect and later perfect is nevertheless not absolute, since what is imperfect is included in the genus of what is perfect "by reduction" *(per reductionem).*[20] This interpretation of generation as an intensive process of perfecting a subject is in line with the way in which Thomas applies the Aristotelian doctrine of potency to the explanation of the process of substantial generation.[21] Now, although the embryo is included in the human species only "by reduction," nevertheless we are entitled to say that the

---

18. See *Sent.,* IV, d. 12, q. 1, a. 2, q.la 4; a. 3, q.la 1, ad 3; d. 44, q. 1, a. 1, q.la 5, ad 3.

19. See, e.g., QDV, q. 14, a. 7, ad 6, vol. 2, 457–458, lin. 139–145,: "Ad sextum dicendum quod fides informis et formata non dicuntur diversa in genere quasi in diversis generibus existentia, sed sicut perfectum quod attingit ad rationem generis et imperfectum quod nondum attingit; unde non oportet quod numero differant, sicut nec embryo et animal." See also ST, I–II, q. 67 a. 6, and II–II, q. 4, a. 4, ad 1: "Tunc enim oportet quod, adveniente perfecto, imperfectum excludatur. [. . .] Sed quando imperfectio non est de ratione imperfectae, tunc illud numero idem quod erat imperfectum fit perfectum: sicut pueritia non est de ratione hominis, et ideo idem numero qui erat puer fit vir."

20. See QDP, q. 3, a. 9, ad 10, 68a: "Ad decimum dicendum, quod embrio antequam habeat animam rationalem non est ens perfectum, sed in via ad perfectionem; unde non est in genere vel specie nisi per reductionem sicut incompletum reducitur ad genus vel speciem completi."

21. See *Exp. Met.,* IX, lec. 8, n. 1856: "Dicit ergo primo, quod non solum actus est prior potentia et ratione et tempore *sed substantia,* idest perfectione. Nomine enim substantiae consuevit forma significari per quam aliquid est perfectum. Et hoc quidem primum apparet tali ratione: quia ea quae sunt posteriora in generatione, sunt *priora secundum substantiam et speciem,* idest perfectione, quia generatio semper procedit ab imperfecto ad perfectum, sicut vir est posterior generatione quam puer, nam ex puero fit vir, et homo posterius generatione quam sperma. Et hoc ideo quia vir et homo iam habent speciem perfectam, puer autem et sperma nondum. Cum igitur in eodem secundum numerum actus generatione et tempore sit posterior potentia, ut ex superioribus patet, sequitur quod actus sit prior potentia substantia et ratione."

embryo is in some way included in the human species. But the fact that it is included precisely "by reduction" leads us to say more cautiously that the embryo *as such* is not included in the human species.

To say that something belongs to a certain genus by reduction can be understood in many senses. Normally, Thomas uses this expression when he wants to indicate that something is classifiable under a certain genus only if there is a procedure that allows us to trace the thing back to that genus, even if that thing of itself is not classifiable directly under that genus. For example, God of himself is not included in any category, but can be made to be included in the category of substance by reduction, insofar as God is the cause *of* substance. Similarly, something negative can be made to be included in the genus of what is positive, since the negation can be traced back to an affirmation inasmuch as it is the negation *of* an affirmation.[22] In the same way, principles or parts of substance (as matter and form, or even the hand) or of quantity (as the point with respect to the line) can be made to be included, respectively, in the genus of substance and of quantity by reduction inasmuch as they are parts or principles *of* substance or *of* quantity.[23] In brief, something *x* belongs to a certain genus G by reduction if (1) *x* is not of itself G, but (2) *x* is in some relevant relation (as being a proper part or a principle) with something that is of itself G, such that there is a procedure that allows us to trace *x* back to G.

In the case at hand, the traceability of what is imperfect to what is perfect is strong, since not only is it presupposed that the two entities are the same entity but also that the imperfect entity is in some measure

---

22. See *Sent.,* I, d. 26, q. 2, a. 3.

23. See, e.g., DEE, ch. 5; *Sent.,* I, d. 28, q. 1, a. 1, ad 3: "Ad tertium dicendum quod in genere continetur aliquid dupliciter, vel per se et proprie, sicut species et ea quae recipiunt praedicationem generis, vel per reductionem, sicut principia generis, ut materia et forma ad substantiam et unitas et punctus ad quantitatem, quamvis neutrum sit quantitas. Ita etiam nulla negatio vel privatio est in genere per se, quia non habet aliquam quidditatem nec esse, sed reducitur ad genus affirmationis secundum quod in non esse intelligitur esse et in negatione affirmatio, ut dicit Philosophus, quia omnis privatio per habitum cognoscitur et remotio per positionem; et sic etiam non relatio est in genere relationis, quamvis ea de quibus dicitur ista negatio, non sint in illo genere"; *Sent.,* I, d. 35, q. 1, a. 3, ad 1; *Sent.,* IV, d. 1, q. 1, a. 4, q.la 2, ad 1.

existent.[24] The continuity of the subject allows Thomas to speak in a coherent way of *the conception of a human being.*[25] It also allows him to deny that an embryo-animal destined to become a human being is identical to an embryo-animal destined to become a horse, as we have said. In addition, the consideration that generation is a case of movement allows Thomas to describe the relation between an embryo and a human being in the same terms as the relation between what is in movement and the end-stage of motion, and so reinforcing the impression of the identity of subject of the embryo.[26]

In the end, then, Thomas seems to have two convictions regarding the nature of embryos that are not yet formed. In the first place, there is a substantial numerical identity or identity of subject between what is at first an embryo and later will become a human being, and in the second place, in each of its stages the embryo always has an imperfect and incomplete form of being, a fact that prevents us from considering the embryo from conception as a genuine human being. If for some reason the process of generating a human being were interrupted, one would find something that is lacking the species of human being, something that is no longer human and not yet a human being. It is only as existing within the process of generation that the embryo assumes a "human" identity, an identity that it maintains as long as a true and proper human being is not formed, but the price that the embryo pays for its being human only as existing within a process of generation is that it never has of itself, insofar as it is an embryo, a stable species. As we have seen, this is a consequence of the way in which Thomas systematically orders certain notions of Aristotelian biology in the description and account of the process of human generation.

This status of the embryo is a source of perplexity for interpreters. The embryo that is not yet formed and the formed embryo *are the same*

---

24. A thing's imperfect existence is not the same as its possibility to exist. See, e.g., QDP, q. 5, a. 5, ad 7, 144a: "Ad septimum dicendum, quod res non dicitur esse imperfecta, quacumque potentia in ipsa non reducta ad actum, sed solum quando per reductionem in actum res suum consequitur complementum. Non enim homo qui est in potentia ut sit in India, imperfectus erit, si ibi non fuerit; sed imperfectus dicitur, si scientia vel virtute careat, qua natus est perfici."

25. See, e.g., *Sent.*, III, d. 4, q. 1, a. 1, q.la 3, ad 1.

26. See, e.g., *Exp. Phys.*, III, lec. 5, n. 324.

subject, and so it does not appear correct to say, as some interpreters have upheld, that the human being that now exists has never been an embryo.[27] Nevertheless, the embryo and the human being *are not numerically the same subject,* for if the species of the subject ceases, the numerical unity that characterizes it also ceases. The difficulty of defining the nature of the embryo in itself, which is something that is continually changing, is fundamentally a result of the way in which generation is described. According to Thomas's interpretation at the start of the first book of *De generatione et corruptione,* Aristotle responds to the objection of one who attempts to show that generation is an inexplicable process, since it cannot start from what is absolutely non-being nor from what is absolutely being. According to Thomas, Aristotle reprises briefly what he had shown at length in the *Physics,* namely, that what is generated derives both from nonbeing and from being: what preexists is being in potency, but it is nonbeing in act with respect to the final form that it will acquire.[28]

This obviously is the case for prime matter with respect to the first substantial form, but it can also be applied to the case of the embryo, since the embryo, like prime matter though in a more advanced stage, is in a state of privation with respect to the successive forms and to the final form. And generation is precisely the passage from a matter that possesses a form, which is also the privation of the successive form, to a form that represents the ceasing of the privation of the preceding form.[29] In this way, an embryo takes on during its history a multiplicity

---

27. Robert Pasnau puts strong emphasis on the radical discontinuity between the embryo and the human being in *Thomas Aquinas on Human Nature: A Philosophical Study of* Summa Theologiae, *Ia 75–89* (Cambridge: Cambridge University Press, 2002), 123.

28. See *Exp. Gen.,* I, lec. 6, nn. 48–51: "Deinde cum dicit: *De his quidem* etc., solvit praedictam dubitationem. Et dicit quod de ista materia etiam in aliis libris, scilicet in I *Physic., amplius,* idest diffusius, et dubitationes positae sunt et determinationes. Et ideo nunc brevius est dicendum, quod simpliciter generatur aliquid quodam modo ex non ente, alio modo ex ente: oportet enim illud quod praeexistit generationi, esse potentia ens, actu autem non ens. Et ita verum est quod dicitur utroque modo: scilicet quod generatio simpliciter sit ex ente, et ex non ente."

29. See *Exp. Gen.,* I, lec. 7, n. 57: "Nam generatio per se quidem est ex ente in potentia, idest ex materia, quae est sicut subiectum rerum naturalium: accidit enim materiae ex qua aliquid generatur, quod sit subiecta alteri formae, secundum quam est ens actu, et privationi formae inducendae, secundum quam est non ens actu."

of forms and as such a multiplicity of privations that are the condition for passing to a successive form that eliminates the privation, perfecting the preceding form. The process stops with the realization of generation and the introduction of the final form.

As has been seen, this explanation attempts to bring into accord certain Aristotelian assumptions, as the idea in the *Categories* that substance cannot admit of degrees, or the idea that substances are fixed entities, as numbers, so that any formal variation implies a process of corruption of the substance and the generation of a new substance.[30] If one accepts the idea that generation is a process of attributing *new* being to something that must not already possess it (for otherwise there would not be a generation *simpliciter*),[31] then the embryo possesses a certain degree of being, insofar as it is endowed with a form that renders it in potency to its being a human being, but it also has an absolute form of nonbeing as regards its being a human being. It is in fact part of the essence of generation that what is generated derives, as to form, from nonbeing: in particular, that in which a process of corruption terminates is the same as that from which a process of generation begins.[32] Nevertheless, the embryo must have a certain degree of being,

---

30. See *Exp. Gen.*, I, lec. 8, n. 62: "Omnes enim formae substantiales differunt secundum magis et minus perfectum: unde in VIII *Metaphys.* dicitur quod species rerum sunt sicut numeri, quorum species variantur secundum additionem et subtractionem. Potest etiam dubitari de hoc quod dicit, quod cuius differentiae magis significant hoc aliquid, magis est substantia: cum tamen dicatur in *Praedicamentis* quod substantia non suscipit magis et minus.—Sed dicendum quod per hoc non intendit significare intensionem et remissionem substantiae in praedicamento substantiae; sed maiorem vel minorem perfectionem in speciebus substantiae, secundum dictam formarum differentiam."

31. See *Exp. Gen.*, I, lec. 9, n. 68: "Illa ergo quae non significant substantiam, sed qualitatem aut aliquid aliorum, non dicuntur generari simpliciter, sed secundum quid: quae vero significant substantiam, dicuntur generari simpliciter. Cuius ratio est, quia generatio est via de non esse ad esse: et ideo illud simpliciter generatur, quod acquirit esse cui non praesupponitur aliud esse. Non enim fit quod est: unde quod iam est, non potest generari simpliciter, sed secundum quid."

32. See *Exp. Gen.*, I, lec. 9, n. 70: "Deinde cum dicit: *Sed nunc quaerere oportet* etc., determinat tres quaestiones consequentes. Quarum prima est, quare semper generatur aliquid ex corruptis: quod supponit in hoc quod dixit, quod generatio unius est corruptio alterius. Et solvit hanc quaestionem, dicens: quia corruptio tendit in non ens, et generatio est ex non ente, ideo oportet quod generatio sit ex corruptis. [. . .] Patet ergo quod, secundum hunc modum, id quod est terminus corruptionis, est principium generationis. Sive ergo sit aliquod subiectum ex quo est generatio, sive non, semper oportet quod generatio eius sit ex non ente, quod est terminus corruptionis: hoc enim

for if generation presupposes an alternation of generations and corruptions, this in turn presupposes that the subject has some form that can be described in turn as privation of another and subsequent form. This guarantees a kind of continuity to the process of generation and of identity to its subject.[33]

3. Some Bioethical Consequences: Abortion, Homicide, and the Suppression of Life

There are certain consequences that follow from the fact that before their complete formation embryos are entities that are not rationally ensouled and are to some degree nonbeing in comparison with the being of humans. Among other consequences, theologically Thomas takes the position that embryos that are not yet ensouled by a rational soul are excluded from certain cases: from participating in the final resurrection,[34] from the benefit of having a personal guardian angel,[35] and from the possibility of sanctification.[36] In addition, such embryos are immune from original sin and all effects connected with it.[37]

---

est de ratione generationis, quod sit ex non ente; quod autem illud non ens adiungatur alteri existenti, accidit generationi. Quare patet quod simul aliquid generatur ex non ente, et corrumpitur in non ens, qualitercumque dicatur non ens. Sic igitur idem est in quod terminatur corruptio, et ex quo est generatio: et propter hoc generatio est ex corruptis. Convenienter ergo non deficit successio generationis et corruptionis, ut supra dictum est: quia generatio est quaedam corruptio non entis, et corruptio est quaedam generatio non entis; et ita unum eorum semper adiungitur alteri, cum in id ex quo unum incipit, aliud terminetur."

33. See *Exp. Gen.*, I, lec. 9, n. 69: "Et etiam dictum est quod causa continuitatis generationis, per modum materiae, est subiectum, quod transmutatur in contraria. Ex hoc enim contingit quod semper in substantiis alterius generatio est alterius corruptio, et e converso: nunquam enim materia est sub privatione unius formae, sine alia forma."

34. See, e.g., *Sent.*, IV, d. 44, q. 1, a. 2, q.la 4, ad 5: "Ad quintum dicendum quod embrya non pertinent ad resurrectionem ante animationem per animam rationalem, in quo statu iam multum advenit supra substantiam seminis de substantia nutrimenti, qua puer in utero matris nutritur"; *Sup. Iob,* ch. 3. Augustine too endorsed this position: see *Enchiridion ad Laurentium,* 85, E. Evans, ed., *Corpus Christianorum Latinorum Series Latina,* t. 46 (Turnhout, Belgium: Brepols, 1969), 95–96.

35. See, e.g., *Sent.*, II, d. 11, q. 1, a. 3, ad 3; ST, I, q. 113, a. 5, ad 3.

36. See ST, III, q. 27, a. 1, ad 4; *In Jer.*, ch. 1, lec. 3.

37. See *Sent.*, II, d. 31, q. 1, a. 1, ad 4: "Ad quartum dicendum quod illa infectio quae est in semine sicut non habet rationem culpae, proprie loquendo, ante infusionem animae, ita nec poenae: oportet enim esse idem subiectum culpae et poenae; et ideo sicut in rebus irrationalibus non proprie est poena, quae de se ordinem ad culpam habet, ita etiam nec in semine poena potest esse"; ST, III,

Juridically, Thomas follows a rather widespread position in his day (based on a passage from *Exodus*)[38] and holds that an act that causes an abortion of an unformed embryo, performed directly or indirectly, knowingly or not, cannot in any way be equated with homicide, even if this does not change the fact that it is a morally reprehensible act, against nature, and, theologically, a mortal sin:[39]

> This sin [i.e., an act that can cause an abortion] however much it is grave and is to be included among the maleficious acts and is against nature, since even the beasts look forward to bringing forth their offspring, still is less than a homicide, since conceiving could still have been impeded in another way. Nor should such an act be judged irregular unless it causes the abortion of an unborn child that is already formed.[40]

This passage, from his early Commentary on the *Sentences*, does not leave much room for doubt about Thomas's position concerning the equivalence between abortion and homicide.

---

q. 27, a. 2. This qualification is useful for understanding Thomas's position on the Immaculate Conception. One argument that Thomas uses for denying the Immaculate Conception is that original sin is transmitted through the father's formative power; but both the full acquisition of the taint of original sin and its sanctification and purification, which can be obtained only by means of divine grace, requires the presence of the rational soul, which for women occurs at about the third month of pregnancy. On this argument, see *Sent.*, III, d. 3, q. 1, a. 1, q.la 1, and ST, III, q. 27, a. 2. For an introduction to medieval theories of generation, with particular attention to cases of extraordinary generation, see Maaike van der Lugt, *Le ver, le démon et la vierge: Les théories médiévales de la généra-tion extraordinaire* (Paris: Les Belles Lettres, 2004).

38. See *Exodus*, 21, 22–25.

39. For a characterization of what constitutes mortal sin, see ST, I–II, q. 72, a. 5.

40. See *Sent.*, IV, d. 31, q. 2, a. 3, *expositio textus:* "Hoc peccatum quamvis sit grave, et inter maleficia computandum, et contra naturam, quia etiam bestiae fetus expectant; tamen est minus quam homicidium; quia adhuc poterat alio modo impediri conceptus. Nec est iudicandus talis irregularis, nisi iam formato puerperio abortum procuret. *Semina paulatim formantur* et cetera. De hoc habitum est in III, distinctione III. *Et postquam venter uxoris intumuerit, non perdant filios.* Quamvis enim matrix post impraegnationem claudatur; tamen ex delectatione, ut Avicenna dicit, movetur et aperitur; et ex hoc imminet periculum abortus; et ideo Hieronymus vituperat accessum viri ad uxorem impraegnatam; non tamen ita quod semper sit peccatum mortale; nisi forte quando probabiliter timetur de periculo abortus." See also ST, II–II, q. 64, a. 8, ad 2: "Ad secundum dicendum quod ille qui percutit mulierem praegnantem dat operam rei illicitae. Et ideo si sequatur mors vel mulieris vel *puerperii animati,* non effugiet homicidii crimen, praecipue cum ex tali

Two things can be noted about this passage, however. In the first place, we can note that Thomas makes the characteristic of abortion's being an act against nature depend on the fact that in nature no animal species has recourse to abortion. There are two ways one could contest this argument. One could show that there are exceptions also in the animal world, for example, by proving that some animal species practice abortion just as there are animal species that practice infanticide. Or one could argue that the condition of an activity simply being found in nature is too weak, for just as generation is to be found in nature, which depends always on an act of will, so also the interruption of pregnancy is to be found in nature, which equally depends on an act of will. To prevent such criticisms, the naturalness of generation seems more convincing bioethically if one explicates it in terms of the automatic nature and necessity of the generative process once it is set in motion.

This passage of Thomas also claims that an act that can cause abortion is not equivalent to an act of homicide, and even here Thomas's position is nuanced. First, such mentioning of abortion and homicide together appears only in this passage of his Commentary on the *Sentences,* and it appears rather indirectly in the context of the explanation of the text of Peter Lombard, the author of the *Sentences.* On the other hand, in a text from the final phase of his career *(Super Primam Epistolam ad Timotheum Lectura),* Thomas associates, if only in passing, abortion and killing, understood as the suppression of a human life.[41] But we should not make too much of the difference between these two passages. Thomas is relying on juridical norms well-defined in his day, according to which an act that can cause abortion, if ending the life of an embryo not yet rationally ensouled, cannot be classified as a

---

percussione in promptu sit quod mors sequatur" (my emphasis). This position, rather common in Aquinas's days, as was said, was endorsed by Albert the Great as well; see his *Commentarius in quattuor libros Sententiarum,* IV, d. 31, a. 18, A. Borgnet, ed., in Alberti Magni *Opera Omnia,* t. 12 (Paris: Vivès, 1894), 250–251.

41. See *Sup. Tim.,* ch. 5, lec. 2, nn. 207–208: "Et ideo subdit: *Melius est nubere quam uri.* Et ideo in quo casu loquitur, videndum est, quia in hoc, ne primam fidem faciant irritam, et ideo quod hic dicit *volo,* intelligitur non ex principali intentione. *Filios procreare,* et non eos occulte occidere per abortum."

homicide. This is not incompatible with considering an act of abortion as an act of killing, understood generically as the suppression of a life (which is, in the case of a human embryo, potentially human). On this, one should note that the above-cited passage of Thomas's Commentary on the *First Letter to Timothy* of St. Paul does not explicitly distinguish between rationally ensouled and nonensouled embryos, and so there is nothing preventing it being understood as referring to offspring already formed in the mother's womb.

However that may be, the absolute equivalence between killing, or the suppression of a life, and homicide is to be rejected. Thomas himself distinguishes them. To kill an innocent child, if it is commanded by God, is not a homicide, and so Abraham who was getting ready to kill Isaac would not have been liable to be condemned if he had killed his son.[42] Similarly, one can kill another in legitimate self-defense or involuntarily.[43] One can also kill a tyrant who is undermining the republic, again, without being charged with the crime of homicide.[44] Also, while unmotivated killing of animals is of no use and is morally reprehensible, if animals are killed for some just purpose the action is morally licit.[45] Certainly there remains some doubt whether the suppression of embryonic life in order to avoid an unwanted pregnancy can be excluded from the fifth commandment, "Thou shalt not kill." But for Thomas this seems to be the case, since that commandment seems to apply only to completely formed human beings.

The characterizations of homicide that Thomas gives in his works are not fixed, nor are all such characterizations relevant to the case we are examining. A rather extended treatment is found in the *Summa theologiae,* II-II, q. 64, where he dedicates eight articles to homicide. Earlier in the *Summa theologiae,* I-II, q. 88, a. 6, ad 3, homicide is characterized

---

42. See ST, I–II, q. 100, a. 8, ad 3.

43. See *Sent.,* IV, d. 25, q. 2, a. 2, q.la 2, ad 3.

44. See, e.g., ST, I–II, q. 100, a. 8, ad 3. For a clear formulation of the difference between homicide and the killing of a human being, see *Quodl.,* VIII, q. 6, a. 4, ad 1. Homicide designates a "disordered killing" *(indebita occisio)* of a human being, and for this reason a homicide is never licit, while killing someone sometimes may be.

45. See, e.g., *Sent.,* IV, d. 1, q. 1, a. 5, q.la 2, ad 2.

with an ethical connotation as "the killing of an innocent" *(occisio innocentis)*.[46] Such killing in the early Commentary on the *Sentences* was characterized as an act "contrary to the law of nature" *(contra legem naturae)*.[47] This characterization could be applied also to the embryo that is not rationally ensouled, although someone could object that such an embryo, insofar as it is lacking a rational soul, cannot properly be said to be innocent or guilty. Again in the *Summa theologiae*, in I-II, q. 100, a. 6, more significantly Thomas defines homicide as "the suppression of the life of a human being already existing" *(homicidium, per quod tollitur vita hominis iam existentis)*, and it is contrasted with the gravity of the sin of adultery, which when committed only prevents the "certain identification" *(certitudo)* of the unborn child.[48] Based on this characterization, an embryo not yet rationally ensouled could not be included among the entities whose suppression is considered an act of homicide. This last clause, i.e., "a human being already existing," becomes narrower in the *Summa theologiae*, II-II, q. 154, a. 3, where homicide is said to be "a sin against the life of a human being already born" *(peccatum quod est contra vitam hominis iam nati, sicut est homicidium)*, and this to such an extent that in his reply to the third argument Thomas observes that homicide is graver than fornication, since the first is directed against the essence of a species that exists in act, while the second is against something that is only a human being in potency.[49] In this case, not even the killing of a rationally ensouled embryo could be considered unconditionally a homicide.

I do not believe that these characterizations should be too easily generalized since each has been shaped by specific contexts. But it is

---

46. See ST, I–II, q. 88, a. 6, ad 3.

47. See *Sent.*, I, d. 47, q. 1, a. 4, ad 2.

48. See ST, I–II, q. 100, a. 6.

49. See ST, II–II, q. 154, a. 3 and ad 3. See also ST, II–II, q. 64, a. 8, ad 2; ST, II–II, q. 73, a. 3; ST, III, q. 68, a. 11; QDM, q. 2, a. 10, 57, 55–63: "Inter peccata autem que sunt in proximum tanto aliqua sunt aliis grauiora quanto maiori bono proximi opponuntur. Maximum autem bonum proximi est ipsa persona hominis, cui opponitur peccatum homicidii, quod tollit actualem hominis uitam, et peccatum luxurie, quod opponitur uite hominis in potentia, quia est inordinatio quedam circa actum generationis humane"; SCG, III, ch. 122, n. 2955.

nevertheless clear that Thomas does not consider an act that can cause an abortion before the infusion of the rational soul as a homicide, for also nature produces fetuses that often abort naturally, and it is unthinkable that nature would generate entities endowed with a rational soul in order to then suppress them.[50] This does not alter the fact, as mentioned earlier, that Thomas considers abortion ethically a mortal sin since it impinges on a natural process that would lead of itself to a human life and theologically an "act of wickedness" *(maleficium)* since it is among the class of acts that are explicitly directed toward evil and in the accomplishment of which one cannot exclude the hidden intervention of the Devil.[51]

In the question of the *Summa theologiae* dedicated to homicide, Thomas makes a few clarifications on these points. In the first article, while debating the question "whether killing any type of living being is illicit," Thomas recalls that to use a thing for the end for which the thing exists is not a sin.[52] In nature, imperfect things are for the sake of perfect things. Thomas emphasizes that this order holds both in the

---

50. For a definition of "abortive fetus," see *Sup. Cor.,* ch. 15, lec. 1, n. 904. On the distinction between rationally ensouled and not-ensouled fetuses, see *Sup. Iob,* ch. 3, 24, 387–402. As was said, Thomas uses this argument to deny that the rational soul is already present in the male semen, for otherwise, in the case of involuntary emission of semen, there would be a useless proliferation of rational souls. In general, Thomas's argument is not particularly conclusive, for it is obvious that also fetuses after the fortieth day, although a small percentage, can be naturally aborted.

51. On the theological significance of the word "act of wickedness" *(maleficium),* see *Sent.,* IV, d. 34, q. 1, a. 3, and *Quodl.,* XI, q. 9, a. 1. Note that in the *Summa contra Gentiles,* III, ch. 106, Thomas counts among the malefic acts also theft and homicide. From this point of view, there seems to be no significant difference between abortion and homicide. In general, Thomas seems to consider respect for nature, understood as a manifestation of the Divine Being, as a sufficient condition for removing from the class of morally licit acts a number of acts, such as abortion, adultery, and the emission of semen not directed to procreation. In this last case, Thomas considers each relevant potentiality for becoming a human being—both remote and proximate—a sufficient condition for attributing to the male semen and the human embryo a certain "divine," sacred character. See QDM, q. 15, a. 2, 274, 198–209: "Uidemus enim quod peccatum mortale est non solum homicidium, per quod uita hominis tollitur, set etiam furtum, per quod subtrahuntur exteriora bona que ad uitam hominis sustentandam ordinantur; unde dicitur Eccli. XXXIV 'Panis egentium uita pauperis, qui defraudat illum homo sanguinis est.' Propinquius autem ordinatur ad uitam hominis semen humanum in quo est homo in potentia quam quecumque res exteriores; unde et Philosophus in sua Politica dicit in semine hominis esse quiddam diuinum, in quantum scilicet est homo in potentia."

52. See ST, II–II, q. 64, a. 1 *(Utrum occidere quaecumque viventia sit illicitum):* "Respondeo dicendum quod nullus peccat ex hoc quod utitur re aliqua ad hoc ad quod est."

case of human generation, with the passage from an imperfect thing to a perfect thing, and more generally in the case of nature, where organisms that are only vegetative, as plants, are for the sake of animal organisms, and these latter are for the sake of human beings. The purpose of this arrangement comes from *the utility* that things have for preserving their own species and, as a final purpose, for preserving the human species: animals make use of plants as food for nourishment, and human beings in their turn make use of plants to feed animals and they make use of animals for their own nourishment.[53]

Dwelling on this point for a moment, someone could incidentally point out that this text leaves room for attributing to plants or animals some right of their own, although it confines itself to expressing a natural hierarchic subordination that is valid only with respect to a given end. Passages from other works of Thomas, where it is denied that someone could do away with a plant or an animal simply from the desire to do away with it, could confirm this impression. Nevertheless, if one continues the reading of the text of the *Summa* passage we are examining, one can ascertain that the vague criterion of life is not enough to extend any fundamental ethical rights to animals and plants. In his response to the third argument against his position—which mentions that killing another's animal is sanctioned by the divine law, based on *Exodus* 22,1—Thomas argues that if someone kills another's ox, the person does not commit a sin because he kills an ox, but simply

---

53. See ST, II–II, q. 64, a. 1: "In rerum autem ordine imperfectiora sunt propter perfectiora: sicut etiam in generationis via natura ab imperfectis ad perfecta procedit. Et inde est quod sicut in generatione hominis prius est vivum, deinde animal, ultimo autem homo; ita etiam ea quae tantum vivunt, ut plantae, sunt communiter propter omnia animalia, et animalia sunt propter hominem. Et ideo si homo utatur plantis ad utilitatem animalium, et animalibus ad utilitatem hominum, non est illicitum, ut etiam per Philosophum patet, in I *Polit.* Inter alios autem usus maxime necessarius esse videtur ut animalia plantis utantur in cibum, et homines animalibus: quod sine mortificatione eorum fieri non potest. Et ideo licitum est et plantas mortificare in usum animalium, et animalia in usum hominum, ex ipsa ordinatione divina." See also ST, I, q. 96, a. 1: "Omnia auem animalia sunt homini naturaliter subiecta. Quod apparet ex tribus. Primo quidem, ex ipso naturae processu. Sicut enim in generatione rerum intelligitur quidam ordo quo proceditur de imperfecto ad perfectum (nam materia est propter formam, et forma imperfectior propter perfectiorem), ita etiam est in usu rerum naturalium, nam imperfectiora cedunt in usum perfectorum; plantae enim utuntur terra ad sui nutrimentum, animalia vero plantis, et homines plantis et animalibus. Unde naturaliter homo dominatur animalibus."

because he damages another person, so much so that such a killing cannot be classified in this instance as homicide, but rather as theft or robbery.[54] The reason is that plants and animals, insofar as they are lacking in rationality, are moved only by a natural impulse, and so they are to be considered in all respects as natural slaves and "available for the use of others" *(aliorum usibus accomodata)*.[55] The criterion of being alive is not of itself a sufficient condition for prohibiting acts directed at making vegetative or animal life available for the use of others.

How are we to understand this "availability" of lower forms of life? How is this availability applicable to embryos? In other words, in the case of human generation what does it mean that imperfect entities are for the sake of perfect entities? In the case of the relation between human beings and animals, Thomas observes that "among the other uses" the most necessary comes from the search after food for survival. What are the other uses? It is plausible to think that, in the case of vegetative organisms, plants can also be used to provide wood for build-ings or for still other purposes, and this usage is also a function of the supreme good of human survival. Animals, instead, can be employed for work in the fields, and also in this case the explanation is similar. If the parallel between imperfect entities of human generation and plants-animals is taken literally, this text allows us to say that embryos are for the sake of the perfect entities that come after: human beings. What is involved in holding that embryos are for the sake of human beings?

Unfortunately, Thomas does not give examples to clarify this par-allel, but even if he had, they would certainly have been disappointing to anyone looking at this problem from the standpoint of contempo-rary bioethical debates. When we speak today of the availability of life, we are referring to the permissibility of using particular forms of life for

---

54. See ST, II–II, q. 64, a. 1, ad 3: "Ad tertium dicendum quod ille qui occidit bovem alterius peccat quidem, non quia occidit bovem, sed quia damnificat hominem in re sua. Unde non continetur sub peccato homicidii, sed sub peccato furti vel rapinae."

55. See ST, II–II, q. 64, a. 1, ad 1 and ad 2: "Ad primum ergo dicendum quod ex ordinatione divina conservatur vita animalium et plantarum non propter seipsam, sed propter hominem. [. . .] Ad secundum dicendum quod animalia bruta et plante non habent vitam rationalem, per quam a se ipsis agantur, sed semper aguntur quasi ab alio, naturali quodam impulsu. Et hoc est signum quod sunt naturaliter serva, et aliorum usibus accomodata."

ends (mostly medical) that are not strictly connected to the nature of such forms. In the case of embryos, for example, one uses the term "available" to refer to the possibility of some intervention, that is, to modifying or multiplying embryos, to creating them artificially or suppressing them, for ends that do not concern the being or well-being of the embryos themselves, but for extrinsic ends such as fertilization, medical cures or the prevention of genetic diseases. Obviously, Thomas could not have had in mind such cases, at his time technically unachievable. Probably Thomas meant that embryos have not been created to be or to remain embryos, but to generate human beings, and this is a sign of their natural subordination. In the case of human generation, it is not the human being, but a still nobler agent, as nature, that uses one being for the sake of another. The instrumental character of embryos should be understood, in my opinion, precisely in the light of this consideration, that a human being conceives to have other human beings. Embryos are not the end of a generative process, and so Thomas would never think of discussing a procedure intentionally directed to generating embryos. This strict sense of availability could not be a question for him.

Still, one could hold that there is a wider sense of availability at play here. Since for Thomas it seems that embryos can be used for no other purpose than generation and, in an obvious sense, are not among the entities that serve nutritional ends, someone could maintain that the only availability that embryos can have is negative, that is, that of being able to be suppressed. In other words, although Thomas could not have envisaged alternative procedures, natural or artificial, that lead to bringing embryos into existence, he could envisage and admit procedures (even if firmly regulated) that, given the existence of an embryo, lead to its suppression. It is undeniable that the text of the *Summa,* given how Thomas expresses himself, can be read in this way. As plants and animals, so embryos are lacking a rational life and in addition are not endowed with a vegetative or animal life so that they might exercise it as such, but rather so that they can become human beings. Suppressing them, therefore, can be included among those things "for the utility of human beings" *(ad utilitatem hominum)* which Thomas mentions. But it must be clear that this "bland availability" has to be evaluated with respect to a teleology that, as a rule that provides for exceptions, characterizes the being of each created thing. To be specific, for an embryo the only tenable end is that of generating a human being. If so, although he could not imagine medical practices that produce and manipulate embryos, still Thomas could in principle not be against (i) medical interventions on embryos already in existence for the purpose of improving them or curing them in order to generate humans substantially more improved or more healthy, and (ii) procedures regarding maternity that could improve it or even make it possible for someone.

In conclusion, based on what we presented in the introduction as a bioethical theory that insists on *properties,* that is, a theory that takes as central to the debate on the beginning of life the ascertaining of certain properties relevant for defining a human being and human life, it is undeniable that for Thomas embryos that are not yet rationally ensouled cannot be treated as complete and perfect human beings. They must of course be protected insofar as they are the potential presupposed for the existence of human beings, but as such they come under a differentiated protection. It is not by chance that in an ethical conflict between the good of the mother and that of the unborn child, Thomas has no doubts that the first is to be favored over the second. Similarly, Thomas thinks that pregnancy should be interrupted if either the mother or the unborn child are in peril of death, allowing the child to be baptized and so saved from eternal death.[56] But on the other hand, based on what we have characterized as a bioethical theory that insists on *the subject,* namely a theory that takes as central to the debate on the beginning of life the ascertaining of certain properties relevant for defining the identity and continuity of a given subject, one could hold that the embryo be seen as the same entity that will later be the human being that derives from it. Still, someone could insist on precision here: for

---

56. See *Sent.,* IV, d. 6, q. 1, a. 1, q.la 1 *(Utrum nativitas ex utero in baptizando sit expectanda),* arg. 4 and ad 4: "Praeterea, mors aeterna peior est quam mors corporalis in infinitum. Sed de duobus malis eligendum est minus malum. Ergo debet mater scindi et extrahi puer, ut baptizatus a morte aeterna liberetur et non expectari nativitas ex utero. [. . .] Ad quartum dicendum quod non sunt facienda mala ut veniant bona, sicut dicitur *Rom.* 3, et ideo homo potius debet dimittere perire infantem quam ipse pereat, homicidii crimen in matre committens."

Thomas, an embryo and a human being are not in any case *exactly* the same entity. This can be admitted: an embryo and a human being are not exactly the same entity, for they are not numerically the same entity. But that does not change the fact that for Thomas there is continuity between that embryo and that human being, and this continuity could be taken as a sufficient metaphysical basis for developing a bioethical theory that is not ready to accept in a generalized way, or at least in an unregulated way, human intervention on embryos that relies on the distinction between a prehuman phase and a properly human phase of the embryos. The continuity between the male semen and the human embryo, and between this latter and the human being, is a sufficient condition, for Thomas, for attributing to whatever is in some relevant potency to a human being a certain "divine," sacred character.[57]

---

57. See above, note 51, the text from the *Quaestiones de malo*.

CHAPTER SEVEN

The Beginning and End of Human Life

IN CONTEMPORARY TERMS, Thomas's position concerning ensoulment of the embryo can be classified among those that maintain *delayed hominization*. As we have seen, the basic idea of Thomas is that until the fortieth day the embryo is not rationally ensouled, but possesses a form of animal ensoulment quite inchoate and imperfect. Until the fortieth day the embryo is only the biological material of a human being, and until that time the embryo cannot be considered a subject of theologically and ethically relevant acts. Perhaps the most interesting philosophical aspect of the thesis of the embryo's delayed hominization is the idea that the property "being human" indicates a capacity for exercising the rational faculty (summarized by the property of "being rational" in the definition of man), which can be actually exercised only with organs sufficiently developed. From Thomas's viewpoint, the embryo's possession of rational ensoulment immediately implies the actual capacity to be able to exercise rational operations. The degree of refinement of the exercise of this capacity depends, obviously, on successive developments of the embryo and on the development of the human being after birth.

An interpreter could contest the implicit suggestion of Thomas that the embryo can exercise rational acts as soon as it has formed fundamental vital organs and, on this basis, reverse the usual way of proceeding. Instead of postdating the actual moment of rational ensoulment and establishing it at the fortieth day, one could antedate this moment at the outset, i.e., at the moment of conception. One could support this move by invoking other medical and biological data. For example, many medical professionals today say that even a newborn baby does not have a cerebral cortex that is fully developed and that is able to support higher intellectual activities. If it is not possible for the newborn babies to perform rational acts, with yet stronger reason, this is not possible for the embryos.

These scientific data, however, could not modify to any great extent a philosophical account of embryonic ensoulment as Thomas's, although the implications that can follow from requiring that the organs supporting higher rational activities be only minimally developed or that they be maximally developed differ greatly.[1] Thomas himself, for example, recognizes that a newborn baby is not able completely and fully to exercise intellectual activities due to the consistency of the cerebral mass being still too "moist." But his point is not whether or not the embryo just rationally ensouled actually exercises rational acts (or whether or not the embryo exercises them perfectly), but rather if and when the embryo *could* exercise such acts. In other words, the sufficient condition required for being able to speak of the embryo's rational ensoulment is not given (1) by the possibility of possessing the capacity to reason, nor (2) by the possession of the capacity to actually reason, but (3) by the actual possession of the capacity to reason. Having just been rationally ensouled and so having just become a human being, the embryo possesses this capacity, even if the ambient conditions or other obstacles can impede its full and complete exercise.[2]

---

1. For a more extensive discussion of this point, see Robert Pasnau, *Thomas Aquinas on Human Nature: A Philosophical Study of* Summa Theologiae, *Ia 75–89* (Cambridge: Cambridge University Press, 2002), 118–120. Some doubts remain whether the strategy reconstructed by Pasnau is actually that of Thomas. Rather than reasons of "caution," my impression is that it is the endorsement of a philosophical method and an Aristotelian perspective that leads Thomas to individuate the fortieth day as the moment of the embryo's rational ensoulment.

2. See SCG, II, ch. 59, n. 1369: "Si homo speciem sortitur per hoc quod est rationalis et intellectum habens, quicumque est in specie humana, est rationalis et intellectum habens. Sed puer,

Evidently much more should be said to articulate better this idea of Thomas, which appears as lucid in the abstract as it is difficult to clarify in the concrete. What kind of rational acts, for example, can or does a rationally ensouled embryo carry out? How can we be certain that a rationally ensouled embryo really does or, more precisely, really *could* carry out such acts? A philosophical account of the process of generation cannot give a scientific explanation of these aspects, nor does it intend to do so. A philosophical account as Thomas's rather aims at providing a theoretical framework that is abstractly explanatory of a certain class of phenomena. This framework provides only the general theoretical structure within which individual scientific data can be located. But a philosophical explanation does not give an account of these data. To distinguish between *possession* and *use* of the capacity to reason, then, is useful in philosophically explaining the phases of the embryo's ensoulment, even if this distinction turns out to be difficult to define biologically. How can we be sure that someone has the capacity to reason if not by the exercise of it? The use of a capacity implies its possession, but how can we determine its possession apart from its use?

At times Thomas seems to connect, somewhat imprecisely, the property of "being a human being" to the *use* of the capacity to reason, rather than to its possession.[3] If the starting point of the embryo's human ensoulment coincided with its *first utilization* of the capacity to reason, then any compromising of its use would imply that in fact, if not in principle, the subject of such an impaired capacity could no longer be considered a human being.[4] If we followed this line of thought, the bases for a fixed and univocal definition of rationality would turn out to be rather narrow. For on the one hand, there are exceptional situations that can impede, whether temporarily or permanently, the exercise of rationality.

---

etiam antequam ex utero egrediatur, est in specie humana: in quo tamen nondum sunt phantasmata, quae sint intelligibilia actu. Non igitur est homo intellectum habens per hoc quod intellectus continuatur homini mediante specie intelligibili cuius subiectum est phantasma."

3. For further discussion of this point, see Chapter 8, note 6.

4. See *Sent.,* II, d. 25, q. 1, a. 2, ad 7: "Ad septimum dicendum quod usus liberi arbitrii non impeditur per se, sed per accidens, in quantum scilicet ad usum liberi arbitrii requiritur usus rationis et ad usum rationis requiritur usus imaginativae virtutis, qui per laesionem organi impeditur"; ST, I–II, q. 33, a. 3, ad 3; ST, II–II, q. 154, a. 5, ad 2; QDM, q. 3, aa. 3–4.

Among these Thomas often cites drunkenness, some types of passion, as anger, certain illness, as dementia, and sleep. In these cases, the possibility of once again exercising rationality is not precluded. On the other hand, in the case of an organic lesion, cerebral for example, that permanently impedes the use of reason, the subject of such a lost capacity could not be considered (or could no longer be considered) a human being.[5] To insist on the condition of having formed organs for there to be a human being could have this drawback: if the organs do not form or if they are formed impaired, the embryo could not be considered a human being. This conclusion, however, seems to conflict with experience and common opinion, leaving aside the fact that even from the point of view of Thomas a human being does not cease to be such with the loss of any material organic part, however primary, but only with the onset of biological death. This is based on the conviction that every organ is in principle, if not in fact, able to be repaired, and so the vital function associated with or dependent upon the organ can always be restored.

Of itself, even a serious lesion of a bodily organ, including presumably the brain, does no damage to the essence of the soul. If that organ could be repaired or could be substituted by transplant, the soul would resume exercising its functions properly.[6] No organic lesion that can

---

5. See *Sent.,* II, d. 22, q. 2, a. 2; SCG, III, ch. 48 and ch. 129; QDSC, a. 2, ad 7. On the importance of the brain for sensory activities, see *Sent. De an.,* II, ch. 19, and *Sent. De sensu,* I, lec. 5.

6. See, e.g., SCG, II, ch. 79, n. 1607 (see Aristotle, *De anima,* I, 4, on the connection between replacement of a defective bodily organ and the full restoration of its function); ST, I–II, q. 72, a. 5; q. 87, a. 3: "Pervertit autem aliquis ordinem quandoque quidem reparabiliter, quandoque autem irreparabiliter. Semper enim defectus quo subtrahitur principium, irreparabilis est: si autem salvetur principium, eius virtute defectus reparari possunt. Sicut si corrumpatur principium visivum, non potest fieri visionis reparatio, nisi sola virtute divina: si vero, salvo principio visivo, aliqua impedimenta adveniant visioni, reparari possunt per naturam vel per artem." The disappearance of the use of reason is not an essential defect for the human being. See ST, I–II, q. 67, a. 3: "Et quia perfectum et imperfectum opponuntur, impossibile est quod simul, secundum idem, sit perfectio et imperfectio. Est autem considerandum quod imperfectio quidem quandoque est de ratione rei, et pertinet ad speciem ipsius, sicut defectus rationis pertinet ad rationem speciei equi vel bovis. Et quia unum et idem numero manens non potest transferri de una specie in aliam, inde est quod, tali imperfectione sublata, tollitur species rei, sicut iam non esset bos vel equus, si esset rationalis. Quandoque vero imperfectio non pertinet ad rationem speciei, sed accidit individuo secundum aliquid aliud, sicut alicui homini quandoque accidit defectus rationis, inquantum impeditur in eo rationis usus, propter somnum vel ebrietatem vel aliquid huiusmodi. Patet autem quod, tali imperfectione remota, nihilominus substantia rei manet."

have an effect, even serious, on the *use* of reason is able to deprive a human being of rational ensoulment. For Thomas himself, it is not plausible to associate the property of "being a human being" only with the use of reason, and this apart from the question of what ought to be understood concretely by the term "reason."[7] It is, then, probable that Thomas, in linking the property of "being a human being" with the *use* of the capacity for reasoning, had meant to express chiefly the idea that the degree of exercise of the capacity for reasoning gives us the degree of completeness of being a human being.

For Thomas, the property of "being a human being" does not depend on the use, but on the *possession* of a capacity that can be realized in more or less perfect form, or even never be realized.[8] If so, embryos endowed with defective or nonfunctioning bodily organs ought to be considered the same as human beings, for they possess the same capacity to be able to exercise rational acts. At first, such a capacity is not exercised or is not able to be exercised, but this does not prevent there arising conditions that make possible a repair or substitution of the organs that are necessary for the exercise of rational activity, so allowing that capacity to be actually exercised or to be able to be exercised. That is sufficient for attributing the property of "being a human being" to

---

7. This is not the place to discuss this notion in detail. Nevertheless, we can say that the difference "rational" in the definition of man as "rational animal" designates a complex cognitive activity, characteristic of the human species, which is explicated by means of three fundamental operations: the formation of simple concepts, the combination of simple concepts in propositions, and the combination of propositions in syllogisms and arguments. More generically, rational activity designates an inferential and discursive capacity, linguistically structured and logically regulated. See, e.g., SCG, I, ch. 57, n. 479: "Ratiocinatio autem est quidam motus intellectus transeuntis ab uno in aliud," and ST, I, q. 79, a. 8: "Homines autem ad intelligibilem veritatem cognoscendam perveniunt, procedendo de uno ad aliud, ut ibidem dicitur, et ideo rationales dicuntur. Patet ergo quod ratiocinari comparatur ad intelligere sicut moveri ad quiescere, vel acquirere ad habere, quorum unum est perfecti, aliud autem imperfecti. Et quia motus semper ab immobili procedit, et ad aliquid quietum terminatur; inde est quod ratiocinatio humana, secundum viam inquisitionis vel inventionis, procedit a quibusdam simpliciter intellectis, quae sunt prima principia; et rursus, in via iudicii, resolvendo redit ad prima principia, ad quae inventa examinat." See also ST, I, q. 83, a. 4; ST, I, q. 85, a. 5; ST, III, q. 43, a. 4, ad 3; QDP, q. 9, a. 2, ad 10; QDSC, q. 2, ad 12; *Exp. Met.*, VIII, lec. 2, n. 1697.

8. See ST, I, q. 101, a. 2. Discussing the question whether the insane can be baptized, Thomas distinguishes three senses of the improper use of reason (III, q. 68, a. 12).

such embryos, even if they are in a defective state with regard to the completeness of that property.

Embryos devoid of organs (for example, a fetus lacking a brain) present an apparently different case. Given the characterization that Thomas provides of the human soul, these embryos ought not to be considered human beings. Thomas says little about such cases, limiting himself to classifying them, with Aristotle, as exceptions or irregularities in the process of generation. This would seem to confirm the exclusion of these entities from the class of human beings. But we could hypothesize that the condition given earlier for according the property of "being a human being" to embryos endowed with imperfect organs could also serve here in the case of embryos devoid of organs. The two cases could be treated philosophically in a similar way. Normally, at a certain moment of the process of embryonic development, the organs are formed. At that point, every embryo receives a rational soul. As was said, this moment can be approximately fixed at the fortieth day for males and the ninetieth for females. The point would be that this moment prescinds from whether the organs are actually formed or, if they are formed, whether they are actually functional. Such embryos are in all respects humans. If the organs could later be supplied and integrated in the one case, or be repaired or perfected in the other, such embryos would also become fully human beings.

Also here, the line of reasoning as developed is purely conjectural, since Thomas dedicates little space to the discussion of these limit cases. Still, this proposal could be considered, all in all, a plausible reconstruction of the position of Thomas. Someone could point out, however, once again, that this line of reasoning, apparently straightforward, actually conceals a possible complication. If the fact of *actually* having organs is not a necessary condition for having a rational soul, why could this not hold also at the moment of conception? In other words, why could not conception be seen as a condition sufficient for the embryo to have a rational soul? Thomas does not consider this possible objection, but in light of his embryological account an answer could be proposed: at the moment of conception there are not the conditions for the embryo to *be able* to actually have the organs that support the activities of the rational soul, while around the fortieth day for males, ninetieth for females, there are all the conditions for the embryo to *be able* to actually have such organs, independently, that is, of whether such organs are actually present or not.

This proposal to resolve certain limit cases within Thomas's account and the differentiation of the moment of conception from that of the formation of the organs rests upon a distinction that Thomas makes between the essence of the soul and its powers. According to his mature philosophy of human nature, the capacity to reason, which essentially characterizes a human being, insofar as it is a capacity is a faculty or power of the soul. Every power of the soul, although necessarily dependent on the soul, is still external to the essence of the soul.[9] In terms of the ontology of substance and accidents, the powers of the soul should technically be called accidents of the soul, since they are external to the essence of the soul: the soul is in fact act, while the powers are precisely potentiality, and no potentiality can be part of the essence of what is essentially act. In terms of the categories of Aristotle, the powers belong to the second species of quality; that is, they are acquired habits. But in terms of the five predicables of Porphyry, the powers of the soul are proper and natural properties of the soul, necessarily following from the essence of the soul for they are caused by it. Although they are not part of the essence of the soul, they are still necessary properties, which the soul cannot cease to have (at least in this actual world).[10] Conceptually, although it is possible to define what a soul is without making

---

9. On the powers as quasi-accidents of the soul, see *Sent.*, IV, d. 44, q. 1, a. 1, q.la 2, ad 3; ST, I, q. 77, aa. 1, 5, 6, and 7, ad 1. The relation between the soul and its powers is extensively examined in QDA, qq. 12–13.

10. See ST, I, q. 77, a. 1, ad 5: "Ad quintum dicendum quod, si accidens accipiatur secundum quod dividitur contra substantiam, sic nihil potest esse medium inter substantiam et accidens. [. . .] Et hoc modo, cum potentia animae non sit eius essentia, oportet quod sit accidens: et est in secunda specie Qualitatis.—Si vero accipiatur accidens secundum quod ponitur unum quinque Universalium, sic aliquid est medium inter substantiam et accidens. Quia ad substantiam pertinet quidquid est essentiale rei: non autem quidquid est extra essentiam, potest sic dici accidens, sed solum id quod non causatur ex principiis essentialibus speciei. *Proprium* enim non est de essentia rei, sed ex principiis essentialibus speciei causatur: unde medium est inter essentiam et accidens sic dictum. Et hoc modo potentiae animae possunt dici mediae inter substantiam et accidens, quasi proprietates animae naturales"; also SCG, IV, ch. 81; ST, I–II, q. 100, a. 4, ad 3–4.

reference to such powers, still one cannot conceive that a soul exists without conceiving also of those powers, nor can a soul exist concretely without those powers.[11]

In the *Summa theologiae*, I, q. 77, a. 1, while discussing the question "whether the very essence of the soul is its power," Thomas clarifies the relation between the soul and its powers in the following terms:

> It is impossible to maintain that the soul's essence is its power, even though some have made this claim. For present purposes, this point can be proven by two arguments. First, since potency and act divide being and each genus of being, potency and act have to be referred back to the same genus. And so, if an act is not in the genus of substance, then the potency corresponding to that act cannot be in the genus of substance. But the soul's operation is not in the genus of substance. It is only in the case of God that his operation is his substance; hence God's power, which is a principle of operation, is the very essence of God. But this cannot be true in the soul's case or in the case of other creatures, as was said earlier when discussing the angels. Second, this point seems impossible in the case of the soul. For in its essence the soul is act. Therefore, if the very essence of the soul were the immediate principle of operation, then whatever has a soul would always actually have the vital operations, in the same way that whatever has a soul is always actually alive. For the soul, insofar as it is a form, is not an act ordered toward some further act, but is instead the ultimate aim of generation. Hence, the fact that the soul is in potency with respect to some further act is not something that belongs to it in virtue of its essence, insofar as it is a form, but rather in virtue of its power. And so insofar as the soul itself is the subject of its own power, it is called first act ordered toward a second act. But a thing that has a soul is not always in act with respect to its vital operations. Hence, even in the definition of the soul one says that the

---

11. See QDA, q. 12 and ad 7, 111, 284–287: "Potentie autem anime sunt accidentia sicut proprietates. Vnde licet sine eis intelligitur quid est anima; non autem sine eis animam esse est possibile neque intelligibile." See also QDA, a. 19; QDSC, q. 11; QDM, q. 4, a. 4.

soul is the act of a body that has life potentially, where this potency, however, is not without soul. Therefore, it follows that the soul's essence is not its power. For nothing is in potency in virtue of act, insofar as it is act.[12]

This text of Thomas introduces a fundamental distinction, namely, that between the possession of a rational ensoulment (first act) and the actual functioning of that ensoulment (second act). If the actual exercise of the capacity of reasoning is a quasi-accident of the soul, then, for the human being to be rationally ensouled or something to be a human being, there is only required that there exist a body in such a condition that it is able to support the functions exercised by the rational faculty of the soul, that is, that there be a soul that is able to exercise rational acts (or would have been able to exercise such acts, if the loss or the lesion of certain organs had not in fact impeded their exercise).[13] If one reads again the text of Thomas cited above, one notes how the fact that the soul is a certain type of act has two important consequences. First, what has a soul lives immediately and continually, so that the presence of vital operations in a given body allows us to infer the existence of a

---

12. See ST, I, q. 77, a. 1: "Respondeo dicendum quod impossibile est dicere quod essentia animae sit eius potentia; licet hoc quidam posuerint. Et hoc dupliciter ostenditur, quantum ad praesens. Primo quia, cum potentia et actus dividant ens et quodlibet genus entis, oportet quod ad idem genus referatur potentia et actus. Et ideo, si actus non est in genere substantiae, potentia quae dicitur ad illum actum, non potest esse in genere substantiae. Operatio autem animae non est in genere substantiae; sed in solo Deo, cuius operatio est eius substantia. Unde Dei potentia, quae est operationis principium, est ipsa Dei essentia. Quod non potest esse verum neque in anima, neque in aliqua creatura; ut supra etiam de Angelo dictum est. Secundo, hoc etiam impossibile apparet in anima. Nam anima secundum suam essentiam est actus. Si ergo ipsa essentia animae esset immediatum operationis principium, semper habens animam actu haberet opera vitae; sicut semper habens animam actu est vivum. Non enim, inquantum est forma, est actus ordinatus ad ulteriorem actum, sed est ultimus terminus generationis. Unde quod sit in potentia adhuc ad alium actum, hoc non competit ei secundum suam essentiam, inquantum est forma; sed secundum suam potentiam. Et sic ipsa anima, secundum quod subest suae potentiae, dicitur actus primus, ordinatus ad actum secundum.—Invenitur autem habens animam non semper esse in actu operum vitae. Unde etiam in definitione animae dicitur quod est actus corporis potentia vitam habentis, quae tamen potentia non abiicit animam. Relinquitur ergo quod essentia animae non est eius potentia. Nihil enim est in potentia secundum actum, inquantum est actus."

13. On the distinction between first and second act, see *Sent.,* I, d. 7, q. 1, a. 1, ad 2; *Sent.,* II, d. 35, q. 1, a. 1. On the identification between the rational soul and the first act of a human being, see SCG, II, ch. 61; QDP, q. 1, a. 1; ST, I, q. 76, a. 4, ad 1; ST, I, q. 77, a. 1; also QDV, q. 27, a. 3, ad 25, vol. 3, fasc. 1, 801, 522–529; DUI, ch. 1; and, in greater detail, *Sent. De an.,* II, chs. 1–2.

soul, as we have said in the third chapter. Second, the soul cannot be its powers, for otherwise someone who is alive immediately and continually would have rational acts.

Regarding this distinction, it can be noted that the insane or the wildly angry or, a more extreme case, those generated by monstrous births are partially or entirely deprived of the exercise of reason, but not of the possibility of reasoning, which depends directly on their being ensouled.[14] For this reason, it cannot be said that they are not human beings, although they cannot be said to be completely or perfectly human beings.[15] Thomas's conclusion, then, seems to be that a human being can be called such insofar as he/she possesses a rational soul, and the rational soul is the first act of an organic, physical body that has life potentially, that is, the first act of an organic, physical body that is in potency to the vital operations. Hence, the first being of a human being consists in its having the potency for vital operations. The bringing of this potency to act indicates the very operation that a human being carries out by actually exercising the vital operations.[16]

However, a greater problem for Thomas (i.e., greater than the case of the exercise of the faculty of reasoning) is that of human beings lacking all or some essential organic parts, a situation little discussed by the Dominican master. How are we to consider a human being born without a brain or deprived of the brain while alive? In many passages of his works, Thomas seems to take seriously the Aristotelian idea that the essential organic parts (principally, the heart and brain) are, if not logically prior, at least logically simultaneous with the rational soul.[17]

---

14. See *Sent.,* II, d. 18, q. 1, a. 3, ad 6; SCG, III, ch. 10 and ch. 154.

15. See ST, III, q. 68, a. 12, ad 2: "Ad secundum dicendum quod furiosi vel amentes carent usu rationis per accidens, scilicet propter aliquod impedimentum organi corporalis, non autem propter defectum animae rationalis, sicut bruta animalia. Unde non est de eis similis ratio."

16. See *Sent. Ethic.,* IX, ch. 7.

17. See *Exp. Met.,* VII, lec. 10, n. 1489: "Sed quaedam partes sunt, quae licet non sint priores toto animali hoc modo prioritatis, quia non possunt esse sine eo, sunt tamen secundum hanc considerationem simul; quia sicut ipsae partes non possunt esse sine integro animali, ita nec integrum animal sine eis. Huiusmodi autem sunt partes principales corporis, in quibus primo consistit 'forma,' scilicet anima; scilicet cor, vel cerebrum. Nec ad propositum differt quicquid tale sit"; *Exp. Met.,* VII, lec. 11, n. 1531: "Ex hoc enim homo est homo, quod habet talem animam. Et propter hoc, si homo definitur, oportet quod definiatur per animam, et quod nihilominus in eius definitione ponantur partes corporis, in quibus primo est anima, sicut cor aut cerebrum, ut supra dixit."

This is true to such an extent that the term "human being," for Thomas, as to its formal signification, designates a composite of a certain soul and a certain body, but as to its material signification, it refers to something endowed with organs, without which rational ensoulment cannot take place.[18]

As noted earlier, Thomas does not discuss at length the case of human beings who lack essential organs. Nevertheless, an interpreter of Thomas could generalize from some of his scattered observations about the defective and unnatural character of those generated by "monstrous births" *(monstruosi partus).*[19] Thus, he/she could contest what was argued earlier and deny that such beings, i.e., who lack essential organs, can be considered human beings or, at least, perfect human beings.[20] This conclusion, furthermore, seems in line with Thomas's idea that the essence of a human being is not given only by the formal properties, dependent on the soul, but also by certain specific material properties, dependent on the body.[21] An individual deprived of the soul certainly is not a human being; but an individual that is not composed of flesh and bones,

---

18. See QDP, q. 9, a. 4, 232b–233a: *"Formaliter* quidem significatur per nomen ad id quod significandum nomen est principaliter impositum, quod est ratio nominis; sicut hoc nomen *homo* significat aliquid compositum ex corpore et anima rationali. *Materialiter* vero significatur per nomen illud in quo talis ratio salvatur; sicut hoc nomen *homo* significat aliquid habens cor et cerebrum et huiusmodi partes, sine quibus non potest esse corpus animatum anima rationali. Secundum hoc ergo dicendum est quod hoc nomen *persona* communiter sumpta nihil aliud significat quam substantiam individuam rationalis naturae."

19. See, e.g., *Sent.,* II, d. 1, q. 1, a. 1, ad 3; *Sent.,* II, d. 20, q. 2, a. 3; *Sent.,* II, d. 34, q. 1, a. 3; SCG, III, ch. 5 and ch. 10; *Exp. Met.,* VII, lec. 8, n. 1453: " 'Fit enim femina ex viro' sicut ex agente; et mulus non fit ex mulo, sed ex equo vel asino, in quo tamen est aliqua similitudo, ut supra dixit. Et quod dixit quod a quo est sperma, oportet esse aliqualiter univocum, subiungit, intelligendum est 'si non fuerit orbatio,' idest si non fuerit defectus naturalis virtutis in semine. Tunc enim generat aliquid quod non est simile generanti, sicut patet in monstruosis partubus." Thomas assumes that monstrous births can be caused either by a defect or indisposition of the female matter or by a corruption of the male semen. Thomas never explains such imperfections in detail, but in both cases the imperfection seems principally due to the fact that both the female matter and the male semen did not enter (or did not enter correctly) into the process of digestion. See for example SCG, III, ch. 10, and QDM, q. 1, a. 1, ad 8, and a. 3. For other explanatory factors of monstrous births, see QDV q. 5, a. 9, ad 9; ST II–II, q. 51, a. 4.

20. See, e.g., QDV, q. 23, a. 2.

21. See, e.g., DEE, ch. 1; ST, I, q. 3, a. 3; *Quodl.,* IX, q. 2, a. 1, ad 1; CT, I, ch. 154. On this point, I take the liberty to refer to my "Aristotle, Averroes, and Thomas Aquinas on the Nature of Essence," *Documenti e studi sulla tradizione filosofica medievale* 14 (2003): 79–122.

or that does not have flesh and bones arranged in an organic structure, also cannot be considered a human being. There is no doubt that in Thomas there is a very strong constraint on specifying a certain matter as a necessary condition for the definition of a human being. An interpreter, then, could reverse our earlier conclusion and argue that an individual can no longer be considered a human being not only with the loss of rational ensoulment but also with the loss of some or all of the primary organs necessary for his rational ensoulment (as when one significantly loses the natural matter on which such organs are composed). This holds, evidently, for the embryos that give rise to imperfect human beings, but it also could hold for those terminal cases of human beings who are in a vegetative state of irreversible coma or of brain death.

Even if brief and isolated, discussions of certain grave exceptions concerning the process of the formation of human beings and the beginning of human life are nevertheless present in the texts of Thomas. Much rarer, instead, are texts where Thomas discusses critical cases concerning the end of human life. Considering these cases, however, turns out to be particularly useful for evaluating the limit cases we have been discussing.

Although Thomas very rarely treats cases about the end of life, still the criterion he adopts for defining what a human being is—the ensoulment of a physical body endowed with organs—seems to imply that the process of substantial corruption follows the same phases of the process of generation, but reversed. As an embryo at first lives a plant life, then an animal life, and finally, once the rational soul is added, a human life, so similarly one supposes that a human being at first lives a human life, then, once rational ensoulment is gone, an animal life, and finally a plant life, before corrupting into simple elements. To my knowledge, there is only one text that can be cited explicitly in favor of this conclusion. It is a passage from his Commentary on the *Liber de causis,* lecture 1, a work from the final period of Thomas's literary activity (1272). In this passage, Thomas states that "in the process of substantial corruption" *(in via corruptionis),* when "the use of reason" *(usum rationis)* is lost, the body continues to be alive. It is only with the loss of life that the body can be said to be dead, even if it continues to be in existence:

Besides, it is evident particularly in the process of the generation of a human being that in the material subject at first there is being, then being alive, and there follows being a human being; for it is an animal before it is a human being, as is said in the second book of *De generatione animalium* [II, 3, 736a24]. Again, in the process of corruption, at first a human being loses the use of reason and remains alive and breathing; in a second moment he loses [life] and remains the same entity, since it does not corrupt into nothing.[22]

This short passage from the Commentary on the *Liber de causis* seems to admit the possibility that a human being can lose the capacity to use reason without losing the capacity to live. In general, this statement can be understood in two ways: either the loss of the capacity to use reason implies no longer being a human being or it does not. Each of these consequences is problematic for Thomas.

---

22. See *Sup. De causis,* lec. 1, 5, 26–6, 21: "Exemplum autem videtur pertinere ad causas formales in quibus quanto forma est universalior tanto prior esse videtur. Si igitur accipiamus aliquem *hominem,* forma quidem specifica eius attenditur in hoc quod est rationalis, forma autem generis eius attenditur in hoc quod est *vivum* vel animal; ulterius autem id quod est omnibus commune est *esse.* Manifestum est autem in generatione unius particularis hominis quod in materiali subiecto primo invenitur esse, deinde invenitur vivum, postmodum autem est homo; prius enim ipse est animal quam homo, ut dicitur in II° *De generatione animalium.* Rursumque in via corruptionis primo amittit usum rationis et remanet vivum et spirans, secundo amittit [vitam] et remanet ipsum ens, quia non corrumpitur in nihilum. Et sic potest intelligi hoc exemplum secundum viam generationis et corruptionis alicuius individui. Et haec est eius intentio, quod patet ex hoc quod dicit: *Cum ergo individuum non est homo,* id est secundum actum proprium hominis, *est animal,* quia adhuc remanet in eo operatio animalis quae consistit in motu et sensu; *et,* cum *non est animal, est esse tantum,* quia remanet corpus penitus inanimatum. Verificatur hoc exemplum in ipso rerum ordine: nam priora sunt existentia viventibus et viventia hominibus, quia remoto homine non removetur animal secundum continentiam, sed e contrario quia, si non est animal, non est homo. Et eadem ratio est de animali et esse." Thomas returns to this text from the *Liber de causis* on various occasions. See the following places: *Sent.,* IV, d. 12, q. 1, a. 1, q.la 1: "Respondeo dicendum ad primam quaestionem quod, sicut dicitur prima propositione *Libri de causis,* causa prima est vehementioris impressionis supra causatum causae secundae quam ipsa causa secunda. Unde quando causa secunda removet influentiam suam a causato, adhuc potest remanere influentia causae primae in causatum illud, sicut remoto rationali, remanet vivum, quo remoto, remanet esse"; ST, I–II, q. 67, a. 5, esp. arg. 1 and ad 1: "Videtur quod aliquid fidei vel spei remaneat in gloria. Remoto enim eo quod est proprium, remanet id quod est commune, sicut dicitur in *Libro de causis,* quod, remoto rationali, remanet vivum; et remoto vivo, remanet ens. [. . .] Ad primum ergo dicendum quod, remoto rationali, non remanet vivum idem numero, sed idem genere, ut ex dictis patet."

If the loss of the capacity to use reason does not stop one from being human, then having the capacity to use reason is not a necessary condition for defining a human being. As seen in the previous chapters, however, and as we will see immediately below, this reading is shown to be false by the texts. Hence, the second interpretation remains, namely, that the loss of the capacity to use reason does imply that one ceases to be a human being. As is evident, this interpretation tends to propose again, in reverse order however, the same phases that characterize the passage from embryo to human being. The consequence that follows is that, based on this text, Thomas would not see as problematic a possible distinction between the *end of human life* and the *biological death* of the individual. An individual would cease to be a human being before ceasing to breathe and to exist. There are also other texts that support this reading, texts in which Thomas clearly states that the loss of the capacity to use reason implies ceasing to be a human being, although the individual continues to be alive.[23]

If this were the real position of Thomas, there would be good reasons to hold that Thomas would have rejected considering individuals in a permanent or irreversible vegetative state or embryos lacking fundamental vital organs as genuine human beings. But to decree what for Thomas are the conditions under which one could decide if an individual is or

---

23. See, e.g., *Sent.*, I, d. 26, q. 2, a. 1, ad 3: "Ad tertium dicendum quod quandocumque aliquid quod est de ratione rei tollitur, oportet quod ipsa res auferatur, sicut, remoto rationali, destruitur homo"; QDP, q. 8, a. 4, ad 5 and esp. ad 12, 224b: "Ad ultimum dicendum quod remoto eo *quod* est in aliquo sicut in subiecto, vel sicut in loco, remanet id *in quo* est; non autem remoto eo quod est in aliquo sicut pars essentiae eius. Non enim remoto rationali, remanet homo; et similiter nec remota proprietate, remanet hypostasis"; ST, III, q. 86, a. 4, ad 1: "Ad primum ergo dicendum quod culpa mortalis utrumque habet, et aversionem a Deo et conversionem ad bonum creatum, sed, sicut in secunda parte habitum est, aversio a Deo est ibi sicut formale, conversio autem ad bonum creatum est ibi sicut materiale. Remoto autem formali cuiuscumque rei, tollitur species, sicut, remoto rationali, tollitur species humana"; *Sent. De an.*, II, ch. 28, 189, 108–113: "Deinde cum dicit: *Omnes enim hii intelligere* etc. ostendit causam predicte positionis. Manifestum est autem quod, remota differencia qua aliqua ad inuicem differunt, remanent idem, sicut si rationale auferatur ab homine remanebit de numero irrationabilium animalium." See also the previous note. In contemporary bioethical literature such a distinction is variously discussed and complicated. See, for example, David de Grazia, *Human Identity and Bioethics* (Cambridge: Cambridge University Press, 2005); John P. Lizza, *Person, Humanity, and the Definition of Death* (Baltimore, MD: Johns Hopkins University Press, 2006) and *Defining the Beginning and End of Life: Readings on Personal Identity and Bioethics* (Baltimore, MD: Johns Hopkins University Press, 2009).

is no longer capable of using reason in the abstract is very difficult and in practice almost impossible to determine on the basis of Thomas's texts. Once again, it is difficult to establish when rational ensoulment of the body ceases apart from referring to the actual use of the faculty of reason. How does one verify that the lesion or the death of an organ has effects not only upon the exercise of the corresponding faculty but also upon the principle of ensoulment of the same organ and upon the subject of that faculty? Following this line of thought could lead to different bioethical treatments according to different circumstances: a human being in a state of irreversible coma would not only be different from a human being whose brain is reactive but the former could not, absolutely speaking, even be considered a human being, for the definition of a human being does not apply to him.

The passage from the Commentary on the *Liber de causis* cited above is without doubt difficult to interpret. The most problematic aspect is that it seems to conflict with the basic Aristotelian functionalism that inspires the entire Thomistic conception of human nature. To better understand this point, we could ask: what does rational ensoulment add to the sensitive ensoulment of a human body? It seems to me that, with respect to the body, rational ensoulment is nothing other than the same sensitive ensoulment, given that what is added, namely the capacity to reason, is not a faculty exercised by means of bodily organs. With respect to the body, rational ensoulment expresses only a more complex sensitive ensoulment, for the body now has organs that are more structured and sophisticated. Rational ensoulment, that is, is sensitive ensoulment itself with an added power capable of transcending the body. If rational ensoulment points to the fact that an organic body manifests sensitive and vegetative vital operations and in addition is capable of carrying out rational acts, the loss of rational ensoulment implies immediately the end of being a human being and of being a living being. In addition, this seems to be in line with the Aristotelian idea that with the loss of rationality a human body is said to be human only in an equivocal way.

From this point of view, the symmetry between the process of generation and the process of corruption is only apparent and this for at least two reasons. First, the rational soul does not disappear only after the organs are gone, while, as we have seen, it is added only after the organs are formed. Therefore, with the loss of rational ensoulment, the body ceases immediately to be human and ensouled.[24] Second, as will be recalled, the rational soul does not only replace the preceding sensitive soul, which was also carrying out vegetative functions, but also reabsorbs its functions so that the rational soul is responsible for all the biological functions of the human being. There are many passages that lead us to say that the sequence of the disappearance of forms in the process of substantial corruption—which does not take the form of a regressive succession of forms of ensoulment by weakening and deterioration—follows biological death rather than preceding it.[25] In other words, it does not seem possible to identify a process of progressive corruption of a human being similar though reverse to that of its generation, a process, that is, in which the human being passes from a form of human ensoulment to a form of subhuman ensoulment, gradually more generic and indeterminate, until the onset of biological death. The symmetry that the case of corruption could suggest does not seem to regard the human being, but the body, once it is deprived of the human soul. If this is the case, it is only an apparent symmetry, for in one case there is the generation of a *human being,* and in this process there is an actual succession of forms of different and progressively

---

24. See *Sent.,* III, d. 22, q. 1, a. 1, ad 1.

25. See, e.g., *Sent.,* IV, d. 11, q. 1, a. 1, q.la 3, ad 3; QDV, q. 25, a. 6; QDA, q. 10; QDSC, a. 2; *Quodl.,* III, q. 2, a. 2; ST, I, q. 76, a. 8; DUI, ch. 3; *Sent. De an.,* II, ch. 1; and esp. *Exp. Gen.,* I, lec. 8, n. 60: "Manifestum est enim in generatione compositorum, puta animalis, quod inter principium generationis, quod est semen, et ultimam formam animalis completi, sunt multae generationes mediae, ut Avicenna dicit in sua *Sufficientia;* quas necesse est terminari ad aliquas formas, quarum nulla facit ens completum secundum speciem, sed ens incompletum, quod est via ad speciem aliquam. Similiter etiam ex parte corruptionis sunt multae formae mediae, quae sunt formae incompletae: non enim, separata anima, corpus animalis statim resolvitur in elementa; sed hoc fit per multas corruptiones medias, succedentibus sibi in materia multis formis imperfectis, sicut est forma corporis mortui, et postmodum putrefacti, et sic inde. Quando igitur per corruptionem pervenitur in privationem cui adiungitur talis forma in materia, est corruptio simpliciter: quando vero ex privatione cui adiungitur forma imperfecta, quae erat via generationis, pervenitur ad formam completam, est generatio simpliciter." Note that, once the human soul is lost, the first form that the human body assumes is that of *dead* body.

more complex ensoulment, while in the other case, there is the corruption of a *body*, and this process is triggered only when every ensoulment has already ceased.

Regarding the limit cases discussed earlier, if rational ensoulment expresses nothing other than the vegetative-sensitive ensoulment of a body with the additional capacity for the body to support rational acts, then embryos endowed with imperfect organs or lacking organs also ought to be considered human beings, even if not complete or perfect human beings.

If this is the authentic position of Thomas, an interpreter could attempt to explain the exception found in the Commentary on the *Liber de causis* in two ways. As a first resort, one could argue that Thomas is confining himself to commenting on what the text was saying and was not expressing his own opinion on the matter. This explanation, however, is very weak, since in this case it would become difficult to explain why Thomas referred to this text in other passages of his works.[26] One could, then, follow another line of thought and emphasize that Thomas had talked of the "use of reason" *(usus rationis)* rather than of the *possession* of (the faculty of) reason or of rational ensoulment. It is evident that an individual can lose, even definitively, the possibility to use reason, while nevertheless continuing to remain alive. Nevertheless, the numerical discontinuity that Thomas posits between the living being before and after the possession of the capacity for reasoning could be evidence against this explanation also. Given the numerical discontinuity that Thomas supposes, a human being in a state of irreversible coma (or more radically, of brain death), not only could not be called a human being or the same human being, but could not even be called one and the same living body. Still, as has been said, the case of the loss of the capacity to actually exercise reason is impossible to verify and to differentiate from the case of the loss of the capacity to possibly exercise reason. There is nothing left, then, but to admit that the separation of rational ensoulment from sensitive ensoulment is the

26. See the passages from the Commentary on the *Sentences* and the *Summa theologiae* quoted above, at the end of note 22.

result of nothing more than our separating them conceptually.[27] In any case, apart from the way one attempts to reconcile the passage from the Commentary on the *Liber de causis* with the Aristotelian doctrine of the homonymy between what is dead and what is alive, it seems to me that there are more reasons to include Thomas among those who do not support the distinction between biological death and the end of human life, rather than among those who uphold this distinction.

To conclude, Thomas has identified the fundamental condition for defining a human being as a certain type of biological ensoulment, chiefly as that functioning ensoulment with a corporeal organization that enables the exercise of an incorporeal operation. This seems to allow him to extend the property of "being a human being" in such a way as to encompass also those cases in which, *as a matter of fact,* such bodily organization either is not present or is defective. The fact, that is, that a human being is not that which actually exercises the capacity for reasoning, but is that which is in a state of having or being able to have the capacity for being able to exercise reason, could permit a follower of Thomas to consider a human being in a state of irreversible coma or of brain death as still a human being. Sophisticated techniques of organ transplants could biomedically restore the conditions that would make it possible to consider all those human beings damaged or deprived of some essential vital organ as properly, even if not perfectly, human beings. As imperfect or monstrous embryos, also human beings in a vegetative state or brain dead, when all is said and done, should rather be considered exceptions to a natural rule (that of perfect natural generation) rather than as entities of a different kind that escape that rule.

---

27. See *Sent.,* III, d. 10, q. 1, a. 1, q.la 2, ad 3; ST, I, q. 40, a. 3.

CHAPTER EIGHT

The Contemporary Debate over the Hominization of the Embryo

IN THE EARLIER CHAPTERS, we discussed Thomas's arguments for maintaining the formal discontinuity of the process of generation and the transtemporal identity of the embryo. We reached the conclusion that for Thomas the embryo shows a certain ensoulment from the moment of conception, but it becomes a human being only between the first and third month of gestation (depending on whether the fetus is male or female). Interrupting pregnancy before that date is held by Thomas to be a morally grave act, but not juridically equivalent to homicide. In the last chapter, then, it was concluded that Thomas can be numbered among those upholding the thesis of delayed hominization of the embryo.

As we have noted, even if only in passing, this account of the embryogenetic process has certain important theological consequences, above all the rejection of the doctrine of the Immaculate Conception. Obviously the explanation of the embryogenetic process that we have reconstructed in the earlier chapters is not the only or even the principal reason for rejecting the Immaculate Conception of Mary. Thomas often brings forward other reasons, more theological, among which stands out the universal character of redemption brought about by Christ: redemption does not admit of any exceptions, for otherwise the full dignity of Christ as savior of the human race would be lessened (see, for example, *Summa theologiae*, III, q. 27, a. 2). Nevertheless, Thomas's embryogenetic account provides the general philosophical framework within which is placed the exclusion of the exception represented by the Immaculate Conception of Mary. Since the transmission of original sin and its possible remission, obtained by the action of divine grace, require the presence of the human soul, it follows that the manner of Mary's conception is theologically irrelevant to an explanation and safeguarding of the immaculate nature of Mary. What is more, as a woman conceived in the natural way, Mary can in no way be distinguished from her parents or from other human beings whose nature is vitiated *ab origine* by original sin (see, for example, *Sent.*, III, d. 3, q. 1, q.la 1).

This and other theological consequences (such as the exclusion of embryos not rationally ensouled from the final resurrection, as was mentioned earlier) are the result of the coherent and rigorous application of certain fundamental philosophical assumptions, among which should be recalled the idea that the human soul is the substantial form of a body suitably organized. Bioethically, the principal consequence of this metaphysical approach is that embryos before the fortieth day, as entities not rationally ensouled, are neutral or completely indifferent subjects with respect to any moral evaluation.

Many philosophers and Thomistic interpreters, especially of Catholic inspiration, have noted that Thomas's embryological teaching does not coincide with the present position of the Roman Catholic Church, and so they have felt the need to find a way to reconcile these positions. The literature on this subject is quite vast, and only with difficulty can a unity be imposed upon it. My intention in this last chapter is not to give a complete account of this historiographic debate, whose roots reach back into twentieth-century Neothomist historiography, but only to present and discuss in the abstract two major proposals of reconciliation. In particular, I shall refer to a few recent studies that once again discuss the problem of the relation between the embryological doctrine of Thomas Aquinas and the present teaching of the Roman Catholic Church.

Abstracting from individual variations, it seems to me that the strategies for reconciling these contrasting positions are fundamentally two.

(A) A first line of thought seems to concede that Thomas had admitted that hominization of the embryo takes place after some weeks, but it maintains that Thomas was substantially mistaken in defending delayed hominization of the embryo. The error is not, however, due to any defect in the reasoning of the Dominican master, but to the fact that Thomas had at his disposal scientific data, especially embryological, that was greatly approximate, if not mistaken. No one today would accept many elements of the Aristotelian embryological account, such as the influence of the heavens (above all that of the sun) on the process of human generation, the importance granted to thermodynamic factors (as the theory of the triple vital heat), or the conception of the male semen as what remains from the final stages of the food's digestion. Above all, there has disappeared the mainstay of Aristotelian embryology, namely, the idea that the mother plays no active and formal role in the process of generation, and that only the father is responsible for the process of formation and for the formal identity of the embryo. More generally, contemporary embryology and biology would find completely unscientific the recourse to entities not empirically verifiable, as the soul, and would find ambitious, to say the least, the conviction that it is possible to mark off a definite and fixed set of properties associated with the rational capacity of human beings.[1]

Those who take this line of thought observe that, although scientifically Thomas's embryological account is outdated, the philosophical principles of his analysis still remain valid. What is involved in this claim? The developed argument is the following: since, formally, Thomas's philosophical account is irreproachable, it follows that if Thomas had been aware of certain decisive medical discoveries, as that of the existence of

---

1. These last considerations raise a serious difficulty in Thomas's explanation. Speaking of a soul, however, need not occupy one very much. As was noted, there can be established a definite correspondence between the soul, understood as the principle of the human being's vital operations, on the one hand, and some specific and selected biological operations exercised by the composite man, on the other. In other words, the various kinds of soul could be easily accounted for as kinds and degrees of the exercise of the function of a given material body.

spermatozoa in the male semen (going back, as is well known, to the investigations of the Dutch Johan Ham Van Arnhem in 1677), as that of the female ovum (due to Karl Ernst von Baer in 1827), or more fundamentally as that of the genetic code (whose molecular structure was decoded by James D. Watson and Francis H. Crick only in 1953), he would certainly have modified his position. All this would allow us to say that on the bases of principles in Thomas's philosophy one can coherently hold *today* that the embryo receives human ensoulment at conception. In other words, it seems possible to combine the metaphysical principles of the embryology of Thomas with the most recent discoveries of human and comparative genetics. The following text summarizes clearly, in my opinion, this first line of thought:

> Other scholars maintain, on the other hand, that in the light of new genetic achievements, the principles of Thomas's philosophy lead necessarily to the affirmation of the immediate ensoulment of the embryo: "Naturally, in the light of contemporary biology the same metaphysical reasoning [the necessary proportionality between substantial form and matter] that led Thomas to incline toward a subsequent ensoulment . . . ought to make us affirm today the doctrine that ensoulment by God takes place *simultaneously* with the act of conception. For the discovery of the typically human genetic complement even in the first fertilized cell produced by the act of conception should make us affirm that the embryo from the first instant lives a typically *human* life and is therefore endowed with a human substantial form." And this is the position that we hold is more coherent with the principles of Thomas's philosophy.[2]

---

2. See Claudio A. Testi, "L'embriologia di S. Tommaso d'Aquino e i suoi riflessi sulla bioetica contemporanea," *Divus Thomas* 101/1 (1998): 80–105, at p. 103: "Altri studiosi sostengono invece che, alla luce delle nuove conquiste genetiche, i principi della filosofia di Tommaso portano necessariamente ad affermare l'animazione immediata dell'embrione: 'Naturalmente alla luce della biologia contemporanea il medesimo ragionamento metafisico [la necessaria proporzionalità tra forma sostanziale e materia] che portava Tommaso a propendere per l'animazione successiva [. . .] ci deve far affermare oggi la dottrina dell'animazione *simultanea* da parte di Dio all'atto del concepimento. Infatti la scoperta del corredo genetico tipicamente umano anche nella prima cellula fecondata

This strategy of realignment of Thomas with the present position of the Roman Catholic Church turns out to be particularly problematic. The principal reason is that it is not completely clear what principles of Thomas's philosophy, valid also for today, could lead to a conclusion

prodotta all'atto del concepimento ci deve far affermare che l'embrione fin dal primo istante vive una vita tipicamente *umana* ed è dunque dotato di una forma sostanziale umana.' È questa la posizione che riteniamo più coerente con i principi della filosofia tommasiana." The text quoted by Testi is drawn from Gianfranco Basti, *Filosofia dell'uomo* (Bologna: Edizioni Studio Domenicano, 1995), 356 ff. See also Benedict M. Ashley, "A Critique of the Theory of Delayed Hominization," in Donald McCarthy and Albert S. Moraczewski, eds., *An Ethical Evaluation of Fetal Experimentation: An Interdisciplinary Study* (St. Louis, MO: Pope John XXIII Medical-Moral Research and Education Center, 1976), 115–129. For further discussion, see Joseph F. Donceel, "Immediate Animation and Delayed Hominization," *Theological Studies* 31 (1970): 76–105; James J. Diamond, "Abortion, Animation, and Biological Hominization," *Theological Studies* 36 (1975): 305–324; Eike-Henner W. Kluge, "St. Thomas, Abortion and Euthanasia: Another Look," *Philosophical Research Archives* 7 (1981): 14–72; Mark F. Johnson, "Quaestio Disputata—Delayed Hominization: Reflections on Some Recent Catholic Claims for Delayed Hominization," *Theological Studies* 56 (1995): 743–763; Thomas A. Shannon, "Delayed Hominization: A Response to Mark Johnson," *Theological Studies* 57 (1996): 731–734; Mark F. Johnson, "Quaestio Disputata: Delayed Hominization; A Rejoinder to Thomas Shannon," *Theological Studies* 58 (1997): 708–714; Patrick Lee, "Embryonic Human Beings," *Journal of Contemporary Health Law and Policy* 22 (2006): 424–438 ; and Craig Payne, *Why a Fetus Is a Human Person from the Moment of Conception: A Revisionist Interpretation of Thomas Aquinas's Treatise on Human Nature* (Lewiston, NY: Edwin Mellen Press, 2010) (see there for further bibliographical references). This seems to be the line of thought most followed in the literature. A clear example of this approach is also given by the proceedings of the General Meetings of the Pontifical Academy for Life. See, for example, the contribution of Mario Pangallo, "The Philosophy of Saint Thomas on the Human Embryo," in Elio Sgreccia and Jean Laffitte, eds., *The Human Embryo before Implantation: Scientific Aspects and Bioethical Considerations; Proceedings of the Twelfth Assembly of the Pontifical Academy for Life (Vatican City, February 27–March 1, 2006)* (Vatican City: Editrice Vaticana, 2007), 209–239; also available at www.academiavita.org (accessed May 1, 2012). On the nature of the embryo in particular, see also the contributions contained in Juan de Dios Vial Correa and Elio Sgreggia, eds., *The Identity and Status of the Human Embryo: Proceedings of Third Assembly of the Pontifical Academy for Life (Vatican City, February 14–16, 1997)* (Vatican City: Editrice Vaticana, 1999). A good state of the art example of this type of literature can be found in John Haldane and Patrick Lee, "Aquinas on Human Ensoulment, Abortion and the Value of Life," *Philosophy* 78 (2003): 255–278, see 258 ff., to which I refer for further bibliographical references. As Jean Porter well summarizes, "Defenders of what is currently the dominant Catholic view are scandalized that we ever took an alternative position, according to which the human embryo only attains full human status after a period of development. They are even more troubled by the fact that no less a theologian than Aquinas defends this view. Much ink has been spilled to show that this view is an aberration, or at best a reflection of Aquinas's imperfect knowledge of human biology. If Aquinas knew what we know about the development of the embryo, he too would defend the official Catholic view—that at least is the argument. In this way, it is suggested that what looks like a real diversity of views within the Catholic tradition is not really an instance of diversity at all; the earlier view is dismissed as the result of ignorance about facts"; I cite from "Is the Embryo a Person?" www.pfaith .org/catholic.htm (accessed May 1, 2012).

opposed to that actually reached and argued for by Thomas. Leaving aside the advisability of revising for one reason or another what Thomas actually held, it seems to me that this attempt at reconciliation should be rejected philosophically for at least two reasons.

The first is that Thomas consciously keeps distinct the plane of scientific analysis of the process of human generation from that of his philosophical explanation. As we have seen, Thomas was aware of alternative interpretations of Aristotelian embryology that argued in favor of the immediate hominization of the embryo. Nevertheless, Thomas holds that these accounts are insufficient on the basis of certain philosophical rather than biological arguments, arguments that the discovery of the genetic code and other relevant biological data accepted today could not invalidate. With or without the genetic code, and independently of whether or not one is inclined to see the "formative power" *(virtus formativa)* of the male semen as something approaching the genetic code, the philosophical intuition of Thomas seems to be that the female matter just fertilized by the male semen is already the embryonic matter. As such the embryonic matter is biologically distinct from that of the mother and is already potentially predisposed toward the formation of a human being. In other words, the female matter just fertilized seems to be considered by Thomas as already a matter "typically human." This, however, must be read not in the sense that the embryonic matter is already the matter of a human being (we have seen, in fact, that for Thomas it is only a *disposition* toward the matter of a human being), but in the sense that, while being the development of a matter that is already human, namely, the matter constituted by the female menstrual blood, it is oriented to become, after a suitable development, the matter of a complete and perfect human being.

It is difficult to say, *per impossibile,* what Thomas would have thought of the genetic code. It is reasonable to hypothesize that the possible discovery of the genetic code would have reinforced Thomas in a conviction that he already had and perhaps have persuaded him to concede something to those who claim that a more active role should be accorded to the woman. But probably, greater theoretical clarity on the potentiality of the matter just fertilized would not have altered Thomas's conviction that the substantial form requires a body organized in such a way that it can support the functions that the form is called upon to perform. From this point of view, the presence of the genetic code does not seem able to provide those conditions that Thomas requires for there to be a human being.

As one can see, although Thomas's explanation unlike its clear formulation is hardly obvious, the plane on which it is developed is not biological but philosophical. The task of a philosophical explanation of the phenomena of human generation seems to be for Thomas that of constructing a theoretical framework that is abstractly explanatory of the phenomena connected with embryogenesis and at the same time is capable of giving an account of the data that medical science provides. An enrichment of these data of itself does not falsify a philosophical explanation, which turns upon the identification of certain macroscopic connections existing among the observed phenomena, or at least the scientific enrichment does not falsify the explanation as long as the scientific data does not bring about a redefinition of the very phenomena observed. To be more specific, the genetic code could yet be paraphrased and handled with the Aristotelian conceptual apparatus. From this viewpoint, contemporary biology could not significantly support or deny the embryological account of Thomas for the simple fact that Thomas is not engaged in developing a strictly biological account of the phenomenon of human generation.

The second reason, more persuasive, for rejecting this attempt at reconciliation is that Thomas denies that any materialistic description, however refined and based upon empirical observations or experiments, could explain the nonmaterial nature of the human soul. A deepening of our scientific knowledge concerning the material dimension of the process, which knowledge includes also the discovery of the genetic code, does not appear to be able to explain in any way the presence and origin of the human soul. As a theologian, Thomas rejects an "emergentist" conception of human rationality. If no material and bodily organization, however highly specialized, can give an account of itself of rationality, the genetic code of the embryo or the fusion of the parents' genetic codes in the zygote cannot be taken as a criterion for fixing the human, or typically human, identity of the embryo. If being a human being depends on having a soul infused by God, the presence of the genetic code in the zygote does not prove or help to prove that the zygote has the property of "being a human being," for otherwise the infusion of the soul would play no role in identifying the embryo as a human being.[3]

Someone could find this argument telling, but not decisive. For the supporters of immediate hominization could reply that the presence of the genetic code in the zygote is not of itself responsible for the embryo being a human being, but the presence of a unique and unrepeatable genetic code for a given embryo *furnishes* all the necessary and sufficient conditions so that that embryo can be a human being, that is, receive a human soul from God.

But even with this response, the admission that the moment of conception is the occasion that God awaits to infuse the human soul seems equally indefensible. For if one assumes that the occasion is given by *conception* as such, such a choice seems completely arbitrary on the part of God and entirely detached from any possibility we have of explaining it rationally. From this standpoint, nothing stops one from adopting as the absolute starting point of the embryo's hominization (and more coherently with the embryology of Thomas) the moment when the semen is detached from the father.

If, on the other hand, the suggestion of the moment of conception depends upon the fact that from then on there is the genetic code of the embryo, such a condition would, from Thomas's viewpoint, be entirely irrelevant. In other words, to account for the occasion for which God awaits to infuse the human soul, one cannot insist on a description, however elaborate, of the matter. The fundamental flaw with this approach is that it tends to reverse the explanatory relation that for Thomas holds between matter and form. Thomas is of the opinion that one must not start from any description of the matter to establish when the rational soul arrives, but, vice versa, one must start from a given definition of the rational soul and from there move to specify the conditions under which the matter can be considered in near potency to being rationally ensouled. In the *Summa theologiae*, I, q. 76, a. 5, while

---

3. The argument is well clarified and championed by Robert Pasnau, *Thomas Aquinas on Human Nature: A Philosophical Study of* Summa Theologiae, *Ia 75–89* (Cambridge: Cambridge University Press, 2002), 109.

discussing the question "To what sort of body does the soul appropriately unite itself?" Thomas expresses this point clearly:

> I respond saying that since form does not exist for the sake of matter, but rather matter exists for the sake of form, it is necessary to draw the reason why the matter is as it is from the form and not vice versa. . . . To the second argument it should be said that the body is not suited to the intellective soul because of the intellectual operation considered in its own right, but because of the sensitive capacity which requires an organ equally articulated. And so it was necessary that the intellective soul be united to such a body and not to a simple element or a mixed body.[4]

Since the rational soul must carry out certain specific functions, there is required a matter that is organized in a way that can guarantee them. As we have repeated many times, Thomas seems to argue in favor of thesis (P) that the rational soul is added when the formative power has predisposed the organs in such a way that they can support the functions carried out by the rational soul.

Still, our hypothetical opponent could continue to object to this conclusion pointing out that the conclusion is not incompatible with

---

4. See ST, I, q. 76, a. 5 and ad 2: "Respondeo dicendum quod, cum forma non sit propter materiam, sed potius materia propter formam; ex forma oportet rationem accipere quare materia sit talis, et non e converso. [. . .] Ad secundum dicendum quod animae intellectivae non debetur corpus propter ipsam intellectualem operationem secundum se; sed propter sensitivam virtutem, quae requirit organum aequaliter complexionatum. Et ideo oportuit animam intellectivam tali corpori uniri, et non simplici elemento, vel corpori mixto." Thomas extensively deals with this issue in QDA, q. 8. See also Sent. De an., II, ch. 1, 71, 265–288; SCG, II, ch. 89, n. 1752: "Quod vero sexto obiicitur, patet quod non de necessitate concludit. Etsi enim detur quod corpus hominis formetur prius quam anima creetur, aut e converso, non sequitur quod idem homo sit prior seipso: non enim homo est suum corpus, neque sua anima. Sequitur autem quod aliqua pars eius sit altera prior. Quod non est inconveniens: nam materia tempore est prior forma; materiam dico secundum quod est in potentia ad formam, non secundum quod actu est per formam perfecta, sic enim est simul cum forma. Corpus igitur humanum, secundum quod est in potentia ad animam, utpote cum nondum habet animam, est prius tempore quam anima: tunc autem non est humanum actu, sed potentia tantum. Cum vero est humanum actu, quasi per animam humanam perfectum, non est prius neque posterius anima, sed simul cum ea."

the thesis of the immediate hominization of the embryo, since thesis (P) could be understood in at least two ways:

(P1) the introduction of the rational soul requires the presence of organs sufficiently and suitably developed to support the functions of the rational soul;

(P2) the introduction of the rational soul requires the presence of a material organization sufficient and suitable for the development of organs that can support the functions of the rational soul.

Interpreters that have attempted to reconcile Thomas's doctrine with the thesis of the immediate hominization of the embryo have proposed (P2) as the correct understanding of the interpretation that Thomas advances of the Aristotelian characterization of the soul. Even if he expressed himself as if he intended to uphold (P1), Thomas could not have meant (P1) since it is evident that even the formed embryo cannot, though endowed with organs, support the functions of the rational soul, at least in the sense of actually or perfectly exercising them.[5] Similarly, as has been said, not even a newly born baby is able to support them.[6] Nor are all those who, because of whatever impediment, are

---

5. For this reply, see Haldane-Lee, "Aquinas on Human Ensoulment," 267–268; Pangallo, "The Philosophy of Saint Thomas." One of the arguments invoked in favor of this interpretation is that the embryo fulfills operations according to an *immanent* principle. As was said, this is the argument that Thomas invokes for rejecting the view that the soul of the mother is the cause of the embryo's ensoulment. According to the argument, the embryo turns out to be ensouled right from conception. See on this the anonymous contribution "De animatione foetus," *Nouvelle Revue Théologique* 11 (1879): 163–268, which started a long series of studies on this topic. Note, however, that this argument only proves that the embryo is *ensouled* right from conception, not that it is *rationally ensouled* from conception.

6. There is a sense in which not only the formed embryo but also the newborn child before reaching the *use* of reason can be said to be not actually different from nonrational animals. This qualification is meaningful for the law, but not for metaphysics. My impression is that, for Thomas, the actual *possession* of a structure that makes possible the use of the capacity of reasoning is the necessary and sufficient condition for having a human being; nevertheless it is the capacity of actually exercising reason that in fact discriminates a human being from a nonrational animal. See ST, II–II, q. 10, a. 12: "Et primo quidem a parentibus non distinguitur secundum corpus, quandiu in

deprived temporarily or permanently of their rational capacity. As a consequence, those who follow this interpretation maintain that the soul should not be understood as the form of a physical body that already has formed organs, since an organic physical body does not exist before the coming of the soul, but rather as the form of a corporeal matter that, guided by the soul, is oriented to the formation of organs.

More generally, the distinction between (P1) and (P2) tends to distinguish the interpretative problem from the theoretical problem. This allows interpreters to argue that the admission that (P1) is or may be the correct interpretation of what Thomas says in his texts does not rule out that, by adopting Thomas's embryological principles, (P2) can also be admitted. Better yet, this should be what is authentically meant by Thomas. Undoubtedly there are passages where Thomas seems to deny that there are intermediate forms between the form of the mixture, which the body possesses before beginning the process of generation and of being informed, and the rational form.[7] The interpretation of (P2) seems to find its plausibility in light of these passages, as also in light of certain assumptions of contemporary biology and of certain difficulties that the interpretation of (P1) could, in the abstract, encounter. Nevertheless, my opinion is that this distinction misses Thomas's point in two ways.

In the first place, the distinction between the interpretative problem and the theoretical problem is not acceptable. If (P1) is the correct interpretation of what Thomas is saying in his texts, then (P1) is also the philosophical proposal that a follower of Thomas ought to take, especially since (P1) is introduced by Thomas in opposition to an embryological account very close to (P2). For recall that Thomas argues

---

matris utero continetur. Postmodum vero, postquam ab utero egreditur, antequam usum liberi arbitrii habeat, continetur sub parentum cura sicut sub quodam spirituali utero. Quandiu enim usum rationis non habet puer, non differt ab animali irrationali. Unde sicut bos vel equus est alicuius ut utatur eo cum voluerit, secundum ius civile, sicut proprio instrumento; ita de iure naturali est quod filius, antequam habeat usum rationis, sit sub cura patris"; also *Quodl.*, II, q. 4, a. 2, and *Sent. Ethic.*, VII, ch. 6, 406–407, 202–209. As was said, Thomas himself recognizes that children at the beginning of their life cannot perfectly exercise reason because of excessive cerebral moisture (e.g., *Sent.*, II, d. 20, q. 2, a. 2 and ad 4; ST, I, q. 101, a. 2).

7. See, e.g., *Sent.*, IV, d. 44, q. 1, a. 1, q.la 1, ad 4; QDP, q. 3, a. 12.

against the idea, going back to Gregory of Nyssa, that the rational soul is the principle that guides the organization of matter from conception toward the formation of organs.

In the second place, the upholders of this interpretation seem to underestimate the fact that Thomas's embryological account is not based only on the Aristotelian characterization of the soul as the form of an organic physical body having life potentially but even, more generally, it takes up the Aristotelian explanation of animal and human generation. Based on the way Thomas explains the term "generation," there exists something that can be called "the generated" only at the end of the process of generation. It is true that, for Thomas, there is not an organic body before the coming of the rational soul, but it is also true that the body that has already begun to organize itself and has almost brought to term this organization under the stimulus of the father's formative power is that which will later be identified with the organic body. The claim that the rational soul is infused by God at the moment of conception conflicts with the empirical datum that that act of infusion does not transform the mother's menstrual blood into an organic matter. Nor is it enough to say that it transforms it into a matter that *can* be or become organic (or that manifests the primordia of such organization), for this is due to the menstrual blood of the mother independently of the rational soul as a direct consequence of the fact that the formative power of the male semen has started the process of actualizing that potentiality to be organized and ensouled that the female menstrual blood possesses of itself. In sum, Thomas seems to see no problem with assuming that an embryo is a *human* embryo right from conception. For him, the primal action of the male semen on the female material, just like the contemporary understanding of the human embryo's genetic identity from conception, is able to support the inference that such an embryo possesses from conception an intrinsic and natural active potentiality to develop the requisite organic structures for rational activity. Such an assumption, however, is unable to support the further inference that such an embryo is a *human being* right from conception, for the embryo does not actually possess at that time such requisite organic structures for rational activity. If this is Thomas's doctrine, it follows that the contemporary understanding of the embryo's genetic identity cannot mitigate the arbitrary nature of the claim that God infuses a rational soul into a human embryo at conception.

I believe, then, that (P1) is to be the preferred interpretation. There are numerous passages in which Thomas requires the actual presence of a suitable bodily organization in order to have rational ensoulment, and he presents it as the intrinsic end of substantial generation.[8] Whether it is only logical or also ontological, there is no doubt that, for Thomas, a suitable bodily organization must *precede* the infusion of the rational soul.[9] Even where Thomas contrasts the entirely unensouled state of the semen with the ensoulment of an organic body, such passages could be called upon to extend the nonensoulment of the embryo up to the formation of the organs rather than to advance the time of the organization of the organs back to the moment of conception.[10]

(B) A second line of reconciliation, not completely distinct from the first, seems to prefer to revise the traditional judgment and so to deny that Thomas had claimed delayed hominization of the embryo. As a consequence, Thomas comes to be classified as an upholder of immediate hominization. Texts that might support this interpretation are not lacking. For example, someone could note that Thomas, when discussing a counterposition to the infusion of the human soul at the fortieth day, does not bring up the infusion of the human soul at the moment of conception, but almost always the preexistence of the human soul in the male semen.[11] In other words, Thomas normally

---

8. See, e.g., *Sent.*, II, d. 19, q. 1, a. 4, ad 1; *Sent.*, III, d. 3, q. 2, a. 1; QDV, q. 8, a. 3; *Quodl.*, IX, q. 5, a. 1. On this debate, see also Pasnau, *Thomas Aquinas on Human Nature*, 111 ff. For a recent attempt at reconciliation see Jason T. Eberl, "Aquinas on the Nature of Human Beings," *Review of Metaphysics* 58.2 (2004): 333–365, and especially "Aquinas's Account of Human Embryogenesis and Recent Interpretations," *Journal of Medicine and Philosophy* 30/4 (2005): 379–394.

9. See, e.g., SCG, IV, ch. 44, n. 3814b–c: "Similiter autem anima requirit propriam materiam: sicut et quaelibet alia forma naturalis. Est autem propria materia animae corpus organizatum: est enim anima *entelechia corporis organici physici potentia vitam habentis*. Si igitur anima a principio conceptionis corpori fuit unita, ut ostensum est, necessarium fuit ut corpus a principio conceptionis organizatum et formatum esset. Et etiam organizatio corporis ordine generationis praecedit animae rationalis introductionem. Unde posito posteriori, necesse fuit et ponere prius."

10. See, e.g., SCG, II, ch. 89, n. 1737 (see also the following note).

11. See, e.g., SCG, II, ch. 89, n. 1737: "Neque tamen potest dici quod in semine ad ipso principio sit anima secundum suam essentiam completam, cuius tamen operationes non appareant propter

discusses a contrast between what happens in the male semen before conception and what happens after conception.[12] And so all the texts in which it is stated that the rational soul requires a suitable organization of the body could be read as texts in which it is affirmed, more simply, that the rational soul requires a matter that *can* be suitably organized.[13] The Aristotelian characterization of the soul, that is, would furnish not so much a constraint on a factual condition of the matter, but rather on the type of matter required, namely on the potentiality of a certain matter to be organized in a given way. The contrast, then, would be between the female matter before and after fertilization. As we have said, this proposal is based on interpretation (P2) of the Aristotelian characterization of the soul. John Haldane and Patrick Lee summarize this proposal as follows:

> Rather, Aquinas's argument only shows, and he surely only held,
> that the beginnings, or *primordial,* of such organs, and in partic-
> ular, the *primordium* of the brain, must be present. . . . We have
> shown that Aquinas did not hold P. 1 [namely, the thesis that the
> presence of actual organs, sufficiently developed, is necessary for

---

organorum defectum. Nam, cum anima uniatur corpori ut forma, non unitur nisi corpori cuius est proprie actus. Est autem anima actus corporis organici. Non est igitur ante organizationem corporis in semine anima actu, sed solum potentia sive virtute. Unde et Aristoteles dicit, in II *De anima,* quod semen et fructus sic sunt potentia vitam habentia quod abiiciunt animam, idest anima carent: cum tamen id cuius anima est actus, sit potentia vitam habens, non tamen abiiciens animam"; QDP, q. 3, a. 9, ad 9, 66b A). In the quoted text from the *Summa contra Gentiles,* for example, Thomas contrasts the organization of the body with the state of the male semen before the female material has been fertilized. This could lead an interpreter to hold that the body's organization formally occurs, for Thomas, at the moment of conception, since one of the reasons given by Thomas for rejecting the view that the human soul is actually in the male semen is precisely the lack of organs (see SCG, II, ch. 89, n. 1740). This possible reading seems to be due to the fact that in Thomas's embryology, as has been said, only the male plays a formal role in the generation of a human being: it is the semen that transmits the form to the one generated, hence justifying the full formal identity between father and son.

12. See, e.g., QDP, q. 3, a. 11, ad 1. It is curious that the supporters of the immediate hominization of the embryo scarcely emphasize such an opposition.

13. See, e.g., ST, I, q. 76, a. 5. If the texts of Thomas are reread in this way, Robert Pasnau's argument (see *Thomas Aquinas on Human Nature,* 115–116) that the thesis of the immediate hominization
of the embryo is plausible only if one holds (1) that the human soul exist as a substance independent
of the body and (2) that the human being be none other than the soul turns out to be groundless.

having a rational soul], though he did apparently require the presence of visible organs. But more importantly, given the embryological facts as we now know them, Aquinas's principles actually lead to P. 2 [namely, to the thesis that for having a rational soul a material organization sufficient for the development of such organs is necessary].[14]

In this text, the two proposals for reconciliation that we have proposed to distinguish tend to merge. For on the one hand, Haldane and Lee argue that even if the texts of Thomas seem to say the contrary, the principles of his metaphysics and the arguments employed lead Thomas toward (P2) rather than toward (P1). But on the other hand, they state that "more importantly" the discoveries of contemporary genetics actually confirm their interpretation. But it is evident that establishing what the exact position of Thomas is and what it could have been are different questions.

Compared to the first proposal of reconciliation, this second appears to me more difficult to uphold. Surely Thomas claims that the embryo has one of its ensoulments from the moment of conception, but he seems to be quite unequivocal in denying that this ensoulment is already human (i.e., rational). This second line of interpretation, which holds otherwise, conflicts with the texts. Thomas knew of the thesis of the rational ensoulment of the embryo from conception, and this thesis was somehow upheld, as far as we know, by Robert Grosseteste and the anonymous author of Van Steenberghen.[15] But Thomas rejects it on a number of occasions. Although this second line of interpretation could help, above all, with the problem of the identity of the embryo, it seems to provide

---

14. See Haldane-Lee, "Aquinas on Human Ensoulment," 267–268. For more on this strategy, see Jason T. Eberl, *Thomistic Principles and Bioethics* (London: Routledge, 2006) and Craig Payne, "Would Aquinas Change His Mind on Hominization Today?" in Joseph W. Koterski, ed., *Life and Learning XVIII: Proceedings of the Eighteenth University Faculty for Life Conference at Marquette University, 2008* (Bronx, NY: University Faculty for Life, 2011), 229–248; see there for other references.

15. See Richard C. Dales, *The Problem of the Rational Soul in the Thirteenth Century* (Leiden: Brill, 1995), 38–39, 57, 164–166, 202. Among the Fathers of the Church, the ensoulment of the embryo from the moment of conception *(a conceptionis principio)* was endorsed at least by Maximus the Confessor, in his *Ambigua*, for the sake of preserving the parallel with Christ.

an insufficient explanation of the process of generation. As will be recalled, the argument of Thomas had been that if the embryo did have a rational soul from the moment of conception, generation would have to be declared concluded already with conception, and this is unacceptable. What is more, there would be confusion between what generates and what is generated. Aristotle's reference in the general characterization of the soul to bodily organization is valid, for Thomas, only if one assumes the existence of organs already fully formed. If this were not the interpretation that Thomas provides of the Aristotelian characterization of the soul, certain data could not be explained: first, why Thomas explicitly establishes the beginning of rational ensoulment of males at the fortieth day, with Aristotle, or at the forty-sixth day, with Augustine; second, and more importantly, why Thomas contrasts the case of Christ, formed and rationally ensouled "from the moment of conception" *(a conceptionis principio),* with that of other human beings.[16]

On the other hand, the contrast between the female material before and after fertilization should not be particularly surprising when taken within an embryological theory such as that of Thomas. For the moment

---

16. See exemplarily ST, III, q. 33. Thomas thinks that the embryo can receive the rational soul only after it has acquired a "suitable quantity" of matter. See ST, III, q. 33, a. 1 and a. 2, ad 1 and ad 2: "Ad secundum dicendum quod anima requirit debitam quantitatem in materia cui infunditur: sed ista quantitas quandam latitudinem habet, quia et in maiori et minori quantitate salvatur." Such suitable quantity of matter is not what the embryo has at the moment of conception. See ST, I, q. 78, a. 2 and ad 3: "Vegetativum enim, ut dictum est, habet pro obiecto ipsum corpus vivens per animam: ad quod quidem corpus triplex animae operatio est necessaria. Una quidem, per quam esse acquirat, et ad hoc ordinatur potentia generativa. Alia vero, per quam corpus vivum acquirit debitam quantitatem, et ad hoc ordinatur vis augmentativa. Alia vero, per quam corpus viventis salvatur et in esse, et in quantitate debita, et ad hoc ordinatur vis nutritiva. [. . .] Ad tertium dicendum quod, quia generatio viventium est ex aliquo semine, oportet quod in principio animal generetur parvae quantitatis. Et propter hoc necesse est quod habeat potentiam animae, per quam ad debitam quantitatem perducatur." See also *Sent.,* III, d. 3, q. 5, a. 2, ad 3: "Maxima autem quantitas in aliquo individuo est in ultimo termino augmenti, et sicut maximum differt in diversis, ita etiam proportionaliter illud minimum. Potuit ergo esse ut corpus Christi in primo instanti conceptionis perfecte figuratum haberet quantitatem sufficientem suae speciei, minorem tamen quam sibi deberetur in principio suae humanitatis si naturaliter conceptus esset, respectu quantitatis quam habuit in completa aetate proportionaliter aliis hominibus; ita quod usque ad quadragesimum aut quadragesimum sextum diem crescendo pervenerit usque ad quantitatem illam quae in eo debuit esse minima proportionaliter aliis hominibus; et deinceps crevit sicut et alii homines crescunt; ita quod totum tempus quo in utero matris fuit, augmento corporis eius servivit, quod in aliis servit conversioni, figurationi, animationi, et augmento"; SCG, IV, ch. 44.

of conception does not constitute the point of departure for the generative process. If only the father is responsible for the formal aspects of the process of generation, it follows that, within the framework of the ordinary and natural process of reproduction, such a process has its beginning with the formation of the male semen and its detachment from the father. This explains (1) why Thomas dwells so much on the question of the preexistence of the human soul in the semen and (2) why in some texts, as the *Summa contra Gentiles,* the form of the semen is said to be, even if inappropriately, the first form that the embryo possesses.[17] We have even seen how in the Commentary on the *Sentences* the material continuant seems to be given *also* by the male semen that, by virtue of the concomitant action of the triple heat, becomes gradually more and more actual, receiving at first the vegetative soul, then the sensitive soul, and finally the rational soul. In the Commentary on the *Sentences,* the formative power of the semen, although it is said to be the moving cause of the process, is defined also as "in some way" *(aliquo modo)* the form of the semen.[18] All this tells us that Thomas did not place particular importance on the moment of conception in the natural process of human generation; in fact, that moment is discussed only in the theological context of the contrast between the ordinary generation of a human being and the extraordinary generation of Christ. If one does not admit that the human soul is infused externally *after* the fundamental vital organs are formed, there is no reason to prefer the moment of conception over that of the detachment of the male semen, and so there is no way to avoid the "traducianist" conclusion that the human soul is transmitted to the embryo directly by the parent.

If what we have proposed is an accurate interpretation of the embryological account of Thomas, it follows that for Thomas, as for the greater part of the Fathers of the Church, the embryo becomes a human being only after a certain time, when the rational soul is introduced by God into a body suitably formed and organized.

---

17. See, e.g., SCG, II, ch. 89, n. 1743: "Species tamen formati non manet eadem: primo habet forma seminis, postea sanguinis, et sic inde quosque veniat ad ultimum complementum."

18. See *Sent.,* II, d. 18, q. 2, a. 3: "Subiectum autem et organum huius virtutis est spiritus vitalis inclusus in semine; unde ad continendum huiusmodi spiritum semen est spumosum et haec est causa albedinis eius. Huic autem spiritui coniungitur virtus formativa, magis per modum motoris quam per modum formae, etsi forma eius aliquo modo sit."

Conclusion

A s we have seen in this study, the embryological account of Thomas Aquinas balances certain theses that in our view appear to be in tension. Probably Thomas did not see things this way and had no difficulty in reconciling the identity of the embryo over time with the discontinuity of the generative process; philosophically, this point is not even particularly troublesome for him. But to emphasize one or another thesis can bring about quite different consequences for one's bioethics. For example, if an interpreter wanted to include Thomas among those who oppose the practice of any form of abortion, she/he could insist on the identity of the subject that Thomas attributes to the embryo in the process of generation rather than seek (not very plausibly, given Thomas's arguments) to extend to the embryo just conceived the property of "being a human being" or even of "being a person."[1] If an interpreter instead wanted to include Thomas among

---

1. From Thomas's perspective, we cannot attribute the property of "being a person" to the non-rationally ensouled embryo, for "being a person" designates a property that logically follows from that of "being a human being," if one endorses the classical characterization of "person" given by Boethius in his *De duabus naturis* (that is, a person is an "individual substance of rational nature").

those who uphold, or at least among those who do not oppose, the practice of abortion, she/he could insist precisely on the discontinuity of the process of human generation. Using a bioethical theory of properties, before the fortieth day the embryo cannot be considered a human being. Using a bioethical theory of the subject, before the fortieth day the embryo can be considered a human being, even if only potentially; in any case, it can be considered the same subject that will be the human being that the embryo will become as long as it is not suppressed.

All the same, it is still difficult to ascertain Thomas's position regarding the type of ensoulment that the embryo has before the coming of the rational soul. As we have seen, sometimes one has the impression that the embryo that is not yet ensouled rationally has an extrinsic ensoulment brought about by the father's soul remaining in it by virtue of the formative power. At other times, Thomas seems led to admit that the embryo has its own principle of ensoulment distinct from the formative power, and that this principle, by passing through various complex replacements, becomes structured over time so that it is capable of carrying out rational operations. In any case, the very fact that there is a distinction between rationally ensouled embryos and those not yet so ensouled (a distinction abolished officially by the Roman Catholic Church only very late by the statement of Pius IX in the Constitution *Apostolicae Sedis* of 1869) speaks in favor of rejecting the attribution of immediate rational ensoulment to the embryo. At the same time, however, it is precisely that distinction that suggests a continuity and identity of the subject that exhibits the properties of "not yet being rationally ensouled" and "being rationally ensouled."

At the end of our investigation, it seems to me that in his embryological account Thomas Aquinas is inspired by genuine good sense and by a certain methodological caution. Even if the *human* embryo cannot

---

This characterization of "person" will be revised by the theologians, especially Franciscans, of the first generation after Thomas. But in Thomas's days it was largely accepted. See *Sent.,* II, d. 3, q. 1, a. 2: "Respondeo dicendum quod personalitas est in angelo alio tamen modo quam in homine. Quod patet, si tria quae sunt de ratione personae considerentur, scilicet subsistere, ratiocinari, et individuum esse"; SCG, IV, ch. 38, n. 3761. On the difference between "being a person" and "being a human being," see also QDP, q. 9, a. 6.

be called a *human being*, by the simple fact that what is potentially a human being is not actually a human being, it is likewise true that the embryo is, in potency, that same identical human being, in act, that the embryo will later become if it is provided with a supportive environment and is otherwise unimpeded. This all suggests that if we should not extend to the embryo considerations and rights that we ascribe to a human being already born, it is still true that we ought to ascribe to the embryo a right that is specifically its own.[2]

Certainly, many aspects of the embryological account of Thomas seem so antiquated and unacceptable today that one might want to reject his entire theory, pointing out among other things his constant use of terms such a "spirit" or "formative power" that lack explanatory force. In general, this is certainly a good reason to reject from a scientific point of view a philosophical or biological account. But this would hold here only if Thomas had intended to attribute to these terms real explanatory value within his theory. In fact, one has the impression reading the texts of Thomas that he is not using the technical terms of medieval biology and medicine in this way. As Robert Pasnau has opportunely observed, "Not all descriptions are intended to be explanatory. Sometimes we attach a label to a thing not because that helps us to understand it any better, but simply because we want a placeholder for a feature that we know it has but we cannot explain."[3]

It seems to me that Pasnau's considerations are quite appropriate for understanding what Thomas is doing here. As has been emphasized many times, Thomas's is a philosophical account, not a biological account,

---

2. See *Sent.*, II, d. 1, q. 1, a. 5: "Et hoc significant verba Philosophi dicentis quod sunt quaedam problemata de quibus rationem non habemus, ut utrum mundus sit aeternus; unde hoc ipse demonstrare nunquam intendit. Quod patet ex suo modo procedendi, quia ubicumque hanc quaestionem pertractat, semper adiungit aliquam persuasionem vel ex opinione plurium vel approbatione rationum, quod nullo modo ad demonstratorem pertinet. Causa autem quare demonstrari non potest est ista, quia natura rei variatur secundum quod est in esse perfecto et secundum quod est in primo suo fieri, secundum quod exit a causa; sicut alia natura est hominis iam nati et eius secundum quod est adhuc in materno utero. Unde si quis ex conditionibus hominis nati et perfecti vellet argumentari de conditionibus eius secundum quod est imperfectus in utero matris existens, deciperetur, sicut narrat Rabbi Moyses."

3. See Robert Pasnau, *Thomas Aquinas on Human Nature: A Philosophical Study of* Summa Theologiae, *Ia 75–89* (Cambridge: Cambridge University Press, 2002), 104.

of the phenomenon of generation, and like all philosophical accounts, his is confined to ordering phenomena according to certain general forms that claim to conform to and replicate conceptually the causal connections found at the macroscopic level among the observed phenomena.

Regarding the bioethics of his position, despite appearances, it does not seem to me that Thomas's analysis of the human embryogenetic process can be considered as an expression of a weak stand on the value of human life. For this reason, the polemic triggered by some commentators of Thomas against the Roman Catholic Church on the moral equivalence of homicide and abortion seems out of place. Although the attempts to bring Thomas Aquinas into conformity with the present positions of the Roman Catholic Church on abortion have failed, this does not mean that the position of Aquinas must be seen as essentially contrary to that of the Church. The Church herself has highlighted, rightly in my opinion, the fact that there is no logical implication between the thesis of the delayed hominization of the embryo (T1) and the thesis of the moral licitness or acceptability of abortion (T2).[4] One can favor the delayed hominization of the embryo and still be clearly against the practice of abortion (or against its generalized use, for example, as a means of contraception or of demographic control). And one can be in favor of the immediate hominization of the embryo and still be open to evaluating in a discriminating way the various cases

---

4. See, e.g., the well-known Document of the Sacred Congregation for the Doctrine of the Faith, November 18, 1974, "Declaration on Procured Abortion—Quaestio de abortu procurato," II, 7, http://www.vatican.va/roman_curia/congregations/cfaith/documents/rc_con_cfaith_doc_19741118 _declaration-abortion_en.html (accessed May 1, 2012). This document contains a certain tension. If correctly the Declaration does not relate the moral illicitness of an act of abortion to the immediate hominization of the embryo, it is less certain, as it argues, that the Catholic Church has always maintained one and the same position on abortion (for this judgment, see also Paul VI, *Litterae Encyclicae Humanae Vitae,* July 25, 1968, n. 14). If the common doctrine taught by the Fathers and Doctors of the Church is "that human life must always be protected and favored right from its beginning" (II, 6), I think that Thomas can easily be counted among the advocates of such a doctrine. But if the common doctrine of the Church, on the basis of other magisterial pronouncements (see, e.g., John Paul II, *Litterae Encyclicae Evangelium Vitae,* March 25, 1995, nn. 13, 54, 58 ff., especially n. 62) and of other affirmations of the same Declaration, is that an act of procured abortion must be considered a crime or a homicide, evidently this was not ever the position unanimously held by the Fathers and Doctors of the Church, because it is not, at least, the position championed by Thomas Aquinas.

involving the interruption of pregnancy, as also one can be clearly against making abortion and homicide morally equivalent in an absolute and unqualified way. Thomas, for example, admits the first thesis (T1), but rejects the second (T2). The sacredness of life—taking "sacredness" as an unconditioned respect for life as it is found naturally—appears to be beyond dispute for Thomas. As a consequence, the concession of Thomas that the embryo becomes human only after a certain period of development cannot be called upon to uphold in a facile way various positions that favor abortion.

The principal purpose of Thomas's analysis seems to be to define exactly the forms and ways in which life reveals itself, attributing to each form a qualified degree of value and so of protection, both ethical and legal. Thomas takes for granted that vegetative and animal life should be respected, insofar as they are forms of life, but it is clear that they cannot have the same respect that is due to human life. As for human life, a central position is given to the existing human being: human life, in its greatest value, belongs to the human being ensouled with a rational soul. An existing human being is not confined to being alive, but lives fully a typically human life. The embryo, on the other hand, is alive from conception, but does not live fully from conception a typically human life. Nevertheless, vegetative life, which the embryo lives right from conception, can be considered higher than the vegetative life of any plant, if one admits that the embryo exercises vegetative functions comparatively more sophisticated than those of plants. However, in light of this functional analogy between an embryo just conceived and a plant, taking the property "being alive" as morally relevant in the discussion of abortion is too generic a condition. But if one takes the more restrictive property of "being a human being," the human embryo ought to be considered a moral subject that is in an intermediate position between that of a plant or animal and that of a completely perfected human being: it is not yet a human being, but nevertheless it is a human being in the making; it lives a plant life or an animal life, but nevertheless it is neither a plant nor an animal. What, then, is the ethical respect due to a human embryo? If the life of a human being is sacred, then it should be respected by the simple fact that it is present. To respect human life implies that human life is considered as maximally precious, and so should be maximally preserved. And for a different but related reason, all that prepares for human life and follows from it, therefore, ought to be preciously defended. As Pasnau, again, illustrates well:

> In a world where water is precious, it would be immoral not only to destroy water but also to destroy the hydrogen and oxygen used to make the water. One need not equate the raw materials with the finished product in order to see the great value of the raw materials. We believe that human life is precious, and so it is entirely appropriate that we value not only living human beings but also the developing embryos and fetuses that will become human beings. The closer we come to an actual human being, the higher that value rises. . . . These values are entirely intelligible without appealing to any dubious identification between the embryo and a human being.[5]

Once it is conceded that life is sacred and once the problem of abortion is posed in these terms, an embryo receives ethical value insofar as it is the indispensible *presupposition* for human life, and it receives metaphysical value as the *subject* of the process of generation that will lead it to becoming a human being. If what is the potential presupposition of a human being is not different, by identity of subject, from that human being, the embryo is to be safeguarded without exceptions insofar as it is, in potency, that same thing that will later actually be a human being. On this Aristotelian metaphysical machinery, it seems difficult to establish as securely other decisions concerning the embryo, however reasonable. The fundamental stipulation that there be identity of subject between what is in potency and what is in act is the metaphysical basis on which hinges the Thomistic conception of the human embryo.[6]

---

5. See Pasnau, *Thomas Aquinas on Human Nature*, 125.

6. Contemporary genetics could call into question even this principle of Thomas's embryological account, pointing out, for example, that before the second day the parents' genetic codes

Commenting on the book of *Job* for his fellow Dominicans at Orvieto (1261–1265), Thomas recapitulates the temporally successive stages that characterize the process of human generation. Given what we have said, no one can be surprised that the final condition he mentions concerns the necessity to conserve life both inside and outside womb, and that Thomas talks of such conservation after the release of the semen, the compressing of the bodily mass, the formation of the organs, and above all after the rational ensoulment of the embryo.

> And since it was also said to the first human being, *You are dust and unto dust you shall return,* he says as a consequence, *and you will grind me into dust,* which also befits natural matter. For

---

do not merge, so that before that time one cannot properly speak of something that is individual and so in potency to a human being. Contemporary genetics can also note that until the fourteenth day the zygote is undifferentiated and totipotent, so that one cannot properly speak of identity of subject if the possibility of monozygotic twinning or of production of chimeras has not been excluded. Certainly, both arguments seriously complicate the picture, perhaps excessively simple, that arises from Thomas's embryological account. But it is clear that the fact that Thomas does not discuss such cases forces us to stop here, that is, not to propose any hypothesis as to what *would have been* Thomas's reply to these complications. In the abstract, however, it can be noted that the argument from monozygotic twinning does not affect very much the embryo's potentiality for being a human being, since the embryo's being in potency to one, two, or more human beings (as well as to something that will not realize itself as a human being) does not prevent the embryo from being in potency to a human being. In other words, the fact that at the beginning one does not know whether x will give rise to only y or y and z or also to nothing, does not entail that once y or y and z are present, one can deny that the process of derivation has been continuous and that x is the same entity that y or y and z are now. This case could be considered as philosophically very similar to that of Eve (which Thomas discusses on several occasions), who is generated by the detachment of Adam's rib. In this case too, there is only one matter that gives rise to two different individuals. On the other hand, the case of a process that, once activated, does not continue or come to completion could be treated as an exception, with the reason appropriately explained. A similar analysis could be proposed for the argument from totipotency. The case of the delayed fusion of the parents' genetic codes is much more difficult to manage. In this case, one could react by backdating the starting point of the process by identifying it with the actual union of the spermatozoon with the ovum (i.e., the copresence of both genetic codes in one and the same cell material) rather than with the actual fusion of the genetic codes, that is, with the moment in which the process that will involve a given subject is activated rather than with the process in which the subject of the process acquires its own genetic identity. In any case, the case of the delayed fusion of the genetic codes is a problem for those who see the genetic code as the hallmark of the embryo's human identity rather than for those who identify it with the relationship between spermatozoon and ovum.

it follows that what is generated from earth is fittingly, according to nature, resolved back into the earth. . . . Next he treats the forming of humans with reference to the operation of propagation by which a human is generated from a human. Note here that]Job] attributes every work of nature to God, not so as to exclude the operation of nature, but [he attributes them] in the way things done through secondary causes are attributed to the principal agent. In a similar way, the operation of the saw [is attributed] to the carpenter. The very fact that nature operates comes from God who instituted it for that purpose. In the generation of a human, first comes the release of the semen and to express this he says, *Did you not pour me out like milk?* For just as semen is what is left over from nourishment, so too is milk. Secondly, then the bodily mass is compressed in the womb of the woman and so he adds, *and did you not curdle me like cheese?* For the semen of the male is related to the matter that the female furnishes in the generation of a human being and other animals like the coagulant is related to the generation of cheese. Thirdly, then the distinction of the organs takes place. Their strength and consistency comes from the nerves and bones and they are encased externally by skin and flesh. So he says, *With skin and flesh you clothed me, with bones and nerves you knit me together.* Fourthly, then comes the ensoulment of the fetus, and this is especially true in the case of the rational soul, which is not infused until after the organization [of the body]. Certain seeds of virtue are divinely infused together with the rational soul into the human, some common to all and others special to the individual. For this reason, some people are naturally disposed to one virtue, others to another. Job says further on, *Compassion grew in me from my infancy and came forth from the womb with me.* He therefore also says here, *You gave me life and mercy.* Lastly, then comes the conservation of life, as much in the womb of the mother as after leaving the womb. This conservation is partly due to natural principles and partly to gifts of God, which are added over and above nature, whether they pertain to the soul, the body, or exterior goods. Expressing this theme he adds, *and your visitation guarded my spirit*. For according to the language of Scripture, as God is said to draw back from someone when he withdraws his gifts from him, so he is said to visit him when he bestows his gifts on him.[7]

To conclude, the account that Thomas offers of Aristotelian embryology surely has certain bioethical consequences, but of itself it does not give rise to one particular bioethical theory or another. As mentioned earlier, it is a philosophical explanation of the phenomenon of

---

7. See *Sup. Iob,* ch. 10, 70–71, 219–276: "Et quia etiam primo homini dictum est 'Pulvis es et in pulverem reverteris,' consequenter subiungit *et in pulverem reduces me,* quod etiam naturali materiae competit: nam ea quae ex terra generantur consequens est secundum naturae ordinem ut resolvantur in terram. Sed de hoc aliquis mirari potest, cum maius videatur de terra formare hominem quam hominem formatum retinere ne in pulverem redigatur, unde est quod Deus qui hominem de luto formavit eum in pulverem redigi permittit: utrum scilicet hoc sit solum ex necessitate materiae, ut homo in hoc nihil plus habeat aliis quae ex terra formantur, vel hoc sit ex divina providentia aliquam hominis culpam puniente. Consequenter autem tangit factionem hominis quantum ad opus propagationis secundum quod homo ab homine generatur. Ubi considerandum est quod omnia naturae opera Deo attribuit non ut excludat naturae operationem sed eo modo quo principali agenti attribuuntur ea quae per causas secundas aguntur, ut artifici operatio serrae: hoc enim ipsum quod natura operatur a Deo habet, qui ad hoc eam instituit. In hac autem hominis generatione primo occurrit seminis resolutio, et quantum ad hoc dicit *Nonne sicut lac mulsisti me?:* sicut enim semen est superfluum alimenti ita et lac. Secundo autem occurrit compactio massae corporeae in utero mulieris, et quantum ad hoc subdit *et sicut caseum me coagulasti?:* ita enim se habet semen maris ad materiam quam femina ministrat in generatione hominis et aliorum animalium sicut se habet coagulum in generatione casei. Tertio autem occurrit distinctio organorum, quorum quidem consistentia et robur est ex nervis et ossibus, circumdantur autem exterius a pelle et carnibus, unde dicit *Pelle et carnibus vestisti me, ossibus et nervis compegisti me.* Quartum autem est animatio fetus, et praecipue quantum ad animam rationalem quae non infunditur nisi post organizationem; simul autem cum anima rationali infunduntur homini divinitus quaedam seminaria virtutum, aliqua quidem communiter omnibus, aliqua vero specialiter aliquibus secundum quod homines quidam sunt naturaliter dispositi ad unam virtutem, quidam ad aliam: Iob autem dicit infra 'Ab infantia crevit mecum miseratio, et de utero egressa est mecum,' unde et hic dicit *Vitam et misericordiam tribuisti mihi.* Ultimum autem est conservatio vitae tam in materno utero quam post exitum ex utero, quae quidem conservatio est partim quidem per principia naturalia, partim autem per alia Dei beneficia naturae superaddita, sive pertineant ad animam sive ad corpus sive ad exteriora bona, et quantum ad hoc subdit *et visitatio tua custodivit spiritum meum:* sicut enim Deus ab aliquo recedere dicitur in Scripturis quando Deus ab eo sua dona subtrahit, sic eum visitare dicitur quando ei sua dona largitur."

generation mapped out in terms of Aristotelian metaphysics, and as such, it can only be of help in developing a bioethical theory. If a normative bioethical theory requires a metaphysically univocal definition of what is alive and what is a human being, it is likely that no such bioethical theory can be developed in a consistent way. As we have seen, onto an Aristotelian metaphysical explanation of the phenomenon of generation it is possible "to graft" different bioethical choices depending on the importance ascribed to one rather than to another element of that explanation. Thomas's attempt to reconcile the discontinuity of human generation with the continuity of the subject of generation only serves, methodologically, to set boundaries to possible bioethical choices, assuring that they be neither too rigid nor too weak.

On the one hand, the fact that, for Thomas, before the fortieth day the embryo is not able to be considered a human being (or, at least, a complete and perfect human being) allows a follower of Thomas to look in a less dramatic way upon the fate of the embryo just conceived and therefore to approach bioethically certain critical cases with greater adaptability to difficult circumstances (as the interruption of a pregnancy caused by rape or deception, or interruption of gestations that are accidental and without fault) as well as possible situations of ethical conflict (as the choice between the survival of the mother and that of the embryo). The case of the embryo after the fortieth day instead would call for a different moral evaluation, since such an embryo is in every respect a human being. From this moment forward, the type of protection to be accorded the embryo could be decided otherwise, for example, on strictly legal or ethical bases.

On the other hand, the fact that before the fortieth day the embryo can also be considered as that which is a human being even if in an incomplete way—since it is what is becoming a human being, and therefore is the same entity, as subject, that will later be a human being rationally ensouled—leads a follower of Aquinas to hold as ethically unacceptable any voluntary act of interruption or manipulation of this process, as would be unmotivated interruptions of pregnancy, direct or indirect intentional interventions on embryos (one could imagine, in any case, such actions for nontherapeutic purposes), certain lifestyles that could put the embryo in danger, and, in certain respects, some practices of artificial insemination.

In light of these considerations, it seems to me that a follower of Thomas could say that, on Thomas's account, the best bioethical approach to the question of the beginning of human life can be summed up in the phrase "the gradual protection of human life." As any gradual protection, so also the gradual protection of human life takes into consideration the interplay of factors, both circumstantial and contextual, that lie outside a strictly metaphysical and philosophical evaluation. This is the reason, in the end, that the attempts made by some Catholics and exponents of the so-called "analytic Thomism" to bring Thomas into accord with the present position of the Roman Catholic Church on abortion are, in addition to being philosophically and philologically unsatisfying, largely pointless. Philosophically, the main reason (often overlooked) for this is that with a metaphysical theory that gives primacy to the species rather than to the individual, every act that interferes with the natural final end, which is the conservation of the species, is by the very fact of such interference to be excluded from the set of morally licit or acceptable acts. A voluntary interruption of an ordinary and natural pregnancy appears to the eyes of Thomas as seriously wrong not only (or not so much) because it suppresses a subject that would have given rise to an individual human being but also (or most of all) because it subordinates the good of the species to the presumed benefit of an individual. The recognition of the centrality of the species and of the necessity of its conservation is of itself a reasonable and sufficient motive for being against, in principle, every unmotivated or generalized practice of abortion. This is true even if the progressive nature of ensoulment of the fetus is such that no one can be charged with the crime of homicide if, voluntarily or involuntarily, he/she interrupts the process before the embryo has completely assumed the form of a human being.

But at the same time, the centrality accorded to the species could in principle make acceptable an application, however minimal, of the principle of the "availability of life" to the embryo; namely, the principle that assumes that life may be, within well-defined limits, made available for purposes other than the preservation of the life itself.

If, ordinarily, acts directed toward obstructing or interrupting a natural generative process are ethically illicit, and therefore ought to be ethically prohibited for Thomas, nevertheless it is still possible, in principle, that acts directed to *perfecting* the process can be ethically licit, and therefore ethically permitted. And finally, it is possible that in exceptional cases the process can be interrupted, as long as this, once again, is held to be useful or only not harmful to the human species. Of course, all these considerations are merely conjectural, because as we have seen in this study no clear treatment of bioethical cases can be found within Thomas's metaphysical investigation of embryogenesis.

When all is said and done, Thomas's position on the beginning of human life is clear. But as we have seen, with the problem of the end of human life things are more complicated and his position is more difficult to define. Some texts, as his Commentary on the *Liber de causis,* lead an interpreter to believe that Thomas did not see a possible distinction between the end of human life and biological death as problematical. According to these texts, Thomas would not be opposed to holding that a human being ceases to be such when he/she ceases to be rational, even while continuing to breathe and so to exist. Hence, the end of human life would not coincide with the biological death of the organism, and the end of human life would take place only after the human being, lacking the organic structures needed for reasoning, could no longer be considered a human being. This distinction, though easy to formulate in the abstract, is quite difficult to apply in concrete cases, and even today there is great discussion about what features we should consider in defining the irreversible end of all brain activities, i.e., the brain death; Thomas says practically nothing, for example, on how to empirically verify the irreversible loss of the capacity to reason. Nevertheless, the distinction between the two states would open the possibility to combine a bioethical theory of the sacredness of life with a bioethical theory of the quality of life, using the principle introduced earlier of the "gradual protection of human life."

But as we have seen, apart from these few passages (which are in any case difficult to interpret) the major part of Thomas's texts in fact provides evidence against the distinction between the end of human life and biological death. In particular, he does not seem to waver in upholding the basic Aristotelian functionalism, according to which each part of a living organism (and the organism itself in its totality) acquires its identity only by reason of the function that it carries out within the whole (or as a whole). A part of a living organism that lacks its function, for example, a hand without the capacity to grasp objects, immediately becomes inanimate, ceasing to be part of that organism. The same can be said of the human organism taken as a whole. More specifically, in the case of the human organism the principal function is rational activity, but given that the rational soul also carries out the sensitive and vegetative functions, the only possible conclusion is to maintain that a human being lacking a rational soul is no longer animated at all. A probable conclusion, then, is that for Thomas human life ends with the biological death of the organism. In this respect, Thomas's virtual lack of treatment of the case of the end of human life can be taken as a sign that for him the two states in essence coincide. For this reason, the sequence by which the forms disappear in the process of corruption, which mirrors the sequence of the forms' appearance in the process of generation, is triggered *after* biological death rather than before. The symmetry emphasized by some interpreters of Thomas between generation and corruption on the basis of the appearance and disappearance of human souls is, therefore, only apparent.

This radical functionalism is dependent upon two firm beliefs: (1) that the rational soul is a substantial form and the first act of an organic, physical body that has life potentially (that is, that is in potency to the exercise of rational activity), and (2) that rational ensoulment takes up into itself the functions of vegetative and sensitive ensoulment. Such a functionalism appears to prevent one from considering those who are brain dead or in a state of grave impairment of the basic vital organs, whether temporary or permanent, as no longer humans (or as not yet humans in the case of formed embryos with such an impairment). In any case, Thomas appears to consider human organisms in these conditions as exceptions to the rule of perfect, natural generation, and as such, although they can be counted as human beings, they cannot be considered as perfected or completed human beings. Once again, this could allow space for a judicious and discriminating ethical evaluation of individual cases.

Bibliography

Index

Bibliography

Aertsen, Jan A. *Nature and Creature: Thomas Aquinas's Way of Thought.* Leiden: Brill, 1988.

Albert the Great. *Commentarius in quartum librum Sententiarum (dd. 23–50),* ed. A. Borgnet. In Alberti Magni *Opera Omnia,* t. 30. Paris: Vivès, 1894.

———. *De natura et origine animae,* ed. A. Borgnet. In Alberti Magni *Opera Omnia,* t. 9. Paris: Vivès, 1890.

———. *In De animalibus,* ed. A. Borgnet. In Alberti Magni *Opera Omnia,* t. 12. Paris: Vivès, 1891.

———. *Summa de creaturis,* ed. A. Borgnet. In Alberti Magni *Opera Omnia,* t. 35. Paris: Vivès, 1896.

Alliney, Guido. "L'identità del corpo mortale e del corpo glorioso nei dibattiti duecenteschi." *Esercizi filosofici* 3 (1996), 187–197.

Amerini, Fabrizio. "Aristotle, Averroes, and Thomas Aquinas on the Nature of Essence." *Documenti e studi sulla tradizione filosofica medievale* 14 (2003), 79–122.

Anonymous. "De animatione fœtus." *Nouvelle Revue Théologique* 11 (1879), 163–268.

Aquinas, Thomas. *Compendium theologiae,* ed. H.-F. Dondaine. In Sancti Thomae de Aquino *Opera Omnia,* t. 42. Rome: Editori di San Tommaso, 1979.

———. *De ente et essentia,* ed. H.-F. Dondaine. In Sancti Thomae de Aquino *Opera Omnia,* t. 43. Rome: Editori di S. Tommaso, 1976.

———. *De principiis naturae,* ed. H.-F. Dondaine. In Sancti Thomae de Aquino *Opera Omnia,* t. 43. Rome: Editori di S. Tommaso, 1976.

———. *De unitate intellectus,* ed. H.-F. Dondaine. In Sancti Thomae de Aquino *Opera Omnia,* t. 43. Rome: Editori di S. Tommaso, 1976.

———. *Expositio super Iob ad litteram,* ed. A. Dondaine. In Sancti Thomae de Aquino *Opera Omnia,* t. 26. Rome: ad Sanctae Sabinae, 1965.

———. *Expositio super Isaiam ad litteram,* ed. H.-F. Dondaine and L. Reid. In Sancti Thomae de Aquino *Opera Omnia,* t. 28. Roma: Editori di S. Tommaso, 1974.

———. *In Aristotelis libros Meteorologicorum Expositio,* ed. R. Spiazzi. Turin-Rome: Marietti, 1952.

———. *In duodecim libros Metaphysicorum Aristotelis Expositio,* ed. R. Spiazzi. Turin-Rome: Marietti, 1964.

———. *In Jeremiam Prophetam Expositio.* In Sancti Thomae Aquinatis *Opera Omnia,* t. 14. Parma, Italy: Fiaccadori, 1863.

———. *In librum primum Aristotelis De generatione et corruptione Expositio,* ed. R. Spiazzi. Turin-Rome: Marietti, 1952.

———. *In octo libros Physicorum Aristotelis Expositio,* ed. M. Maggiòlo. Turin: Marietti, 1954.

———. *Quaestio disputata de spiritualibus creaturis,* ed. M. Calcaterra and T. S. Centi. In S. Thomae Aquinatis *Quaestiones disputatae,* vol. 2. Turin: Marietti, 1965 (critical edition by J. Cos. In Sancti Thomae de Aquino *Opera Omnia,* t. 24/2. Rome: Commissio Leonina-Les Éditions du Cerf, 2006).

———. *Quaestiones de quolibet,* ed. R.-A. Gauthier. In Sancti Thomae de Aquino *Opera Omnia,* t. 25, 2 vols. Rome: Commissio Leonina-Les Éditions du Cerf, 1996).

———. *Quaestiones disputatae de anima,* ed. B.-C. Bazán. In Sancti Thomae de Aquino *Opera Omnia,* t. 24/1. Rome: Commissio Leonina-Les Éditions du Cerf, 1996.

———. *Quaestiones disputatae de malo,* ed. P.-M. Gills. In Sancti Thomae de Aquino *Opera Omnia,* t. 33. Rome: Commissio Leonina-Vrin, 1982.

———. *Quaestiones disputatae de potentia,* ed. M. Pession. In S. Thomae Aquinatis *Quaestiones disputatae,* vol. 1. Turin: Marietti, 1965.

———. *Quaestiones disputatae de veritate,* ed. A. Dondaine. In Sancti Thomae de Aquino *Opera Omnia,* t. 22, 3 vols., 4 fasc. Rome: Editori di S. Tommaso, 1970–1976.

———. *Quaestiones disputatae de virtutibus,* ed. E. Odetto. In S. Thomae Aquinatis *Quaestiones disputatae,* vol. 2. Turin: Marietti, 1965.

———. *Scriptum super Sententiis magistri Petri Lombardi,* I–II, ed. P. Mandonnet, vols. 1–2. Paris: Lethielleux, 1929.

———. *Scriptum super Sententiis magistri Petri Lombardi,* III–IV, d. 22, ed. M. F. Moos, vols. 3–4. Paris: Lethielleux, 1947 and 1956.

———. *Scriptum super Sententiis magistri Petri Lombardi,* IV, dd. 23–50, t. 7/2. Parma, Italy: Fiaccadori, 1858.

———. *Sentencia libri De anima,* ed. R.-A. Gauthier. In Sancti Thomae de Aquino *Opera Omnia,* t. 45, 1. Rome: Commissio Leonina-Vrin, 1984.

———. *Sentencia libri De sensu et sensato,* ed. R.-A. Gauthier. In Sancti Thomae de Aquino *Opera Omnia,* t. 45, 2. Rome: Commissio Leonina-Vrin, 1984.

———. *Sententia libri Ethicorum,* ed. R.-A. Gauthier. In Sancti Thomae de Aquino *Opera Omnia,* t. 47, 2 vols. Rome: Ad Sanctae Sabinae, 1969.

————. *Summa contra Gentiles,* ed. C. Pera, P. Marc, and P. Caramello. Turin: Marietti, 1961.

————. *Summa theologiae.* In Sancti Thomae de Aquino *Opera omnia iussu impensaque Leonis XIII P. M. edita,* t. 4–12. Rome: Ex Typographia Polyglotta S. C. de Propaganda Fide, 1888–1906.

————. *Super Boetium De Trinitate,* ed. P.-M. J. Gils. In Sancti Thomae de Aquino *Opera Omnia,* t. 50. Rome: Commissio Leonina-Les Éditions du Cerf, 1992.

————. *Super Epistolam ad Ephesios Lectura,* ed. R. Cai. In S. Thomae Aquinatis *Super Epistolas S. Pauli Lectura,* vol. 2. Turin: Marietti, 1953.

————. *Super Epistolam ad Galatas Lectura,* ed. R. Cai. In S. Thomae Aquinatis *Super Epistolas S. Pauli Lectura,* vol. 2. Turin: Marietti, 1953.

————. *Super Evangelium S. Ioannis Lectura,* ed. R. Cai. Turin: Marietti, 1952.

————. *Super librum De causis Expositio,* ed. H. D. Saffrey. Paris: Vrin, 2002 (first ed. Paris: Le Saulchoir, 1952).

————. *Super primam Epistolam ad Corinthios Lectura,* ed. R. Cai. In S. Thomae Aquinatis *Super Epistolas S. Pauli Lectura,* vol. 1. Turin: Marietti, 1953.

————. *Super primam Epistolam ad Timotheum Lectura,* ed. R. Cai. In S. Thomae Aquinatis *Super Epistolas S. Pauli Lectura,* vol. 2. Turin: Marietti, 1953.

Ashley, Benedict M. "A Critique of the Theory of Delayed Hominization." In *An Ethical Evaluation of Fetal Experimentation: An Interdisciplinary Study,* edited by Donald McCarthy and Albert S. Moraczewski. St. Louis, MO: Pope John XXIII Medical-Moral Research and Education Center, 1976, 115–129.

Augustine. *Enchiridion ad Laurentium,* ed. E. Evans. Corpus Christianorum Latinorum Series Latina, t. 46. Turnhout, Belgium: Brepols, 1969.

Averroes. *In De generatione Commentarium.* Venice: Apud Junctas, 1572, t. 6.2.

————. *In Metaphysicam Commentarium.* Venice: Apud Junctas, 1572, t. 8.

Basti, Gianfranco. *Filosofia dell'uomo.* Bologna: Edizioni Studio Domenicano, 1995.

Bastit, Michel. "L'embryologie de Saint Thomas." *Ethique* 3 (1992), 48–59.

Bazán, Bernardo-Carlos. "The Human Soul: Form and Substance? Thomas Aquinas' Critique of Eclectic Aristotelianism." *Archives d'histoire doctrinale et littéraire du Moyen Âge* 64 (1997), 95–126.

————. "La Corporalité selon saint Thomas." *Revue philosophique de Louvain* 81 (1983), 369–409.

————. "Pluralisme de formes ou dualisme de substances?" *Revue philosophique de Louvain* 67 (1969), 30–73.

————. *Préface,* in Sancti Thomae de Aquino *Quaestiones disputatae de anima, Opera Omnia,* t. 24, 1. Rome: Commissio Leonina-Les Éditions du Cerf, 1996, 1*–102*.

Berti, Enrico. "Quando esiste l'uomo in potenza? La tesi di Aristotele." In *Quale statuto per l'embrione umano? Problemi e prospettive,* edited by Maurizio Mori. Milan: Bibliotechne, 1992, 52–58.

Bonaventure. *Commentaria in quattuor libros Sententiarum.* In *Opera Omnia,* t. 2. Quaracchi, Florence: Ex Typographia Collegii S. Bonaventurae, 1885.

Boonin, David. *A Defense of Abortion.* Cambridge: Cambridge University Press, 2003.

Bradley, Denis J. M. " 'To Be or Not To Be?' Pasnau on Aquinas's Immortal Human Soul." *The Thomist* 68 (2004), 1–39.

Brisson, Luc, Marie-Hélène Congourdeau, and Jean-Luc Solère, eds., *L'embryon: Formation et animation; Antiquité grecque et latine, tradition hébraïque, chrétienne et islamique.* Paris: Vrin, 2008.

Cova, Luciano. "Prius animal quam homo: Aspetti dell'embriologia tommasiana." In *Parva Naturalia: Saperi medievali, natura e vita,* edited by Chiara Crisciani, Roberto Lambertini, and Romana Martorelli Vico. Pisa: Istituti Editoriali e Poligrafici Internazionali, 2004, 357–378.

Crisciani, Chiara. "Aspetti del dibattito sull'umido radicale nella cultura del tardo Medioevo (secoli XIII–XV)." In *Arxiu de Textos Catalans Antics 23/24: Actes de la II Trobada Internacional d'Estudis sobre Arnau de Vilanova,* edited by Josep Perarnau. Barcelona: Institut d'Estudios Catalans, 2005, 333–380.

Dales, Richard C. *The Problem of the Rational Soul in the Thirteenth Century.* Leiden: Brill, 1995.

D'Ancona, Cristina. "La trasmissione della filosofia araba dalla Spagna musulmana alle università del XIII secolo." In *Storia della filosofia nell'Islam medievale,* edited by Cristina d'Ancona, 2 vols. Turin: Einaudi, 2005, vol. 2, 783–843.

"Declaration on Procured Abortion—Quaestio de abortu procurato," http://www.vatican .va/roman_curia/congregations/cfaith/documents/rc_con_cfaith_doc_19741118 _declaration-abortion_en.html (accessed May 1, 2012).

De Dios Vial Correa, Juan, and Elio Sgreggia, eds. *The Identity and Status of the Human Embryo: Proceedings of Third Assembly of the Pontifical Academy for Life (Vatican City, February 14–16, 1997).* Vatican City: Editrice Vaticana, 1999.

De Grazia, David. *Human Identity and Bioethics.* Cambridge: Cambridge University Press, 2005.

Demaitre, Luke, and Anthony Travil. "Human Embryology and Development in the Works of Albertus Magnus." In *Albertus Magnus and the Sciences: Commemorative Essays 1980,* edited by James A. Weisheipl. Toronto: Pontifical Institute of Mediaeval Studies, 1980, 405–440.

De Siebenthal, Jean. "L'animation selon Thomas d'Aquin: Peut-on affirmer que l'embryon est d'abord autre chose qu'un homme en s'appuyant sur Thomas d'Aquin?" In *L'Embryon: Un homme,* edited by the Société Suisse de Bioéthique. Lausanne: Société Suisse de Bioéthique, 1986, 91–98.

Diamond, James J. "Abortion, Animation, and Biological Hominization." *Theological Studies* 36 (1975), 305–324.

Donati, Silvia. "La dottrina delle dimensioni indeterminate in Egidio Romano." *Medioevo* 14 (1988), 149–233.

Donceel, Joseph F. "Immediate Animation and Delayed Hominization." *Theological Studies* 31 (1970), 76–105.

Eberl, Jason T. "Aquinas' Account of Human Embryogenesis and Recent Interpretations." *Journal of Medicine and Philosophy* 30/4 (2005), 379–394.

———. "Aquinas on the Nature of Human Beings." *Review of Metaphysics* 58.2 (2004), 333–365.

———. "The Beginning of Personhood: A Thomistic Biological Analysis." *Bioethics* 14.2 (2000), 134–157.

———. *Thomistic Principles and Bioethics.* London: Routledge, 2006.

Engelhardt, H. Tristram. *Foundations of Bioethics.* New York: Oxford University Press, 1996.

Feinberg, Joel, ed. *The Problem of Abortion.* Belmont, CA: Wadsworth, 1984.

Finnis, John. *Natural Law and Natural Rights.* Oxford: Oxford University Press, 1980.

Ford, Norman M. *The Prenatal Person. Ethics from Conception to Birth.* Oxford: Blackwell, 2002.

———. *When Did I Begin? Conception of the Human Individual in History, Philosophy and Science.* Cambridge: Cambridge University Press, 1991.

Galluzzo, Gabriele. "Aquinas on the Genus and Differentia of Separate Substances." *Documenti e studi sulla tradizione filosofica medievale* 18 (2007), 343–361.

Gill, Mary L. *Aristotle on Substance: The Paradox of Unity.* Princeton, NJ: Princeton University Press, 1991.

Gomez-Lobo, Alfonso. *Morality and the Human Goods: An Introduction to Natural Law Ethics.* Washington, DC: Georgetown University Press, 2002.

Haldane, John, and Patrick Lee. "Aquinas on Human Ensoulment, Abortion and the Value of Life." *Philosophy* 78 (2003), 255–278.

———. "Rational Souls and the Beginning of Life: A Reply to Robert Pasnau." *Philosophy* 78 (2003), 532–540.

Harris, John. *Bioethics.* Oxford: Oxford University Press, 2001.

Heaney, Stephen J. "Aquinas and the Presence of the Human Rational Soul in the Early Embryo." *The Thomist* 56 (1992), 19–48.

———, ed. *Abortion: A New Generation of Catholic Responses.* Braintree, MA: Pope John Center, 1992.

Huby, Pamela M. "Soul, Life, Sense, Intellect: Some Thirteenth-Century Problems." In *The Human Embryo: Aristotle and the Arabic and European Traditions,* edited by Gordon R. Dunstan. Exeter, Devon., England: University of Exeter Press, 1990, 113–122.

Hughes, Christopher. "Aquinas on Continuity and Identity." *Medieval Philosophy and Theology* 6 (1997), 93–108.

Isidore of Seville, *Etymologiae,* ed. W. M. Lindsay. Oxford: Clarendon Press, 1911; also available at www2.hs-augsburg.de/~Harsch/Chronologia/Lspost07/Isidorus/isi_et00.html (accessed May 1, 2012).

King, Peter O. "Body and Soul." In *The Oxford Handbook of Medieval Philosoophy,* edited by John Marenbon. Oxford: Oxford University Press, 2012, 505–524.

———. "Why Isn't the Mind-Body Problem Mediaeval." In *Forming the Mind: Essays on the Internal Senses and the Mind-Body Problem from Avicenna to the Medical Enlightenment,* edited by Henrik Lagerlund. Berlin: Springer Verlag, 2007, 187–205; also available at www.individual.utoronto.ca/pking/ (accessed May 1, 2012).

Kluge, Eike-Henner W. "St. Thomas, Abortion and Euthanasia: Another Look." *Philosophical Research Archives* 7 (1981), 14–72.

Kuhse, Helga, and Peter Singer, eds. *A Companion to Bioethics.* Oxford: Blackwell, 1998.

———. *Bioethics: An Anthology.* Oxford: Blackwell, 2006.

Johnson, Mark F. "Quaestio Disputata—Delayed Hominization: Reflections on Some Recent Catholic Claims for Delayed Hominization." *Theological Studies* 56 (1995), 743–763.

———. "Quaestio Disputata—Delayed Hominization: A Rejoinder to Thomas Shannon." *Theological Studies* 58 (1997), 708–714.

Johnston, Eric M. *The Role of Aristotelian Biology in Thomas Aquinas's Theology of Marriage*, Ph.D. dissertation, Catholic University of America, Washington, DC, 2008.

Lee, Patrick. *Abortion: The Unborn Human Life*. Washington, DC: Catholic University of America Press, 1996.

———. "Embryonic Human Beings." *Journal of Contemporary Health Law and Policy* 22 (2006), 424–438.

———. "The Pro-Life Argument from Substantial Identity: A Defense." *Bioethics* 18 (2004), 249–263.

———. "Substantial Identity and the Right to Life: A Rejoinder to Dean Stretton." *Bioethics* 21 (2007), 93–97.

Lenzi, Massimiliano. "Alberto e Tommaso sulla natura dell'anima umana." *Archives d'histoire doctrinale et littéraire du Moyen Âge* 74 (2007), 27–58.

———. *Anima, forma e sostanza: Filosofia e teologia nel dibattito antropologico del XIII secolo*. Spoleto, Italy: CISAM, 2011.

Lisska, Anthony J. *Aquinas's Theory of Natural Law: An Analytic Reconstruction*. Oxford: Clarendon Press, 1996.

Lizza, John P. *Defining the Beginning and End of Life: Readings on Personal Identity and Bioethics*. Baltimore, MD: Johns Hopkins University Press, 2009.

———. *Person, Humanity, and the Definition of Death*. Baltimore, MD: Johns Hopkins University Press, 2006.

———. "Potentiality and Human Embryos." *Bioethics* 21.7 (2007), 379–385.

———. *Potentiality: Metaphysical and Bioethical Dimensions*. Baltimore, MD: Johns Hopkins University Press, forthcoming.

Lottin, Odon. *Psychologie et morale au XIIe et XIIIe siècle*, 2 vols. Leuven: Abbaye du Mont César, 1949.

Loux, Michael J. *Metaphysics: A Contemporary Introduction*. London: Routledge, 2006.

Lowe, E. Jonathan. *A Survey of Metaphysics*. Oxford: Oxford University Press, 2002.

MacDonald, Scott, and Eleonore Stump, eds. *Aquinas's Moral Theory: Essays in Honor of Norman Kretzmann*. Ithaca, NY: Cornell University Press, 1999.

Manninen, Bertha A. "Revisiting the Argument from Fetal Potential." *Philosophy, Ethics, and Humanities in Medicine* 2.7 (2007); also available at www.peh-med.com/content/2/1/7 (accessed May 1, 2012).

Maritain, Jacques. "Verso un'idea tomista dell'evoluzione." In J. Maritain, *Approches sans entraves: Scritti di filosofia cristiana*. Rome: Città Nuova, 1977, vol. 1, 87–153.

Martorelli Vico, Romana. "Anima e corpo nell'embriologia medievale." In *Anima e corpo nella cultura medievale,* edited by Carla Casagrande and Silvana Vecchio. Florence: Sismel-Edizioni del Galluzzo, 1999, 95–106.

———. *Medicina e filosofia: Per una storia dell'embriologia medievale del XIII e XIV secolo*. Naples: Guerini e Associati, 2002.

McDaniel, Matthew G. *De Anima, DNA: A Modified Stump/Aquinas Hylomorphic Model, the Soul and the Identity of Human Persons, Resurrected*. M.A. thesis in Religious Studies, Liberty University, VA, 2010; also available at www.works.bepress.com/matthewgmcdaniel/1 (accessed May 1, 2012).

Mori, Maurizio. "Il feto ha diritto alla vita? Un'analisi filosofica dei vari argomenti in materia, con particolare riguardo a quello di potenzialità." In *Il meritevole di tutela,* edited by Luigi Lombardi-Vallauri. Milan: Giuffré, 1990, 735–839.

Murphy, Mark C. *Natural Law and Practical Rationality.* Cambridge: Cambridge University Press, 2001.

Nardi, Bruno. "L'origine dell'anima umana secondo Dante." *Giornale storico della filosofia italiana* 12 (1931), 433–456, and 13 (1932), 45–56 and 81–102; reprinted in *Studi di filosofia medievale.* Rome: Edizioni di Storia e Letteratura, 1960, 9–68.

———. "Sull'origine dell'anima umana." *Giornale dantesco* 39 (1938), 15–28; reprinted in *Dante e la cultura medievale.* Rome: Laterza, 1983, 207–224.

Needham, Joseph. *A History of Embryology.* Cambridge: Cambridge University Press, 1959.

Owens, Joseph. "Thomas Aquinas: Dimensive Quantity as Individuating Principle." *Mediaeval Studies* 50 (1988), 279–310.

Pangallo, Mario. "The Philosophy of Saint Thomas on the Human Embryo." In *The Human Embryo before Implantation: Scientific Aspects and Bioethical Considerations: Proceedings of the Twelfth Assembly of the Pontifical Academy for Life (Vatican City, February 27–March 1, 2006),* edited by Elio Sgreccia and Jean Laffitte. Vatican City: Editrice Vaticana, 2007, 209–239; also available at www.academiavita.org (accessed May 1, 2012).

Pasnau, Robert. "Mind and Hylomorphism." In *The Oxford Handbook of Medieval Philosophy,* edited by John Marenbon. Oxford: Oxford University Press, 2012, 486–504.

———. "Souls and the Beginning of Life: A Reply to Haldane and Lee." *Philosophy* 78 (2003), 521–531.

———. *Theories of Cognition in the Later Middle Ages.* Cambridge: Cambridge University Press, 1997.

———. *Thomas Aquinas on Human Nature: A Philosophical Study of* Summa Theologiae, *Ia 75–89.* Cambridge: Cambridge University Press, 2002.

Payne, Craig. *Why a Fetus Is a Human Person from the Moment of Conception: A Revisionist Interpretation of Thomas Aquinas's Treatise on Human Nature.* Lewiston, NY: Edwin Mellen Press, 2010.

———. "Would Aquinas Change His Mind on Hominization Today?" In *Life and Learning XVIII.* Proceedings of the Eighteenth University Faculty for Life Conference at Marquette University, 2008, edited by Joseph W. Koterski. Bronx, NY: University Faculty for Life, 2011, 229–248.

Petagine, Antonio. *L'aristotelismo difficile: L'intelletto umano nella prospettiva di Alberto Magno, Tommaso d'Aquino e Sigieri di Brabante.* Milan: Vita e Pensiero, 2004.

Porter, Jean. "Is the Embryo a Person?" www.pfaith.org/catholic.htm (accessed May 1, 2012).

———. *Nature as Reason: A Thomistic Theory of the Natural Law.* Grand Rapids, MI: Eerdmans, 2005.

Potter, Van Rensselaer. *Bioethics: Bridge to the Future.* Englewood Cliffs, NJ: Prentice-Hall, 1971.

Rawls, John. *Theory of Justice.* Oxford: Oxford University Press, 1981.

Reichlin, Massimo. "The Argument from Potential: A Reappraisal." *Bioethics* 11 (1997), 1–23.

Reynolds, Philip L. *Food and the Body: Some Peculiar Questions in High Medieval Theology.* Leiden: Brill, 1999.

Roland-Gosselin, Marie-Dominique. *Le "De ente et essentia" de s. Thomas d'Aquin: Texte etabli d'apres les manuscrits parisiens; Introduction, notes et études historiques.* Paris: Vrin, 1948.

Shannon, Thomas A. "Delayed Hominization: A Response to Mark Johnson." *Theological Studies* 57 (1996), 731–734.

Shields, Christopher J. "Aristotle's Psychology." In *The Stanford Encyclopedia of Philosophy* (winter 2005 ed.), edited by E. N. Zalta, www.plato.stanford.edu (accessed May 1, 2012).

Singer, Peter. *Practical Ethics.* Cambridge: Cambridge University Press, 1979.

Stretton, Dean. "Essential Properties and the Right to Life: A Response to Lee." *Bioethics* 18.3 (2004), 264–282.

Stump, Eleonore. *Aquinas.* London: Routledge, 2003.

———. "Forms and Bodies: The Soul." In *Intellect and Imagination in Medieval Philosophy,* edited by Maria C. Pacheco and José Meirinhos, 4 vols. Turnhout, Belgium: Brepols, 2006, vol. 3, 1379–1387.

———. "Non-Cartesian Substance Dualism and Materialism without Reductionism." *Faith and Philosophy* 12 (1995), 505–531.

———. "Resurrection, Reassembly, and Reconstitution: Aquinas on the Soul." In *Die menschliche Seele: Brauchen wir den Dualismus?* edited by Bruno Niederberger and Edmund Runggaldier. Frankfurt: Ontos Verlag, 2006, 153–174.

———. "Resurrection and the Separated Soul." In *The Oxford Handbook of Aquinas,* edited by Brian Davies and Eleonore Stump. Oxford: Oxford University Press, 2012, 458–466.

Sumner, Leonard W. *Abortion and Moral Theory.* Princeton, NJ: Princeton University Press, 1981.

Taylor, Michael A. *Human Generation in the Thought of Thomas Aquinas: A Case Study on the Role of Biological Fact in Theological Science.* S.T.D. dissertation, Catholic University of America, Washington, DC, 1982.

Testi, Claudio A. "L'embriologia di S. Tommaso d'Aquino e i suoi riflessi sulla bioetica contemporanea." *Divus Thomas* 101/1 (1998), 80–105.

Te Velde, Rudi A. *Participation and Substantiality in Thomas Aquinas.* Leiden: Brill, 1995.

Tooley, Michael, Celia Wolf-Devine, Philip E. Devine, and Alison M. Jaggar. *Abortion: Three Perspectives.* New York: Oxford University Press, 2009.

Torrell, Jean-Pierre. *Initiation à Saint Thomas d'Aquin: Sa personne et son œuvre.* Fribourg: Éditions Universitaires-Les Éditions Du Cerf, 1993.

Van der Lugt, Maaike. *Le ver, le démon et la vierge: Les théories médiévales de la génération extraordinaire.* Paris: Les Belles Lettres, 2004.

Van Dyke, Christina. "Human Identity, Immanent Causal Relations, and the Principle of Non-Repeatability: Thomas Aquinas on the Bodily Resurrection." *Religious Studies* 43 (2007), 373–394.

———. *Metaphysical Amphibians: Aquinas on the Individuation and Identity of Human Beings.* Ph.D. dissertation, Cornell University, Cornell, NY, 2000.

Van Steenberghen, Fernand. *Thomas Aquinas and Radical Aristotelianism.* Washington, DC: Catholic University of America Press, 1980.

Vanni Rovighi, Sofia. *L'antropologia filosofica di san Tommaso d'Aquino.* Milano: Vita e Pensiero, 1972.

Veatch, Robert. *The Basics of Bioethics.* Upper Saddle River, NJ: Prentice-Hall, 2000.

Volek, Peter. "Thomas Aquinas' Views on the Origins of Humans and Contemporary Embryology." *Filozofia* 62/3 (2007), 203–222.

Wade, Francis C. "Potentiality in the Abortion Discussions." *Review of Metaphysics* 29 (1975), 239–255.

Wallace, William A. "Aquinas's Legacy on Individuation, Cogitation and Hominisation." In *Thomas Aquinas and His Legacy,* edited by David M. Gallagher. Washington, DC: Catholic University of America Press, 1994, 173–193.

———. "St. Thomas on the Beginning and Ending of Human Life." In *Sanctus Thomas de Aquino doctor hodiernae humanitatis,* edited by Abelardo Lobato and Daniel Ols. Vatican City: Editrice Vaticana, 1995, pp. 394–407.

Waterlow, Sarah. *Nature, Change, and Agency in Aristotle's Physics.* Oxford: Oxford University Press, 1982.

Wilson, Gordon A. "Thomas Aquinas and Henry of Ghent on the Succession of Substantial Forms and the Origin of Human Life." In *The Ethics of Having Children,* edited by Lawrence P. Schrenk. Washington, D.C.: American Catholic Philosophical Association, 1990, pp. 117–131.

Wippel, John F. *The Metaphysical Thought of Thomas Aquinas. From Finite Being to Uncreated Being.* Washington, D.C.: The Catholic University of America Press, 2000.

Zavalloni, Roberto. *Richard de Mediavilla et la controverse sur la pluralité des formes.* Leuven: Éditions de l'Institut Supérieur de Philosophie, 1951.

Index